"Sarah Sumner's book has the promise to break the divisive deadlock between egalitarians and complementarians that continues to hinder the effectiveness of the church. Sumner's clear, carefully argued message challenges all of us regardless of our position. A must-read for Christian leaders and potential leaders."

LILIAN CALLES BARGER,
PRESIDENT OF THE DAMARIS PROJECT

"Sarah's solid biblical approach clarified several issues for me personally. *Men and Women in the Church* is the 'talking point' book on this subject for this generation."

JIM BURNS, PH.D.,
PRESIDENT, YOUTHBUILDERS

"With courage and honesty, Dr. Sumner explores the biblical and cultural assumptions behind evangelical disagreements over gender and leadership. This book cuts to the heart of Christian anxieties about sexuality and the church. It gives new hope to men and women who have felt torn between their support for women's ministries and their adherence to scriptural norms. I recommend it very highly."

DANA L. ROBERT,
TRUMAN COLLINS PROFESSOR OF WORLD MISSION, BOSTON UNIVERSITY

"Every once in awhile someone enters into a theological skirmish and lifts it to a level where rays of biblical sunshine reveal a whole new way of looking at the issue. Honest male readers will repent—at least, I did—of some thoughts. So will honest female readers. And we'll humbly and joyfully explore the new dimension Sarah has helped us see."

JIM GARLOW,
SENIOR PASTOR, SKYLINE WESLEYAN CHURCH

"Dr. Sumner's book is like a fresh breeze from the New Testament, moving clouds of bias and freeing us to look again at the valuable ministry for women in the kingdom of God."

BARRY MCMURTRIE, SENIOR PASTOR,
CROSSROADS CHRISTIAN CHURCH, CORONA, CALIFORNIA, AND CHAIRMAN,
LONDEN INSTITUTE FOR WORLD EVANGELISM

"Sarah Sumner's practical approach to Scripture offers the church new hope for unity and growth."

PAT VERBAL, FOUNDER,
MINISTRY TO TODAY'S CHILD

"I have felt a deep need for someone to enter the discussion of gender and leadership in the church and provide some fresh perspectives and new approaches. Dr. Sumner has listened well. Her work is done in the context both of careful scholarship and of personal experience within the evangelical community. And, I believe, she provides an important contribution to the life of the church."

GREGORY WAYBRIGHT, PH.D.,
PRESIDENT, TRINITY EVANGELICAL DIVINITY SCHOOL

MEN AND Women
IN THE CHURCH

Building Consensus
on Christian Leadership

SARAH SUMNER, PH.D.
FOREWORD BY PHILLIP E. JOHNSON

InterVarsity Press
Downers Grove, Illinois

InterVarsity Press
P.O. Box 1400, Downers Grove, IL 60515-1426
World Wide Web: www.ivpress.com
E-mail: mail@ivpress.com

InterVarsity Press® *is the book-publishing division of InterVarsity Christian Fellowship/USA*®*, a student movement active on campus at hundreds of universities, colleges and schools of nursing in the United States of America, and a member movement of the International Fellowship of Evangelical Students. For information about local and regional activities, write Public Relations Dept., InterVarsity Christian Fellowship/USA, 6400 Schroeder Rd., P.O. Box 7895, Madison, WI 53707-7895, or visit the IVCF website at <www.ivcf.org>.*

All Scripture quotations, unless otherwise indicated, are taken from the New American Standard Bible, © *1960, 1962, 1963, 1971, 1972, 1973, 1975, 1977 by the Lockman Foundation. Used by permission.*

Cover design: Cindy Kiple

ISBN 0-8308-2391-3

Printed in the United States of America ∞

Library of Congress Cataloging-in-Publication Data

Sumner, Sarah, 1963-
  Men and women in the church: building consensus on Christian leadership/Sarah Sumner.
    p. cm.
Includes bibliographical references and indexes.
  ISBN 0-8303-2391-3 (pbk.: alk. paper)
  1. Christian leadership. 2. Women in church work. I. Title.
  BV652. 1 .S86 2003
  262'.14'082—dc21

                        2002152086

P	18	17	16	15	14	13	12	11	10	9	8	7	6	5	4	3	2	1
Y	17	16	15	14	13	12	11	10	09	08	07	06	05	04	03			

To my husband, Jim,

God's answer to my prayers

CONTENTS

PART 2: BUILDING CONSENSUS ON CHRISTIAN LEADERSHIP

Foreword

When Sarah Sumner was seeking a descriptive title for this book, she told me that one adviser had suggested she title it either the "problem" or the "dilemma" of women in Christian leadership. Many conservative Christians probably frame the subject in one of those terms, but I responded, "You are not writing about a problem, much less a dilemma. You are addressing an opportunity." Sarah's aim is to help us set aside some self-defeating ways of thinking—to allow Christians to move forward in total honesty with ourselves about how we *are* or *are not* welcoming the gifted teachers whom God is making available to us for the more effective proclaiming and teaching of the gospel.

My background in secular universities and mainstream churches has made me wary of feminism but, like Sarah's father, enthusiastically admiring of "women who can get things done." As the founder and leader of the movement I describe in *The Wedge of Truth* (IVP, 2000), I eagerly welcome the participation of any women or men who can help us to bring out the truth, by public speaking, writing or whatever they are gifted to do. When I think of women who are truly making a contribution to the truth, however, I include women who are making that difference in the context of their families as well as those who are called to take a more publicly visible role. When pressed in interviews to name my heroes, I have spontaneously responded that they are "home-schooling mothers!" To me, the heroic mothers who nurture the next generation of faithful Christians are among the leaders of the church, regardless of whether they ever speak in front of a congregation.

One thing I know, however, is that my heroes are nurturing daughters as well as sons, who will step forward bearing gifts of teaching or preaching that we will surely want to call upon as we face the obstacles God is calling us to overcome in the twenty-first century. Like the first century, ours is a time that requires heroes, and we must joyfully welcome the potential heroes whom God provides for us, even if they are not exactly what we might have expected. To be sure, we must faithfully follow the Scriptures, but doing this requires that we distinguish, as Sarah so persuasively does, between an influential cultural tradition, which has often been misogynist, and the actual message of the Bible.

Biblical interpretation is not my profession, but I do have a determination to encourage the gifted young scholars and teachers whom it is my privilege to mentor to produce the very best work of which they are capable, and to step forward in confidence that they have something important to say to a mixed-up world that badly needs to hear it. As that implies, I am equally determined to persuade the world to pay attention.

If as Sarah's friend and mentor I have made any contribution to this book, it is by urging her to put more of herself into her writing, to let the reader see her ideas and arguments in the context of her family background and personal struggle to be accepted in a male world that did not make it easy for her. If some of her teachers warned her not to "show the full color of [her] plume," lest it threaten the men, I told her the opposite. She says that she is a Christian first and last, and not a feminist, and that she wants to write in furtherance of truth and Christ's power, not women's power. Personally, I know that to be true, but I know also that some readers may suspect that there must be some suppressed anger or feminist power-seeking lurking in the background. The best way to correct that kind of mistake is to understand how she related as a child to her father and her mother, and as a young adult to the biblically faithful seminary professors who developed her intellectual and scholarly capacities, but who in some cases were struggling "manfully" (a certain wry irony in the use of this term is fully intended) with the novel concept of a female theologian.

I am certain that the overwhelming majority of faithful Christians agree with me that we would rather hear good teaching from a gifted woman than inferior teaching from a less gifted man, and I am confident that Paul himself would approve of our preference, however much difficulty we may have sorting out all the intricacies of specific statements the great apostle made.

I am equally certain that Sarah fully recognizes that providing opportunities for *anyone* in the church, women included, is not an end in itself but always in furtherance of taking the whole gospel truth to men, women and families. We should never accept some hybrid such as feminist theology on the mistaken assumption that we are thereby pleasing women. We will never truly satisfy women that way, and even if we did, it would not be worth the cost. Our objective must always be to please Christ, and not to please men (yes, that generic term includes both sexes).

Not everyone will agree with all of Dr. Sumner's answers, but I think it more important that impartial readers will agree that she raises the right questions. I remember a distinguished scholar who, informed that I was supporting Sarah's project, assumed that it must be primarily about which church offices should be open to women. That is precisely the wrong question to start with, akin to the wrangling for position that characterized the disciples at their worst. Sarah starts with a much better question. How should men and women regard and treat each other if they are both truly faithful to the gospel of Christ and value truth more than personal power?

If you do not find that question important and fascinating, you ought to. So please move on and start reading Sarah's book, where you will find that question very thoroughly and faithfully answered.

Phillip E. Johnson

Acknowledgments

When I first began to understand my calling to write this book, I made a decision to "go for it" and ask God for the moon. In other words, I decided to ask God to introduce me to Phillip Johnson. Phil has more expertise in logic and argumentation than anyone else I know of. I had learned about Phil from my church history professor at Trinity Evangelical Divinity School, Dr. John Woodbridge, who alluded in class one day to a then-recent book titled *Darwin on Trial*. I went home and read the book right away. After that, I casually started keeping track of Phil's other writings. Over time I gained a tremendous sense of appreciation not only for Phil Johnson's wise approach to the debate on creation and evolution but also for his cheerful attitude. Phil knows how to argue without fighting. He also knows how to befriend his opponents and mobilize people for the sake of a common cause. Thus I was delighted when Phil agreed a few years ago to take a look at the first few pages I produced (all of which were eventually discarded). His involvement in my project was another confirmation that God had entrusted me with something important to say.

Though initially I sought out Phil for the purpose of helping me structure my logic, he helped me instead by challenging me to first convince him that I am not a feminist (he didn't automatically believe me at first) and by prodding me to forfeit my fear of writing about myself in the context of this book. There's a story of how that happened, but I won't tell it here. Suffice

it to say, Phil has been my mentor, and thus it is he whom I want to acknowledge first as I express my heartfelt thanks. My gratitude for Phil Johnson
runs deep, especially for the way he models what it means to seek truth.

I also want to thank the people who read all or parts of the countless early
versions of the manuscript. This includes all those who gave me valuable
feedback, such as my sister, Rebecca Hughes (my most regular encourager in
the project), my father, John S. Chambers, my mother, Zanne Chambers, my
brother, John F. Chambers, and many other helpful people such as Ney
Bailey, Lilian Barger, Colleen Hurley-Bates, Stuart Briscoe, Joe Brown, Jim
Burns, Sally Clingman, Steve and Judy Douglass, Ted Engstrom, Hillary
Evans, Rich Gathro, Daniel Lai, Joel Lehman, Kara Powell, Holly Sheldon,
Knofel Staton, Jenny Vaneerden, Pat Verbal, Roy Wheeler, and my top two
seminary mentors, Harold O. J. Brown and Carl F. H. Henry.

Special thanks go to my cherished friend Andrea Buczynski, who read
more versions than anyone else and constantly offered insightful words of
constructive criticism that helped me to rethink and rewrite and make many
needed changes. Andrea and I share a special bond due to her sacrificial giving and practical wisdom.

I also appreciate all thirty-two women who attended the Newport Gathering in June of 2000. Taking a risk, they flew in from all over the United
States (and Singapore) to California to Johanna Townsend's house to hear
me teach for two and a half days straight, some of them having never even
met me before. Our time spent together marks an historical moment. I'll never
forget that last night when we prayed. This book is a result, in part, of their
faith.

A special word of thanks to my students here at Azusa Pacific University,
especially Halee Scott, who helped compile the index. Thanks also to the Academic Cabinet who awarded me a course reduction during spring 2001 so
that I could focus more on my writing. I am also grateful for my trusted colleagues Lane Scott and Robert Harvey as well as the professors in the ministry department (Enrique, Gordon, Kent, Roger and Steve).

I also thank the members of New Song Church, particularly Dennis Bachman, Norma Bachoura, Julie Burkholder, Amy Davis, Jennifer and Jeremiah Dean, Manuel and Julie Del Gado, Becky Durben, Marilyn Faber, George Haraksin, Dave Johnson, Cindy Mitchell, Frank Selvaggio, Ardath Smith, and Ray and Janice Wheeler, who prayed for me, my husband and this book.

I am grateful as well to the reviewers whom my publisher solicited. All six readers, including my editor Jim Hoover, pointed out flaws in the book that had previously not been drawn to my attention. If it wasn't for them, this book would be less readable, less clear and less reflective of my intent to be respectful to both sides of the debate. The other person from IVP whom I want to mention by name is the marketing director, Jeff Crosby. Jeff's enthusiasm for this book has lifted my spirits time and time again. Perhaps the best way to articulate my thanks to the folks at IVP is to say that I literally prayed consistently for sixteen years for God to connect me to the right publisher. I believe God answered that prayer.

Finally, I acknowledge my husband, Jim Sumner. Jim deserves a chest full of medals for his unselfish willingness to be my number-one supporter. Not once did he complain that I was writing yet again into the wee hours of the night. On the contrary, he championed the project with gusto from the inception until its finish five years later. With that, he granted me full permission to tell any personal story about him or our marriage if it appeared to have the potential to help others. I am so grateful to have a husband who finds his identity in Christ. Certainly Jim's strength plays into the book if for no other reason than that he is the one who urged me to write it in the first place.

PART ONE

MEN AND WOMEN IN THE CHURCH

1

MY STORY

If I perish, I perish.
ESTHER 4:16

Thanks to my upbringing, I am unaware of what life is like apart from my relationship with God. I learned how to pray as soon as I could talk. At eleven months of age, I was given my own Bible to carry. My father was so eager to equip us with resources that would help us understand the proper meaning of the Scriptures that he purchased a full set of Bible commentaries for each of us kids to keep in our bedrooms before any of us were old enough to read. For us, it was normal to think about God because every night at bedtime my mother read us stories from the Bible.

We lived on a ranch in Texas fifteen miles outside of town on the land where my father was raised. Three times a week my family drove to church on bumpy, unpaved roads. I can still remember the struggle of trying to share the back seat with my brother and sister during the long ride there. Sundays were special because right after breakfast Daddy would play records of gospel music (Johnny Cash and Tennessee Ernie Ford) to warm us up for worship and give our mother time to get ready. We enjoyed those moments of waiting on her because Daddy always made it so fun. He would imitate Donald Duck and Yogi Bear and then turn on the music and wink at us and snap his fingers to the beat of the tune.

At church our favorite hymn was the one that reminded us of Daddy. We loved the hymn "Standing on the Promises of God" because we misunderstood it as a song about someone named Stanley. During the chorus all three of us kids would bellow as loudly as we could, "Stanley! Stanley! Stanley on the promises of God my Savior . . ." We had no idea of what that song was about, but every time we sang it, we poured out our hearts proudly singing Daddy's middle name.

I delighted in my dad, and yet for me the love of God could best be described as greater than the love of my mother. Her love and protection shone so brightly on me that I could see God's goodness through her. I can truthfully say that nearly every time I looked at her, she gave me another loving smile. Year after year the warmth in her eyes would greet me anew in almost every passing glance that I had the privilege to receive. She was always so glad to see me, even though she saw me every day. I have countless childhood memories of looking up to find assurance from my mother's loving gaze manufactured just for me over and over again.

My mother was tender, but that doesn't mean she wasn't tough. My mom lived in a state of readiness to protect us kids from harm. On the ranch, if a rattlesnake ever ventured into our yard, it had to deal with my mom. She was brave enough to get the hoe and charge out independently and chop off its head with two or three blows all by herself. Don't assume she was a country girl; she had no prior experience confronting snakes. Her inner drive arose from the depth of her commitment to defend us kids regardless of what it might have meant for her.

I have rarely met anyone as dogged and determined as my mom. After my father left ranching for the oil business, he said that Mother could accomplish more on a part-time basis in his office during one week than could fifteen full-time secretaries. He said she really had a knack for "getting things done." By the time I graduated from college, she had become an aerobics instructor, an airplane pilot and a candidate for a Ph.D. I am so inspired by her efforts to help people. Over the years she has been involved in Sunday school, Girl Scouts, Meals on Wheels, teaching local retarded children and serving as a therapist to members of the Red Cross during unexpected times of disaster. I could write a whole book detailing the things that my mother has done and is doing. Here my intention is to try to explain the impact that her charitable way of life has had on me. Not only have I watched her in action, but also I have noticed my father's glad approval of women who "get things done."

If anything captures my father's attention, it is Christian women getting things done. I think that traces back to his memories of his mother, who died before I was born but whose legacy of service lives on. My grandmother was a woman of hospitality and concern for other people. I have often heard my dad and his two sisters recount how efficient and productive she was. My dad delights when women excel, especially when they're building God's kingdom. I remember when he told me about his discovery of Kay Arthur and "the fabulous way" she teaches people the Scriptures. I also recall the day he phoned me from Palm Springs and said, "Sarah, you've got to drive out here immediately. There's a woman at the Campus Crusade meeting who tells the gospel with more enthusiasm than anyone I've ever seen before. She has planted over three hundred churches!"

My dad has never been paid to be a pastor, but he has a heart for the church. When I was a little girl, he would preach the Sunday sermon sometimes when the preacher was absent. The only problem was that he couldn't always make out what his sermon notes said because he couldn't read his own handwriting. Sometimes he would have to make up something new right there on the spot because his notes were impossible to decipher. After a few times of having that experience, he came up with a plan to prevent that from happening again. And I was his personal solution. Though I was only in fourth grade, my dad gave me the job of writing a legible copy of his sermon. I loved those three or four occasions. My involvement felt so natural that it never occurred to me that I was doing something out of the ordinary.

What did occur to me was something terrible. It was right about that time when a vague sense of fear began to invade my mind. I looked up at Mother one Sunday morning during church and said, "Momma, do you think I'd be a good preacher's wife?" She looked at me softly with encouragement in her eyes and said, "I think you'd be a *great* preacher's wife." Deflated by a response that was not surprising, I groaned inside and muttered, "That's what I figured you'd say."

I could just see it. Sarah the pastor's wife stuck doing all the planning for skating parties and potluck dinners. I didn't want to go to the church skating party, much less have to plan it. My heart's desire was to do something more, but I didn't know how to picture a woman doing more.

During high school, I forgot about my fear of marrying a preacher. By then my plan was to marry a lawyer, have four kids and teach elementary school. But that plan didn't last long. At the age of twenty-one, I saw a film one Sunday night of author and speaker Joyce Landorf. I had never seen a woman teach the full congregation. Watching her, even indirectly by film, dramatically changed my life. Then and there my self-understanding was transformed. Breathlessly, I tapped my mother on the shoulder and said, "Mother, I'm like her. I want to be a Christian speaker." Prior to that experience, it had never entered my mind that I, as a woman, could forward the gospel openly through public ministry.

MY WALK FORWARD

Though I wanted to be a speaker, I had no idea how to transition myself into that line of work. But I had a college degree that enabled me to teach elementary school. So that's what I did for one semester. During that season, my mind was plagued with a flood of anxious thoughts. *How can I become a Christian speaker when no one has ever heard of me? And who's going to listen to a third-grade teacher from Texas? I need credibility.* So I packed my bags and moved to Illinois to pursue a master's degree at Wheaton College.

I went there to major in Bible. But as soon as I arrived, that changed. During orientation, I became informed of something all the other students, who had read their Wheaton mail, already knew. Upon entering the room, I found out that we were all required to pass a written test in Old Testament, New Testament and theology before we could start our degrees. More important, I learned it was time to take the tests right now.

"Right now?"

Yes, right now. So they handed me a pencil, and I took the tests cold turkey. That's when I discovered theology. Out of fifty questions, I knew only one answer. My goodness, at that time I had never even heard of Augustine. In my Bible-focused past, we just read the Scriptures and sang hymns.

Predictably, I aced the Bible tests and failed the test on theology. This marked the turning point for me. The next two days all of us flunkies were funneled into mandatory sessions where we were taught theology at a high-speed-cram-for-your-life pace. I loved it. I felt as though I had entered heaven.

After it was over, I rushed to my advisor and said, "Okay, I want every single elective of mine to be a theology class."

He said, "Then why don't you change your major to theology?"

I said, "How do I do that?"

Victoriously he replied, "You just did. All you have to do is tell me."

One year later I graduated from Wheaton with a master's degree in theology. Having finished early, I considered going on to earn my doctorate, but I felt too impatient to walk the long path of more schooling. It seemed better to capitalize on my new credibility and set out immediately as a full-time professional Christian speaker.

That's when I bumped into reality. Reality said, "Excuse me, ma'am, you are far too unknown to be invited enough places to manage to make a living at that."

At age twenty-four I decided instead to launch a bivocational career. Without consulting any mentors, brilliantly I forged a makeshift plan to sell insurance during the day and write Christian bestsellers at night. There were only two problems: (1) I hated selling insurance and (2) my writing stunk.

Thankfully, those problems prompted me to choose a better path. I reasoned to myself, "C'mon, be realistic. You need to find out if you're truly cut out to write books." (Then I took the appropriate actions.) Within a matter of weeks, I was hired to travel nationally as a sales representative for a Christian publisher. The experience was tremendously positive. But after two or three years of being on the road, my passion for the job began to fade.

One night on a sales trip, I prayed aloud to God, "Lord, people keep saying how well-suited I am for sales. I don't want to *sell* books; I want to *write* books." And then I told him how dissatisfied I was. It was such a time of brokenness for me. It hurt to surrender my high-minded ideas of aspiring into greatness at age twenty-four in an attempt to be like John Calvin, the famous Reformer, who remarkably published a draft of *The Institutes* at age twenty-seven. I remember praying, "God, I want to be a minister of your Word, but look at me. Here I am alone and hidden in a private hotel, and I don't know what to do next."

That's when God interrupted me. *Quit.* Sniffling through my tears, the idea of quitting flashed through my mind, but I ignored it. The word came to mind again. *Quit.* What? I hadn't even considered the option of quitting. What a great idea! It was true that I had completed my commitment to work there for a minimum of two years, but I had forgotten about that. All of a sudden, I couldn't wait to return to Chicago and submit my resignation.

After I quit, I found myself standing alone without a plan. My heart sank into discouragement. In my opinion, I was nothing but an extra on the planet. There wasn't any place for me to go. So there I was, jobless and planless in the presence of God, having finally reached the end of myself.

A few days later my brother said to me, "Well, Sis, have you thought about doing doctoral work?" I'll never forget that moment. Doctoral work. The thing I had avoided for five years. I didn't want to take the trouble to learn Greek, Hebrew, French and German. As a single woman, I was fearful to invest so much in school. What if that perpetually postponed the possibility of marriage? I was already twenty-seven years old. Why should I go back to school now? Why couldn't I be like Joyce Landorf, my first public woman role model, who never went to seminary? Why was my calling so different?

These were my complaints, though I must confess that as soon as my brother offered his casual suggestion, my heart fluttered and leaped. I couldn't stop smiling, no matter how hard I tried. It hit me somewhere deep that God was leading me to go back to school. I said to my brother, "Okay, I'll go. But God will have to open the doors."

For me, the venture of going back to school was long and involved because I had to earn the equivalent of yet another master's degree. In the field of theology, it's not enough to have thirty-six units of graduate credit, which is what I had acquired at Wheaton. Doctoral studies in systematic theology require more preparation than that.

It took fifteen months of full-time schooling for me to qualify just to apply to the program I wanted—with no guarantee that I'd get in. Choosing this route was risky for me because no other woman had ever tried to enter before and because I went there in spite of a warning. A professor I knew from another institution had earlier taken pains to discourage me away from Trinity. Urgently he had told me, "Whatever you do, don't go to Trinity. You will be disparaged as a woman."

I appreciated his concern, but it hardly influenced me. I wasn't worried about being "disparaged as a woman" because I felt confident that none of the professors at Trinity would ever disparage the Bible. As long as the Scriptures outranked the opinions of everybody else, I knew that I'd be fine. God would protect me with his Word.

That spring on campus, I was given old advice: don't apply. This time it was a Trinity professor. He spent a full half-hour trying to convince me that with seventy other applicants, I would never be admitted into the program. His attitude was clearly uninviting.

Just before I left, he said, "So what are you going to do?"

Flatly I told him, "Apply."

Within a week, I was accepted into Trinity Evangelical Divinity School. Later I found out that two of my professors had threatened to quit if a woman was accepted into the program. Bottom line? No one quit, and everything worked out fine. A few years later, I finished my degree, got hired on a church staff, and married my husband, Jim Sumner.

WOMEN WALKING FORWARD IN FAITH

One day out of the blue a professor at Trinity whom I didn't even know walked up to me and said, "Are you angry?" Embarrassed by his question, I answered, "I don't think so. Do I seem angry to you?" He said, "No, not at all. That's what amazes me." He couldn't figure out how I—as a woman in a somewhat unwelcoming environment—could be so happy.

"I have loved being at Trinity," I assured him.

Unconvinced, he said to me, "I want to talk to you in five years. I'll be really curious to see whether or not you're angry in five years."

I stood perplexed at his amazement. From my perspective, there was nothing to be angry about. The Lord called me into doctoral school. I didn't need to be celebrated by every professor in order to be blessed by my doctoral education. The reading and research, the writing of papers, exposure to lectures, conversations with peers, even listening to the prayers of my professors all enriched my relationship with God. My cup overflowed. How could I be angry? I didn't understand how *any* Christian woman could be angry.

Not every professor was glad to see me in the classroom, but three or four of them were glad enough to make the effort to get to know me. Dr. Carl Henry especially took an interest in me. I'll never forget the day I first met him. Both of us were standing in line downstairs at the seminary snack bar. Somehow I found out that Carl F. H. Henry was just three or four people away from me. Eagerly I abandoned my place in line, walked up to him and said, "You're Dr. Henry? I signed up for your class. I'm really looking forward to seeing you again this afternoon." About half grinning, he looked at me with piercing eyes and said with a touch of dry humor, "You must be Sarah. I heard you're trouble." All I could do was laugh. He laughed too, and that was the start of our friendship. About midway through the semester, he said to me after class, "I want you to meet the Mrs." So that day I went home with him and met Dr. Henry's wife, Helga.

The next year Dr. Henry hired me as his assistant. Mostly he involved me in his writing projects, but once he let me lecture in class. I also remember him joking about his age—for he's almost to the day fifty years older than I.

A couple of times on our way to class, he dryly said to me, "Sarah, what are you going to lecture on today if I drop dead before the class time ends?" Both of us chuckled and kept walking. He was so at ease with the thought of being in heaven that it was comfortable, even didactic, for me to watch him come to grips with the fact that he was steadily growing old.

It wasn't until my husband and I sensed God calling us to move that I began to see why someone might anticipate a woman like me becoming angry. Before graduating from doctoral school, I had never really thought about the turbulence I might face in the very near future as a woman in ministry leadership. I didn't realize I had already been facing it for years. Nor did I notice myself reading books on the subject of women in leadership outside of my classroom assignments. I was aware there were gatherings at Trinity where women seminary students came to seek each other's support. But I never could identify with their pain. I remember being persuaded to attend one meeting, but even then, I stayed for only fourteen or fifteen minutes. After that, I never returned. It simply wasn't relevant to me.

Someone might think from hearing all this that things were destined to get worse. Actually, things got better.[1] In 1997 I was hired to teach full time in the graduate school of theology at Azusa Pacific University (APU) in Azusa, California. One year later, the lead pastor of my conservative Baptist church started asking me to preach with him occasionally. Two years later, I received a double promotion at APU. My life in California was rich. My work at APU, my service at church, my husband's development and satisfaction with his life converged into a mighty flowing river. Any spare hours that I could find were devoted to my ongoing writing.

One evening my husband stepped into our bedroom, where I was seated at the computer, undissertationing my doctoral thesis, trying to convert it into a less academic kind of book. Jim knew I had invested hour after hour,

---

[1]That is not to say everything was easy. I encountered various roadblocks and learned what it means for a search committee to say, "You emerged as our top candidate, and we want you to know that we're now looking for a male Sarah Sumner because you line up with our ideal profile person better than anyone else we know. We'll be praying for you."

month after month, trying to produce a well-written book on the biblical view of godly human anger. Twelve long years had slowly elapsed since I had first attempted to become a Christian writer, and yet up to that point, I had not published a thing. Knowing how sensitive the subject was to me, my husband tried to approach me with gentleness.

"Honey, I think you're writing the wrong book," he said in his most supportive voice.

I knew exactly what he meant. The Lord had impressed the same thought on me, but I was evading my conviction.

"You think I'm supposed to be writing about men and women in the church?" I said to him without enthusiasm.

He answered, "Yes, and I think you're going to be published."

After all those years of struggling to write, intuitively I could tell that something real was finally going to happen. Nevertheless, I felt hesitant. I didn't want my first book to be focused on a controversial subject. I didn't want to get involved in the women's issue or even be associated with "that." Yet no matter how hard I tried, I could not deny that Jim was right. God *had* placed a burden on my heart, and I was responsible to bear it.

Due to the circumstances, I already was immersed in studying the subject that I had tried to avoid. But even then I was studying not because I wanted to but because I had been assigned to teach a graduate-level class called "Men and Women in Ministry." To quite frank, it bothered me to teach that class. What bothered me even more is the inner pull the subject had on me. I hated to admit it, but my energy was great. I taught, spoke, read, thought and prayed about women in leadership all the time.

Even so, it was difficult for me to write this book. For months and months, I discarded my work and started the project again. My writing was not relaxed because I was not relaxed. I was too self-conscious and too unresolved within my own mind to express myself freely on the page. I was loath to introduce myself personally in print for fear that my book would then be perceived as nothing but a "woman's testimony." To me, it seemed better— since I am female—to keep myself out of the way. *Load them up with logic and*

Bible. That's what I said to myself. But through a series of events, which I someday hope to write about, I became convicted to "introduce myself and introduce my theology." After that hard-won breakthrough, the ideas in my head cascaded down into paragraph after paragraph finding their form until finally this book was completed.

I changed in the process of writing this book. I am not the same person as I was when I first tried to write it. My dignity is far more intact. Making myself known as a woman theologian, going public with my views, forced me to confront who I am. I am a woman. Prior to my spiritual breakthrough, I wasn't very comfortable owning my femaleness so fully. I didn't want to be associated with all the negative perceptions commonly attached to women in ministry. I didn't want to be seen as a quasi-theologian who is quasi- because of my gender. Nor did I want people to be distracted by the fact that I am a woman and therefore somewhat suspect just from that.

For me, writing this book became an act of repentance. It forced me to repent from the sin of being prejudiced against women. Please understand, I'm not saying I had a problem with self-esteem. Nor am I saying that I was a snob toward women. What I'm saying is that I was a *typical* evangelical Christian in America. Like most other people who honestly believe they haven't any issue with seeing women as inferior, I too believed that mistakenly about myself.

Though it might seem unbelievable, it is nonetheless true that I finally awakened to the plight of Christian women unexpectedly by vicarious means. I was not sensitized to the severity of women's experience until after I started listening to other women. *Their* stories caused to me to adjust my perspective. *Their* tears softened my heart.

It was having a woman say to me, "I just want to hand out a bulletin. Why can't I hand out a bulletin for the Sunday service at my church? I want to smile and greet the people, but at my church, the greeters are all men."

It was hearing another one say, "Why should I bother to get a master's degree in divinity? I'll never get a job. What a waste of money for me!"

It was listening to another one boldly confess, "I don't want to enter the world of theology; I'm afraid of what it might do to me. So many women in seminary are angry, and I don't want to be like them. I wish I wasn't like this because I lose out no matter what choice I make. If I seize the opportunity, I lose out big time by becoming embittered at Christians who refuse to accept me. If I forgo the opportunity, I lose out even more by missing God's call on my life."

These are the cries that arrested my attention and drove me relentlessly to prayer. *Lord, I don't want to be involved in this. It's grievous. And unnecessary. Why can't your people work this out? There's got to be a way for Christians to work this out. O dear God, stir in us a willingness to repent from being selfish and help us be loving instead.*

2
THE PURPOSE OF THIS BOOK

There is none who is righteous, not even one.

ROMANS 3:10

Many Christian women see themselves caught between two undesirable choices: either to flee or to fight. In other words, they can choose to back away from their ministry calling, bow their heads and flee to the refuge of conventional femininity. Or they can march forthrightly into their calling, shake their fists and fight for women's right to be ordained. Most Christian women truly don't want to do either. But what else can they do?

I believe there is an alternative: to go forward. Queen Esther went forward without fighting for her rights or fleeing from her dire situation. Esther went forward by violating the norms of her culture. She had the courage to enter the court of the king in spite of the fact that her presence before him was unsolicited and unlawful.[1] Esther went forward because God called her to go forward. So heartfelt were her convictions that she resolved to risk her very life. "If I perish, I perish," she said (Esther 4:16). The story of Esther fore-

---

[1]See Esther 4:11, "All the king's servants and the people of the king's provinces know that for any man or woman who comes to the king to the inner court who is not summoned, he has but one law, that he be put to death, unless the king holds out to him the golden scepter so that he may live. And I have not been summoned to come to the king for these thirty days."

shadows the story of Christ, who walked forward in obedience, even to the
point of death (Phil 2:8). Jesus healed on the sabbath, ate with sinners and
did many other things that violated cultural protocol. Jesus had the courage
to follow his calling and disregard the voices of dissent.

As a Christian woman leader, I have to ask myself, "Do I have the courage
to violate cultural protocol? Do I have the will to disregard the voices of dissent? How am *I* to walk forward in obedience to Christ?"

WHAT CHRISTIAN WOMEN HEAR

It's confusing to know what going forward means, especially with regard to
what Christian women leaders commonly hear. On the one hand, they are
told they can do all things through Christ (Phil 4:13). A woman can step out
into a foreign mission field and evangelize an unreached people. She can disciple a king, rebuke a false teacher, correct a wayward brother and change the
course of history by her prayers. She can lead or preach to thousands as long
as the appropriate men invite her to. If her leadership is more suited for work
outside the church, then she can become a senator, CEO or even president.
There's really nothing she can't do.

On the other hand, every Christian woman is told not to lead too much.
She can lead women, but she isn't to be called the women's pastor. She can
preach to men in someone's home or in a conference setting but not in a local
sanctuary. She can oversee a big budget in a big government or nonprofit, but
she can't have an official say over the small budget of a small church. Are women
supposed to believe that these vast and pervasive inconsistencies are justified
by orthodox Christian theology? Surely not, for in the words of Mortimer
Adler, "We know that if we contradict ourselves or if we think contradictory
things, we are missing the truth somewhere."[2] It is logically inconsistent to
think that women are designed to be subordinate to men in the home and
church but not necessarily in society. Yet that is what Christian women hear.

When I was a student at Trinity, one of my professors called me into his

---

[2]Mortimer J. Adler, *The Great Ideas* (Peru, Ill.: Open Court, 2000), p. 8.

office and said to me in a warm, fatherly tone, "Sarah, do not show the full color of your plume; it will intimidate the men." My professor sincerely believed he was doing me a favor by telling me not to express myself without also holding back. He liked me, and he didn't want me to become controversial or lose the good favor of the men. I left his office confronted once again by the same recurring question: *Do I have the courage to exercise integrity and be who I am in Christ?*

To be honest, I am the audience this book is targeted for. I am the one who needs to read it. Writing this book has helped me to see that I unknowingly have followed the proverbial advice to be a good woman and hold back. There's a reason why my writing was so bad for many years. The reason was that I held back.

It also took me several years to begin to overcome my longstanding reluctance to write from my whole self. I was slow to realize that I have felt self-conscious about being a woman in ministry. I *have* felt self-conscious because women ministers are controversial. But at this point in my journey, I am repenting from my subconscious fear of being left out because I, as a woman, do not measure up as a man.

I didn't ask God to grant me the grace to enter seminary and complete my doctoral work. That was his idea. He designed the plan; he's the one who saw me through. I did not anticipate becoming the woman I am. Nor would I have guessed that my struggle to be a writer somehow was connected to my ministry. In all those years of pre-authorship, I never once dreamed of writing about my story as a woman theologian. I didn't even know I had a story.

CHRISTIANITY VERSUS FEMINISM

People who know me understand that I am a Christian, not a feminist.[3] Here's what I mean by that. I am a follower of Christ (Mt 16:24). I confess with my mouth that "Jesus [is] Lord" and believe in my heart "that God

---

[3] According to *Webster's Dictionary*, the word *feminist* literally means "one who believes in the principle that women should have political, economic, and social rights equal to those of men."

raised Him from the dead" (Rom 10:9). My vocation is to become like Christ (Rom 8:29). With that, my number one goal is to love God foremost (Mt 22:37). If I were a feminist, my focus would be on women and equality and power.[4] But since I am a Christian, my focus is on Christ and truth and grace (Jn 1:17). As a Christian, I don't function in a feminist paradigm.

Christians don't have to be feminists in order to believe in social justice. Feminism is not something that must be added to Christianity in order for the church to honor women. The gospel itself is pro-women. It is quintessentially Christian to be pro-people. Hence it is just as unnecessary for a Christian to be a feminist as it is for a Christian to be a humanist. There's no need to blend a humanist worldview into a Christian worldview, because Christians already have the highest view of humanity in the world. Our Lord Jesus is himself the all-time greatest Advocate for men and women and children. Anyone who thinks that treating women fairly is a feminist thing to do, not a Christian thing to do, doesn't understand Christianity.

The point of Christianity is to unite the people of God as one in Christ. When any of us squabble about power and personal status, we display a lack of faith in God's plan. God has arranged for each member of the body to make a contribution—though not as the head of the church. Christ is the head of the church (Col 1:18). None of us are the head. The pope is not the head. Billy Graham is not the head. No woman is the head because no man is the head. Christ alone is the head.

And yet, here we are, as members of Christ's body, debating over who can be the head. We're clamoring for power because we keep overlooking God's plan. God's plan is for us to be united to the Head. That's what church is all

---

[4]Writer Anne Atkins expresses a similar perspective: "Christians and feminists are agreed in wanting the job market to be fair, but we are not agreed on the purpose of life itself. . . . There is indeed an essential difference between Christianity and feminism, but it is a difference we have not just with the women's movement but with almost any philosophy in our society. We do not live for the here and now: we believe in a hereafter. We cannot live to please ourselves. . . . We may not simply work for a just society: we have a gospel to proclaim which is even more urgent." See Anne Atkins, *Split Image* (London: Hodder & Stoughton, 1998), p. 253.

about. It's about us being one with Christ. About us growing up "in all aspects into Him who is the head, even Christ" (Eph 4:15). God also has arranged for us to reign (Rev 22:5; 2 Tim 2:12). Someday each of us will reign, but none of will reign as the head.

Until we learn this, until we have it settled in our minds that Christ—and no one else—is the church's head, I don't think we're ready to talk about other matters of church order. For whenever we attempt to inaugurate someone other than Christ to be the head, inadvertently we forfeit an aspect of our freedom. Unwittingly we end up subjecting ourselves to the very yoke of slavery (that is, slavery to sin) from which Christ has effectively released us. Galatians 5:1 says, "It was for freedom that Christ set us free." He did not set us free so that we could attempt to displace him. Christ set us free so that we would be free. Free from death. Free from sin. Free from selfish ambition. Free from deception. Free from dishonesty. Free from religious hypocrisy. God wants us to be free so that we can show the world what it means to be reconciled to God through Christ (2 Cor 5:18).

God also intends for Christian men and women to be fully reconciled to one another. In Christ, we have been made one (Gal 3:28). While to some it may appear that Christian men and women are already fully unified, the indicators say that we are not. If we were unified, we would not be embroiled in such a heated debate about the parameters for women in the church. Instead, we might be focused on mobilizing laborers for the gospel.

This is where repentance comes in. Some of us need to repent from feeling threatened by the giftedness of others. The Bible says, "But if you have bitter jealousy and selfish ambition in your heart, do not be arrogant and lie against the truth. This wisdom is . . . demonic" (Jas 3:14-15). Selfish ambition is of the devil. It is not from God above. I know firsthand how destructive my own selfish ambition can be. As James puts it, where selfish ambition exists, there is "disorder" and "every evil thing" (Jas 3:16). This verse couldn't be more relevant to the subject of women in the church. For if we want to establish church order, then we have to put away the disorder that arises from our selfish ambition. In other words, we have to repent.

To be clear, I am not saying that people must repent from their doctrinal differences. Nor am I saying that diversity of conviction isn't good. Instead, I am saying the mere topic of women in ministry is uncomfortable. Many of us dread it because we know it's complicated; thus we'd just as soon not try to sort it out. I understand. Just as I didn't want to write this book, others may not want to read it. It's painful for the church to consider our sins against women. It's hard to come to terms with what we've done and what we're doing. It is humbling to realize that we have failed to treat men and women lovingly without partiality. I have failed in this. Who hasn't?

Overall, I believe that the debate on women in ministry has been improperly reduced to a debate about roles. The church is prone to say that women should do this and not do that when her activity is not the issue. As I see it, the confusion in the church ultimately stems from a more fundamental question of relationships. The church has not yet learned how to relate to Christian women who, in light of their ministry calling, have chosen to walk an unconventional path. Though I'm getting ahead of myself, let me try to illustrate what I mean.

I have been told that Christian women in Korea feel devastated socially if they turn thirty before marriage. Evidently they feel challenged, even in the church, to find their role. As I see it, the issue of their role is not the problem. The problem, rather, lies in everyone around them who feels at a loss to know how to relate to them as single Christian women. My single female friends in the United States, especially those over the age of forty who have never been married, constantly describe the same ordeal. They feel that many Christians do not know how to relate to them comfortably. Instead, people want to know "how they're coping" with their singleness and lack of motherhood. In other words, they want to know how they're coping with their conventional rolelessness.

Conversely, it seems that Christians also feel uncomfortable when a woman in the church begins to attain an excessive rolefulness, if you will. In other words, we begin to squirm when a woman accepts a visible position of public leadership. Thus we start to wonder about Anne Graham Lotz, a daughter of Billy Graham, because she is a she, and she is a preacher in our midst.

Granted, on the surface the debate about women has to do with proper roles. But underneath, it has to do with the more complex question of the God-given nature of women. Followers of Christ are struggling to figure out how it is that female human beings can be made in the image of God who reveals himself as "he." On top of that, we're arguing about culture and perspectives and the authority of the Bible. In truth, we are arguing about a multitude of things because the question of women's identity inevitably is connected to a multitude of other related factors. So many questions come to mind. For instance, what does it mean to be a woman? What does it mean to be a man? Why do an inordinate number of men avoid the church? Would even fewer men attend if women served as pastors and preachers? What are we going to do about the divorce rate? What about women who feel convicted to stay at home and rear their kids? What about the Bible? What about the church being true to obey God's Word?

In light of this, our foremost concern, at least in conversation, is to raise the red flag of 1 Timothy 2:12-14, which is usually translated, "But I do not allow a woman to teach or exercise authority over a man, but to remain quiet. For it was Adam who was first created, and then Eve. And it was not Adam who was deceived, but the woman being deceived, fell into transgression."

No doubt this passage is prominent in the debate. In fact, it is mentioned so often throughout the rest of the book that I refer to it and the verses that surround it as 1 Timothy 2. Nevertheless, I do not believe that the "problem" of women in ministry boils down to a collision between feminist theology and the timeless teaching of Paul. In my view, the problem is more basic than that.

TACKLING A TOUGH PROBLEM IN THE CHURCH

Most of us are aware of the global trends of feminism spreading throughout the world and seeping sometimes into the church. At the extreme end of the movement, women are claiming the right to be sexually promiscuous, to live as lesbians and to abort their unborn children. I agree that it is not God's way for women to come barreling in making personal demands for themselves. But I would like to add that it's not God's way for men either. It's not God's way for women to interact as mutual lovers, but it's not God's way for men either. It is not God's way for mothers to abandon their children either born or unborn. And yet, it's not God's way for fathers either. In the kingdom of God, there is no double standard. All of us are responsible to live for God, and yet all of us are guilty of living primarily for ourselves.

The apostle Paul put it plainly: "There is none righteous, not even one. There is none who understands. There is none who seeks for God. All have turned aside, together they have become useless. There is none who does good. There is not even one" (Rom 3:10-12).

Christians know that God's way is offensive to the world. But sometimes we forget that God's way can also be offensive to us Christians. None of us is naturally inclined toward God. All of us stand in constant need of correction. For obvious reasons, I cannot say with integrity, "Get it right as I have it right," but I can say, "Repent as I repent." All of us are contributors to the problems between men and women; thus all of us are part of the solution.

I am writing this book because I have hope that men and women in the church can build new bridges of trust (1 Cor 13:8). I think it's realistic to believe that we can change. We *can* repent and build more integrity within ourselves as well as in our local church communities. We can also seek to heal our relationships. But in order to do this, we have to come to grips with our current condition and engage in some unsettling conversations. We also have to lean on God in prayer.

THE PURPOSE OF THIS BOOK

This book introduces a theology of women woven into the narrative of my story. It expresses my rendition of a complex issue that is weighing down heavily upon the church. Notice I didn't say it's an issue that is weighing down heavily upon women. No, this issue is everybody's issue, because it has to do with women and men. It is true that motherhood is strictly a women's issue. But it's not true that parenthood is. Nor is it true that women in church leadership pertains only to women. Church leadership is a general subject; hence it involves the whole church.

Unlike some reference books that are written on this topic, my book is not meant for pick-up-and-put-down use. Instead, it represents one author's attempt to challenge believers along with myself to examine our assumptions about women and men and see if they're biblical or not. It is also meant to interpret the debate in evangelicalism and explain why the two sides collide.

For the record, it is not my goal to mirror everybody who reads this. Instead, my aim is to communicate true stories that typify men and women in the church. If you find yourself thinking, *This doesn't describe me,* then consider that it probably describes someone else. If you find yourself feeling convicted, then you are similar to me. I am not an innocent party when it comes to this debate. Perhaps that is why my overall conviction is to stimulate Christians to face the truth, even if the truth indicts us.

To offer a sneak preview, I can tell you twelve assertions in this book:

1. Both sides of the debate are radically revising church tradition. The notion of women being equal in personhood to men is a relatively novel idea, or rather, a biblical one that only recently has been renewed.

2. Both sides of the debate are trying to be biblical.

3. Both sides are also mixed. Complementarian thought is usually a mix of Bible and traditionalism. Egalitarian thought is usually a mix of Bible and feminism.

4. It is possible to affirm women leaders in the church without becoming a feminist. Feminism is about women's power. Christianity is about Christ's power.

5. It is possible to believe in complementarity of the sexes without reaffirming church tradition. Church tradition says that women are inferior; Christianity does not.

6. The Scriptures nowhere say to pursue "biblical manhood" or "biblical womanhood." The Bible commands us rather to become like Christ (Phil 2:5-11; I Pet 2:21-23).

7. There are no problem verses in the Bible. First Timothy 2 is inspired by God and therefore not a problem per se.

8. Neither side of the debate promotes a straightforward reading of I Timothy 2:12-15. Instead, both nuance their interpretations of the passage.

9. The word *head* in Ephesians 5 ("the husband is the head of the wife") does not mean "authority" or "source" or "covering."

10. Many Christians, such as myself, have sinned by being prejudiced against women and partial to men. This kind of behavior is contrary to the teachings of Scripture (Mk 12:14; I Tim 5:21; Rom 2:11).

11. The only way that Christians can resolve this debate is for each one of us to repent from our own sins.

12. Men and women in the church can begin to build consensus, but only through relationships of trust (I Cor 13:8).

There are questions at the end of each remaining chapter. I wrote them for the purpose of facilitating discussion among my readers. There are also many footnotes included. If you're the type of reader who would rather move past them, then do so. Footnotes aren't for everyone. My philosophy is that even if you feel burdened by footnotes, there's a benefit to having them—because when you *ignore* them, you get to turn the page a little sooner. (Psychologically it's sort of like swimming with flippers. You get the feeling with flippers that you can swim faster. Likewise, skipping footnotes makes you feel like you can read faster.) If, by contrast, you're the type of reader who savors footnotes, then perhaps you will be happy that they are nicely set before you rather than packaged less accessibly as endnotes.

THE CHALLENGE OF THIS BOOK

From the start of my research, I have felt convicted by a well-known passage in 1 Peter:

> For you have been called for this purpose, since Christ also suffered for you, leaving you an example for you to follow in His steps, who committed no sin, nor was any deceit found in His mouth; and while being reviled, He did not revile in return; while suffering he uttered no threats, but kept entrusting Himself to Him who judges righteously. (1 Pet 2:21-23)

Every time I read this, I see the word *you*. God has called "you," meaning me, for this purpose, since Christ suffered for "you," meaning me, and left me an example for me to follow in his steps.

Though many people might still argue that women are entitled to the political right to lead in the realm of church government, I do not concur. Within the kingdom of God, people have only one right. The Bible says that all who receive Christ as Savior and Lord, to them God gives "the right" to become children of God (Jn 1:12). That one right is sufficient. As long as I have the right to be a child of God, then my identity on earth cannot be threatened. I am God's child, an heir of the kingdom, empowered by the Spirit of the Lord.

Indeed, all Christians easily can afford to confess that we don't have rights in the democratic sense of the word. For instance, it is not my right to be loved by other people. It is the duty of all others to love me, because God commands other individuals to love me as they love themselves (Mt 22:39). But duties are distinguished from rights.[5] Thus Christian feminists who insistently proclaim that women have the right to be ordained or the right to be treated fairly have no biblical basis on which to stand. No Christian has the right to lead. No Christian is entitled to demand such a right for our-

---

[5]The Enlightenment philosopher Immanuel Kant is the one who persuaded Western culture to believe that rights are defined by others' duties. To learn the difference between Kantian ethics and Christian ethics, see Steve Wilkens, *Beyond Bumper Sticker Ethics* (Downers Grove, Ill.: InterVarsity Press, 1995), pp. 99-115.

selves. The Bible does not say to lead one another. It says to "love one another." Once we do that, we won't have a thought about clamoring for our
positions anymore. Instead, we'll be like him who came to serve (Mk 9:34;
10:35-45).

In closing, I acknowledge that God has not commissioned me to enter
this debate and settle the matter conclusively. He has called me to something
higher and more painful. He has called me to repent from my sins, speak the
truth, suffer for his sake, love other people and entrust myself to him who
judges righteously. This is his call to all believers. In the past we have failed
to follow in his steps. But that is no excuse. It's not too late to make a better
decision.

DISCUSSION QUESTIONS

1. Which chapter in this book are you most excited to read? What interests
   you about it?

2. Why are you reading this book? What are some of your most pressing
   questions regarding men and women in the church? What are you hoping
   to learn?

3. What do women in your local church hear? What are they told about
   their participation in the church?

4. What does it mean to "show the full color of your plume"? Do you think
   it's wise to advise Christian women not show the full color of their
   plumes? Why or why not?

3

THE PRIMACY OF SCRIPTURE

The grass withers, the flower fades,
But the word of our God stands forever.
ISAIAH 40:8

On a national level, conservative evangelicals have begun to polarize into two incompatible groups: complementarians and egalitarians. For example, Rebecca Merrill Groothuis[1] is an egalitarian. She believes that ministry roles are interchangeable for men and women who are suitably gifted. Though not a professor herself, she is scholarly and well-studied, having written two books.[2] She also is a strict inerrantist.

Wayne Grudem is a complementarian. He believes that certain ministry roles, such as pastor, preacher and elder, should be filled only by men. Like Groothuis, Grudem upholds the doctrine of inerrancy in the sense that he believes all Scripture is authoritative and true and inerrant in the original manuscripts.[3] Currently he serves as a professor of theology at Phoenix Seminary. Before that, he was one of my teachers at Trinity Evangelical Divinity

---

[1]Douglas Groothuis, her husband, currently serves on the faculty of Denver Seminary.

[2]Rebecca Merrill Groothuis, *Women Caught in the Conflict* (Grand Rapids, Mich.: Baker, 1994) and *Good News for Women* (Grand Rapids, Mich.: Baker, 1997). She has another book coedited with Ron Pierce, to be published by InterVarsity Press in 2004.

[3]For a more in-depth discussion, see Norman L. Geisler, ed., *Inerrancy* (Grand Rapids, Mich.: Zondervan, 1980).

School.[4] By my request, he played the role of second reader for my doctoral dissertation. I benefited greatly from his input. Thanks in part to Dr. Grudem, I became Dr. Sarah Sumner.

In 1995 Wayne Grudem copioneered the Council on Biblical Manhood and Womanhood (CBMW). He also cofounded a newsletter called the *CBMW News*, which later became the *Journal for Biblical Manhood and Womanhood (JBMW)*.[5] With John Piper, he also coedited an extensive book entitled *Recovering Biblical Manhood and Womanhood*.[6] Though Piper and Grudem have been extremely influential in Southern Baptist circles, neither is Southern Baptist. John Piper is Baptist, but he belongs to the Baptist General Conference. Wayne Grudem is a Vineyard charismatic who believes that women can prophesy and speak in tongues at church as long as they don't preach the Sunday sermon or teach men. Not all complementarians agree with everything said by Piper and Grudem, the two leading voices for that group. But there is a strong consensus among many complementarian leaders that God has established gender-based roles for marriage and ministry.

Egalitarians are organized in a group called Christians for Biblical Equality (CBE). Conservative Christian scholars such as Ron Pierce and Gordon Fee are members of CBE; they and many others have a built a biblical case for women in leadership. I am not a member of CBE.

EVALUATING CHURCH TRADITION

As one might expect, complementarians and egalitarians are often caricatured. For example, complementarians are tagged as legalistic (insensitive to

---

[4]When I was Wayne Grudem's student, he and I engaged sometimes in fairly lively discussions during his class. Yet both of us were able to refrain from personalizing the other's argument. I remember being in K-41 lecture hall one afternoon in a class of seventy or eighty students when Dr. Grudem and I bantered back and forth in front of everyone in hearty disagreement about the mystery of predestination and free will. After class Dr. Grudem and I rushed to make sure that neither felt offended by the other. And we didn't.

[5]Wayne Grudem has written other books as well, most notably *Systematic Theology* (Grand Rapids, Mich.: Zondervan, 1994).

[6]I have met John Piper only once for approximately fifteen minutes when I chauffeured him to the train station near Trinity.

the spirit of the law), and egalitarians are labeled as lax (inattentive to the letter of the law). Both accusations may to some extent manifest an element of truth, but neither is entirely fair.

Unfortunately, complementarians are often referred to as "traditionalists" rather than as "complementarians." Egalitarians, in turn, are frequently labeled as "feminists" rather than "egalitarians." It's true that most egalitarians consider themselves to be evangelical feminists, but that is not the same as being a radical feminist or a secular feminist who holds a low view of the Bible. Egalitarians, then, are evangelical feminists, ones who hold a high view of the Word.

One more thing every reader needs to know—complementarians and egalitarians are conservative Protestants.[7] That is, both sides believe in the primacy of Scripture. In other words, both sides agree that the authority of Scripture is higher than the authority of church tradition.[8] While tradition is duly honored, it should always be subjected to the God-inspired authority of the Word. Practically speaking, then, Scripture should prevail if tradition ever seems to contradict it.

Curiously, the current debate has not been focused on evaluating the biblical accuracy of the tradition. In fact, most born-again believers apprised of this debate are unapprised of the influence of tradition. Very few conservatives have been taught to consider the biases against women that tradition has taught us to bring into our reading of the text. On the contrary, we have been assured that the Spirit will be faithful to prevent us from such error. Unfortunately that assumption is mistaken.

Think about it. If the Spirit of God guided everyone's reading such that none of us ever made errors, then Spirit-filled Christians would all agree on

---

[7]There may be Christians outside the evangelical Protestant camp who would see themselves as complementarians or egalitarians. But for the most part this is an in-house debate.

[8]John Wesley preached the rule of testing all tradition (along with reason and experience) against the Bible. Wesley said, "I allow no other rule, whether faith or practice, than the Holy Scriptures." Wesley counted reason, experience and tradition as secondary sources that serve to confirm, evaluate and apply what is found in Scripture. See Don Thorsen, *The Wesleyan Quadrilateral* (Grand Rapids, Mich.: Zondervan, 1990), p. 127.

what is the right interpretation. In reality, fellow elders sitting side by side on the same church board don't always see eye to eye. The Spirit guides our reading and enlightens our understanding, but he doesn't grant us perfect comprehension. Nor does he prevent us from being partial. It is our responsibility, therefore, to test our assumptions against the biblical text as we try to understand the text itself.

THE TRADITIONAL VIEW OF WOMEN

Most Christians don't know it, but complementarians and egalitarians have something else in common. Both are trying hard to bring reform to the church's view of women. But they are doing it in two different ways. Whereas complementarians want Christians to believe that women's *worth* is equal to men's, egalitarians want Christians to believe that women's *rights* are equal to men's.[9] Both are revising church tradition.

Church tradition says that women are by nature lower than men. Indeed, most of the church fathers promoted this traditional belief. For instance, in the third century A.D. Tertullian wrote a poignant treatise entitled "On the Dress of Women" and presented it to a female audience. The treatise includes these exhortations:

> If there dwelt upon earth a faith as great as is the reward of faith which is expected in the heavens, no one of you at all, best beloved sisters, from the time that she had first "known the Lord," and learned (the truth) concerning her own (that is woman's) condition, would have desired too gladsome (not to say too ostentatious) a style of dress; so as not to go about in humble garb, and rather to affect meanness of appearance, walking about as Eve mourning and repentant, in order that by every garb of penitence she might the more fully expiate that which she derives from Eve,—the ignominy, I mean, of the first sin, and the odium (attaching to her as the cause) of human perdition. . . .
>
> And do you not know that you are (each) an Eve? The sentence of God on

---

[9]Egalitarians very much agree that women's worth is equal to men's. But as they see it, her worth entitles her to exercise equal rights.

this sex of yours lives in this age: the guilt must of necessity live too. *You* are the devil's gateway: *you* are the unsealer of that (forbidden) tree: *you* are the first deserter of the divine law: *you* are she who persuaded him whom the devil was not valiant enough to attack. *You* destroyed so easily God's image, man. On account of *your* desert—that is, death—even the Son of God had to die. And you think about adorning yourself over and above your "tunics of skins" (Gen 3:21)?[10]

The influence of Tertullian is incalculable. This is the same theologian who coined the word *Trinity*, developed certain aspects of the doctrine of original sin and defended the two natures of Christ. Yet it was he who believed that women are to blame for the entrance of sin into the world. Tertullian is famous for having uttered the words "God's judgment of this sex lives on."

When one pastor heard me say this, he responded defensively, "The teaching of Tertullian is way too distant and removed to have any bearing on what contemporary Christians think of women." In one sense, I agree. Today hardly a believer would ever want to say that women "must of necessity" bear "the guilt" of original sin. Neither Piper nor Grudem would ever want to say that either. Today we're not arguing about women's perpetual guilt for the fall of humankind because conservative evangelicals don't believe that. As Christians, we trust in the atonement of Christ to take away the sins of all who put their faith in the Messiah. With that, we tell ourselves that we do not believe that women are inferior to men. But as I will try to show throughout the rest of this book, our theology of women is not so pure.

Let's take another look at Tertullian. As a matter of principle, Tertullian considered it impossible to believe that Paul the apostle ever would have allowed a Christian woman—"this sex"—to baptize any person, much less teach a man. In his treatise "On Baptism" he interjects, "For how credible would it seem, that he who has not permitted a woman even to learn with

---

[10]Tertullian, "On the Dress of Women," trans. S. Thelwall, *Ante-Nicene Fathers*, ed. Alexander Roberts, 10 vols. (Peabody, Mass.: Hendrickson, 1994), 4:14.

over-boldness, should give a female the power of teaching and of baptizing!
'Let them be silent,' he says, 'and at home consult their own husbands' (I Cor
14:34-35)."[11]

Is it fair for us to imagine that Tertullian may have been biased? I say it is.
For if everyone agreed with Tertullian's point of view, then women would be
forbidden even to "learn with over-boldness." I suppose that would mean
that women could not attend seminary or study the Bible privately too much.
Instead, women would be required to hold back.

HOW THE TRADITIONAL VIEW
OF WOMEN IS BEING REVISED

Of all the seminaries in the United States, I chose to attend Trinity Evangelical Divinity School in Deerfield, Illinois, specifically because the men on the
faculty maintain a very high view of Scripture. For five years I had the privilege to study with professors such as Dr. Wayne Grudem, Dr. Douglas
Moo,[12] Dr. Ray Ortlund Jr.[13] and others. All three of these professors are
strict complementarians; that is, all of them believe in limited roles for women
in church leadership. Yet none of them are forwarding Tertullian's belief that
women should be prohibited from learning.

In contradistinction from church tradition, the award-winning book *Recovering Biblical Manhood and Womanhood,* edited by John Piper and Wayne Grudem, says it is misrepresentative for anyone to say that complementarians
believe women should not be privileged to study the Scriptures. As one contributor puts it, "There are no role distinctions for learning from Christ . . .
certainly women *are* to learn and apply the Word of God. This is vitally important."[14] Moo agrees. Commenting on I Timothy 2:11, he goes on to say,
"That Paul wants Christian women to learn is an important point, for such

---

[11]Tertullian, "On Baptism," trans. S. Thelwall, *Ante-Nicene Fathers,* ed. Alexander Roberts, 10 vols. (Pea-
    body, Mass.: Hendrickson, 1994), 3:677.
[12]Dr. Moo now teaches at Wheaton College.
[13]Dr. Ray Ortlund Jr. now serves as a senior pastor in Atlanta.
[14]James Borland, "Women in the Life and Teachings of Jesus," in *Recovering Biblical Manhood and Womanhood,*
    ed. John Piper and Wayne Grudem (Wheaton, Ill.: Crossway, 1991), p. 118.

a practice was not generally encouraged by the Jews."[15]

As you can see, each man openly counters church tradition. Indeed, for the most part, nearly all evangelicals have dramatically departed from Tertullian's way of thinking about women. We have also departed from the traditional views of three other luminaries of the past: Ambrose, Augustine and Aquinas. There's a noticeable difference between the views of these church fathers and the views of my complementarian professors at Trinity.

Consider Ambrose, the bishop of Milan from 374 to 397. In his treatise "On Paradise," Ambrose wrote, "In fact, even though the man was created outside Paradise (i.e., in an inferior place), he is found to be superior, while woman, though created in a better place (i.e., inside Paradise) is found inferior."[16] Apparently, for Ambrose, no qualification needs to be made. To him, it was a brute fact of nature that men are superior to women. But for Ortlund, it is not. Ortlund proclaims that the equality of personhood, value and dignity for the entire human race is a brute fact of Christian theology.[17] Or to quote Piper, "boasting in either sex as superior to the other is folly."[18]

Next, take Augustine—probably the most renowned theologian in church history. Augustine believed that God did not create the woman for any reason other than procreation. Explicitly he said:

> If it were not the case that the woman was created to be man's helper specifically for the production of children, then why would she have been created as a "helper" (Gen. 2:18)? Was it so that she might work the land with him? No

---

[15]At the same time, Moo says the apostle Paul's point is to explain the manner in which women should learn. See Douglas Moo, "What Does It Mean Not to Teach or Have Authority Over Men? I Timothy 2:11-15" in *Recovering Biblical Manhood and Womanhood*, ed. John Piper and Wayne Grudem (Wheaton, Ill.: Crossway, 1991), p. 183.

[16]Ambrose, "On Paradise," quoted in Elizabeth A. Clark, *Women in the Early Church*, ed. Thomas Halton, Message of the Fathers of the Church 13 (Collegeville, Minn.: Liturgical Press, 1983), p. 30.

[17]See Ray Ortlund Jr., "Male-Female Equality and Male Headship: Genesis 1—3" in *Recovering Biblical Manhood and Womanhood*, ed. John Piper and Wayne Grudem (Wheaton, Ill.: Crossway, 1991), p. 100.

[18]See John Piper, "A Vision of Biblical Complementarity: Manhood and Womanhood Defined According to the Bible" in *Recovering Biblical Manhood and Womanhood*, ed. John Piper and Wayne Grudem (Wheaton, Ill.: Crossway, 1991), p. 49.

because there did not yet exist any such labor for which he needed a helper, and even if such work had been required, a male would have made a better assistant. One can also posit that the reason for her creation as a helper had to do with the companionship she could provide for the man, if perhaps he got bored with his solitude. Yet for company and conversation, how much more agreeable it is for two male friends to dwell together than for a man and a woman! . . . I cannot think of any reason for woman's being made as man's helper, if we dismiss the reason of procreation.[19]

I cannot overemphasize how dissimilar this view is from today's conservative views on both sides of the debate.

I remember one day in the library when Wayne Grudem asked me in a puzzled tone of voice, "What are you going to do when you graduate?" I told him, "I don't know." Politely he conveyed that I might not be able to find a job for myself that would utilize my theological training, but never did he suggest that my purpose in life was strictly for procreation.

Third, it is revealing to read a line from Thomas Aquinas.[20] He said that women are dominated by sexual appetite and that men are ruled by reason.[21] (How true is that?) Another thing Thomas said was that women depend on men for everything in life while men depend on women only for procreation.[22] Obviously things have changed. Many pastors today heavily depend on women to do most of the work. Women are the ones who usually care for the poor and visit the sick and pray for those in need. Women run the nurseries, answer the church phone and organize most church events. Contemporary pastors rely so much on women that many Christian women feel used. Aquinas did not have a category for using Christian

[19]Augustine, "Literal Commentary on Genesis," quoted in *Women in the Early Church*, pp. 28-29. I use Clark's wording because her translation of Augustine is relatively easy to understand.
[20]Though Aquinas is often associated with Roman Catholic thinking, it is unreasonable to imagine that his influence in Christendom is neatly contained within the confines of the walls of the Catholic church. For one thing, he predates the Reformation by three hundred years; for another thing, his Aristotelian theology was celebrated throughout the Western church.
[21]See Ruth Tucker and Walter L. Liefeld, *Daughters of the Church* (Grand Rapids, Mich.: Zondervan, 1987), p. 164. Tucker and Liefeld use the language of Will Durant, who in turn summarizes Aquinas.
[22]Ibid.

women, because he did not see women as useful. Aquinas went even further, reducing the value of women as mothers. He said, "Children ought to love their father more than their mother."[23] Though many conservative pastors think it's good to be traditional in their thinking about women, surely we can see that it is not. If anyone ever dared to preach a truly traditional sermon on the nature of women, they would instantly be judged as bigoted and unfit to teach the Word.

Piper and Grudem understand this. In the preface of their book, they insert as an opening caveat, "We are uncomfortable with the term 'traditionalist' because it implies an unwillingness to let Scripture challenge traditional patterns of behavior."[24]

TWO NOVEL IDEAS

If the church fathers were prejudiced against women, and we know it, then we should be careful not to absorb their bias. Traditional Christian thinking is not the same thing as biblical thinking about women. Even someone as conservative as Daniel Doriani says that Tertullian's rhetoric is "loaded with . . . misogyny."[25] Thus I pose the question, Why would anyone look to a misogynist for help in discerning the biblical teaching on women? Misogynists are called misogynists because of their degrading view of women. The word *misogyny* literally means "hatred of women."

It is unwise to enshrine Tertullian as a leading authority on the proper role of women in the church. And yet, certain professors seem to do this. William Weinrich, for instance, argues for an all-male pastorate partly on the basis of

---

[23]The full quote is: "Strictly speaking, however, the father should be loved more than the mother. For the father and mother are loved as principles of our natural origin. Now the father is principle in a more excellent way than the mother, because he is the active principle, while the mother is a passive and material principle. Consequently, strictly speaking, the father is to be loved more." See Thomas Aquinas, *Summa Theologica,* quoted by Sister Prudence Allen, *The Concept of Woman: The Aristotelian Revolution 750 B.C.-A.D. 1250* (Grand Rapids, Mich.: Eerdmans, 1985), p. 405.

[24]Piper and Grudem, *Recovering Biblical Manhood and Womanhood,* p. xiv.

[25]Daniel Doriani, "Appendix I: History of the Interpretation of 1 Timothy 2" in *Women in the Church,* ed. Andreas Köstenberger, Thomas R. Schreiner and H. Scott Baldwin (Grand Rapids, Mich.: Baker, 1995), pp. 222-26.

church tradition.[26] He recognizes that "misogynous remarks and opinions of inferiority do exist" within the tradition.[27] But he summarily dismisses those misogynous remarks.[28] He cites Tertullian as a "representative voice" of the viewpoint that contends that "to men alone" it is given "to be pastors and sacramental ministers."[29]

It's critical for Christians to embrace church tradition, but not when it is unbiblical. When it comes to core issues of doctrinal truth, such as the doctrine of the Trinity, the teachings of the church fathers are instructive. But when it comes to other issues, such as the identity of Christian women, which are far less developed—and far less grounded in Scripture—the teachings of the church fathers need to be reconsidered and reformed.

It was customary, not biblical, for the church fathers to denounce the nature of women.[30] Most people in their culture did the same.[31] Women were

---

[26]For instance, he cites the *Statuta Ecclesiai antiqua* written by Gennadius of Marseilles (c. A.D. 480), which says, "A woman, however learned and holy, may not presume to teach men in the assembly" *(in conventu)*. See William Weinrich, "Women in the History of the Church: Learned and Holy, But Not Pastors," in *Recovering Biblical Manhood and Womanhood*, ed. John Piper and Wayne Grudem (Wheaton, Ill.: Crossway, 1991), p. 277.

[27]Ibid.

[28]Ibid. Weinrich argues that the language of the Gennadius' *Statuta*—"however learned and holy"—as well as the exaggerated language Innocent III used of Jesus' mother—"that Mary stands higher than all the apostles"—indicates that ultimately and officially considerations of intellect and sanctity were not surprising nor affirming of women in leadership. Throughout church history, Mary has been praised for her motherhood and faith in God. She is not representative of women in church leadership. Similarly, for it to be said that even learned and holy women "may not presume to teach men in the assembly" does not decisively indicate that Gennadius respected women as equals of men. He might have been saying that even when a woman is holy and learned, she is inferior to men. This kind of attitude is prevalent, not unusual.

[29]Weinrich, "Women in the History of the Church," p. 273.

[30]Tertullian, for instance, lived in a Roman culture conditioned by Cynics, Stoics, Neo-Pythagoreans, Neo-Platonists and Gnostics—all of whom practiced asceticism. In an ascetic culture, virginity is praised whereas marriage and women are degraded. See M. Rosamond Nugent, *Portrait of the Consecrated Woman in Greek Christian Literature of the First Four Centuries* (Washington, D.C.: Catholic University of America Press, 1941), pp. 1-5.

[31]Much of early Christian thought was shaped by some combination of the dissimilar influences of Plato and Aristotle, neither of whom was Christian. Whereas Plato believed that men and women were of the same nature and could act out the same virtues and functions, Aristotle believed women are a "privation of man" and thus are passive and irrational in relation to men and thus unequal in virtue. See Allen, *The Concept of Woman*, pp. 79-88.

seen as gullible and seductive and inferior.[32] Today this might sound crazy, almost fabricated, as if some radical, godless feminist made it up. But it's true, and Christians need to know it. In the past, the question of women's place in the church was a no-brainer. Women were assigned to subordinate roles because women themselves were thought to be essentially inferior.

Today we have rejected this idea. Today both sides of the current debate insist that women are not inferior to men. It's important for us to hear this because the concern keeps being raised that women in church leadership is a novel idea in church history. What I'm trying to say is that *women's equal worth* is a novel idea in church history. Both ideas are relatively new to Christian thinking. The commonly known phrase that men and women are "equal before God in personhood" did not come up until recently.[33] In that sense, evangelical feminism is no more revolutionary than the very conservative teachings of Grudem.

It's embarrassing for us to talk about this since most of us aren't informed about our history. No one ever told us that our Christian heritage is filled with awful ideas about women. No one ever told us about the residue of tradition and how it might be tainting our opinions. It's tough news to discover that our reading of the Scripture may not be as objective as we think.

Besides that, it's a little overwhelming to process the suggestion that God might desire to use the likes of us to reform a long tradition of the past. Most of us don't even read history, much less expect God to use us to make history. How many of us today are thinking about the way that our generation fits into the universal schema of church history? It's probably no big deal when any of us find out about historical transitions in the church. We can read about Luther and the Protestant Reformation without being riveted inside.

---

[32]There were exceptions. In A.D. 404, for example, Jerome said of a woman named Paula, "no talent was ever more tractable than hers. She was slow at speaking and quick at listening. . . . She had memorized the Scriptures . . . but even more she followed the spiritual understanding of Scripture. . . . She chanted the Psalms in Hebrew and her diction echoed no trace of the distinctive Latin character of the Latin language." See Jerome, Epistle 108, as translated and quoted by Clark, *Women in the Early Church*, pp. 163-64.

[33]To view the Danvers Statement, see <www.cbmw.org/AboutCBMW>.

But it takes faith to believe that God might be calling our generation to move the church into a more biblical practice.

Of course the Bible has not changed, nor has the timelessness of its truth. What has changed is our confidence in the tradition.

DISCUSSION QUESTIONS

1. What was your initial reaction when you read the excerpts from Tertullian, Ambrose, Augustine and Aquinas?

2. What is the difference between a biblical view of women and a traditional view of women?

3. What do you think about the church being informed by men such as Tertullian, whose writing about women is "loaded with misogyny"? Do you trust the early church fathers to have passed down a right interpretation of verses in the Scripture about women?

4. In what sense is the teaching of "women's equal worth" a revolutionary idea in the church?

4

EXCEPTIONAL WOMEN

*It is neither useful nor becoming
to await the result of slow remedies.*
JOHN CALVIN

Every generation produces gifted women who minister effectively to women and men. This book deals with the problem of relating to those women. How should we respond to the evidence of their fruitfulness and the passion they express for Jesus Christ?

It's hard to dismiss them. It's also hard for us to treat them as peers with Christian men because according to church tradition, the Bible plainly says women should be prohibited from preaching and pastoring and teaching the Bible to men. As the familiar argument goes, God created women to be followers, not leaders.

To be clear, it's not that conservative evangelicals prohibit Christian women from being leaders of other women and children, although that happens. Nor is it that conservative evangelicals fail to value women as members of the kingdom of God. Christian women *are* valued as mothers and wives and helpers of men and church members and teachers of children. They're regularly counted as mainstream members of the church. Women are baptized the same and preached to the same as the men are. Women, moreover, are equally invited to partake of the Lord's Supper if their conscience before God is clear.

No one is debating whether or not women can be full-fledged Christians (Gal 3:28). The debate has to do with women being able to use their spiritual gifts in the presence of the full congregation. To be more specific, the argument is about women and spiritual authority. Followers of Christ are arguing over the question of whether it's biblical or not for a woman to be permitted to exercise authority over men.

CONTRADICTIONS IN THE CHRISTIAN COMMUNITY

Carefully sorting out what conservatives believe can often be confusing, especially if one compares what is verbally said with what is promoted. For example, Anne Graham Lotz, a daughter of Billy Graham, is regularly invited to expound the Scriptures to groups that include Christian men. Even Southern Baptist Theological Seminary in Louisville, Kentucky, invited her to preach in chapel to a group of graduate students who are regularly being taught that it's wrong for a woman to proclaim the gospel publicly to men. She was also invited to preach to men at a pastors' conference where many of the participants physically turned their backs to her in the middle of her sermon.

They were pastors—not new Christians—who had signed up for a conference at which she was a speaker, paid their fees, traveled to get there, then decided on the premises to protest collectively against her. Why did they bother to come? And why didn't they just leave? And how could they accuse her of sinning on them when they sat there listening to her? When she stood up to preach, they may have turned their backs, but they did not walk away. So Anne Graham Lotz zealously preached to their backs.[1] There they sat, making a moot point by showing up and staying in the room

Why do Christian women keep proclaiming God's Word to crowds of conservative believers? Because we invite them to. We pay them honorariums

---

[1]Wendy Murray Zoba, "Angel in the Pulpit," *Christianity Today*, April 5, 1999, p. 58.

and arrange for them to join us because we don't want to miss their awesome sermons. Not too long ago Elisabeth Elliot drew the largest crowd of any chapel service in the history of Azusa Pacific University (APU). We had to open six sites because so many people drove in locally or flew in from other states to hear what she had to say—about the Word of God.

ProWomen, Yet Antifeminism

Most Christians want to welcome women in ministry, though not apart from exercising a certain measure of caution. While many Christian leaders oppose feminist theology, some of those same people champion Christian women. For example, Dr. Carl F. H. Henry, a world-class theologian known for his fierce conservatism, wrote a letter of recommendation for me to be hired to teach theology as an adjunct professor at Wheaton College. Two years later, he recommended me again, this time for my post at Azusa Pacific University, where I currently serve as chair of the department of ministry in Haggard Graduate School of Theology. Dr. Henry has been a friend and mentor to me ever since I met him in 1990.

One day Dr. Henry said to me tongue in cheek with a gleam in his eye, "You know, doing this goes against my beliefs."

I asked, "Then how come you're helping me?"

He answered, "Because I believe God is calling you to minister."

Dr. Henry serves on the Board of Reference for the Council on Biblical Manhood and Womanhood (CBMW), a coalition of conservatives that strongly opposes all types of feminism, but that doesn't mean he is unsupportive of women.[2] For more than ten years, Dr. Henry has consistently exhorted me to "be a voice in the kingdom!" The last time he said this to me was in a personal letter written on September 21, 2001. Seven years before that, Dr. Henry gave me a handwritten list of things he predicted I might do. Among the things he listed were serving as a full-time teaching pastor in a

---

[2]Dr. Henry is an antifeminist insofar as he abhors the things associated with secular feminism such as abortion, lesbianism and goddess worship. To hear directly from him, see one portion of his magnum opus, Carl F. H. Henry, *God, Revelation and Authority*, 6 vols. (Waco, Tex.: Word, 1979), 5:157-64.

local church, working as a professor of theology, traveling as an itinerant circuit speaker and becoming a prolific Christian author. Dr. Henry encouraged me to pursue any combination of these things. What is more, Dr. Henry let me lecture in his class, edit his writing and work for him as his assistant.

Though Dr. Henry stands out as being especially supportive, his way of reaching out to me by no means was unique. For example, a different member of the CBMW board counseled me not to retract from participating in the role of paid pastoral leadership. I once had an appointment scheduled with him one hour before he was to leave for his sabbatical overseas. The weather in Chicago was terrible that day; it was snowy and dreary and windy. As I drove toward the seminary, I began to realize that I wasn't going to make it in time. Knowing my opportunity to speak with him had dwindled to approximately twenty minutes, I decided to stop and call him from a pay phone outside of a local gas station. I'll always remember that definitive winter moment, shivering in the snow with an icy phone pressed against my ear.

With no time to spare, point blank I asked him what he thought about me joining the staff at Willow Creek, in which part of my role was to serve as a leader over men. Plainly he answered, "God calls certain women to be a Priscilla."

Taking courage from that, I asked him further, "Then what am I supposed to do?"

He said, "Be Priscilla. I think you're a Priscilla."

The New Testament describes Priscilla as a prominent woman in the early church in Ephesus. She and her husband, Aquila, planted a church "in their house" (Rom 16:5), where presumably she taught the Bible, even to other pastors and leaders. In fact, Priscilla is famous along with her husband for having tutored a man named Apollos. Apollos was not an unbeliever. On the contrary, Apollos was "mighty in the Scriptures" and "fervent in spirit," a man who taught "accurately" the facts about the ministry of Jesus (Acts 18:24-25). It's significant that Priscilla taught a man who had already been "instructed in the way of the Lord" (Acts 18:25). As my professor put it, Priscilla represents the gifted Christian women who are used by God in atypical ways. He said that some Christian women, like Priscilla, are "exceptional."[3]

When I hung up the phone, I realized my professor had given me the green light to serve on the church staff as freely as if I were a man. So there you have it again—an example of an antifeminist who isn't anti-women-in-ministry. I believe this represents the mindset of the majority of evangelical Christians. So many Christians sincerely desire to promote women ministers in the name of Jesus Christ. But they also want to refrain from compromising Scripture or advocating the feminist cause.[4]

I am here to testify that prominent Christian leaders such as Dr. Henry and Dr. Bill Bright are genuinely for Christian women. Bill Bright, founder of Campus Crusade for Christ, has told me face to face that Christian women leaders should have more latitude. He is so forthright that, without hesitation, he openly confesses that he hasn't helped women enough. He also told me recently that one of his top goals is to mobilize more women for the gospel.

REVISING CHURCH TRADITION

Over the years I have come to conclude that evangelicals are in conflict with each other because we are conflicted within ourselves. For instance, some of us are eager for one or two women to speak at church but hesitant to endorse a woman as a pastoral leader. Others of us are saying, "On a biblical level, I agree with the complementarians, but on a practical level, I agree with the egalitarians." Still others are saying, "I just don't like the feeling I get when women are allowed to speak in a formal church setting." Granted, there are those such as Groothuis and Grudem who don't appear to be conflicted.

---

[3]The idea of putting gifted women in a special category traces back at least as far as John Calvin. In reference to Deborah, Philip's daughters, Abigail, and other female prophets and teachers, Calvin said their cases are "extraordinary" and "do not overturn the ordinary rules of government by which he [God] intended we be bound." See John Calvin, *Commentaries on the Epistles to Timothy, Titus and Philemon* (Grand Rapids, Mich.: Baker, 1979), p. 67. Already one can see that Calvin's belief in "extraordinary" women precludes the idea that I Timothy presents a universal principle that prohibits all women from teaching and leading Christian men.

[4]I use the word *feminist* generically here to represent the blending of Christianity and feminism.

Groothuis believes that qualified women ought to be included at all levels of leadership. Grudem says they should not. But not all of us enjoy such clarity.

At stake is our conception of God. If God affirms women in church leadership, then why did he allow the tradition to exclude them for so long? Why didn't God intervene with correction any sooner? Church history demonstrates that in God's providence Christian women in the world have been leading and teaching since the time of Pentecost.[5] But church tradition, as we have seen, does not affirm that. Consequently, some of us get the feeling that if we question church tradition, we're questioning God.

I agree that church tradition should be honored.[6] But with that, I would say that tradition should continually be reformed. It is good for prayerful Christians to revise the tradition as long as we make it more biblical. But it's unsettling to let go of church tradition. It seems presumptuous to break away from part of our inherited past. Besides that, change is just plain hard.

Change is hard, even when we yearn for improvement.

To put this in perspective, past changes in the church have always been hard to effect. In every generation, reform is difficult, even for those who catalyze the changes. Look at the apostle Paul. He suffered in his efforts to get Gentiles included in the church. It was hard for him to expand the Jewish mind. Many of the early Jewish Christians resented Paul's understanding of the gospel. They didn't want to share the church with all the other believers in the world. Reread the book of Acts, and you will be reminded that Paul was a controversial person.

During the Reformation, John Calvin was controversial too. Calvin com-

---

[5]For an extensive account of women's participation in various forms of church leadership, see the bibliography of Ruth Tucker and Walter L. Liefeld, *Daughters of the Church* (Grand Rapids, Mich.: Zondervan, 1987), pp. 511-40, and of Dana L. Robert, *American Women in Mission* (Macon, Ga.: Mercer University Press, 1997), pp. 419-44.

[6] The Wesleyan quadrilateral, often referred to now as the Protestant quadrilateral, says that while Scripture alone is divinely inspired, it is not the only source of truth. Scripture is the primary source, and yet truth can also be identified outside of the Bible instrumentally through tradition, reason and experience. As Arthur Holmes puts it, "All truth is God's truth." See Arthur L. Holmes, *All Truth Is God's Truth* (Grand Rapids, Mich.: Eerdmans, 1977). Cf. Donald Thorsen, *The Wesleyan Quadrilateral* (Grand Rapids, Mich.: Zondervan, 1990).

plained that accusations came his way not because of any impropriety on his part but rather because he took the initiative to announce the need for change. Though Calvin is a hero to Protestants today, in the sixteenth century he and his associates were unsparingly accused of "rash and impious innovation."[7]

But what if God has decided yet again that it's time for another change within the church? What if all this hardship is leading to something?[8]

Could it be that the global trends of feminism coincide with God's plan to reform the way the church treats women?[9] After all, there is biblical precedent for God to use pagans to make his name known and act on behalf of the oppressed. Cyrus, king of Persia, was chosen of the Lord in spite of his false beliefs (Is 45:4). God used Cyrus to bring Israel back from Babylon. Would it be so unlike God to use the waves of feminism to reform the way that people experience church?

In 1544 Calvin wrote *The Necessity of Reforming the Church*, in which he said, "The question is not, Whether the Church labors under diseases both numerous and grievous, (this is admitted even by all the moderate judges,) but whether the diseases are of a kind the cure of which admits not of longer delay, and as to which, therefore, it is neither useful nor becoming to await the result of slow remedies."[10]

For almost two thousand years, the church's view of women, among many other things, has been "diseased." By God's providence, within the last cen-

---

[7]John Calvin, *The Necessity of Reforming the Church* (Chicago: Moody Press, 1994), p. 3.

[8]For anyone worried that church reform regarding women ultimately might lead to acceptance of homosexual practices among Christians, see William Webb, *Slaves, Women and Homosexuals* (Downers Grove, Ill.: InterVarsity Press, 2001). Webb offers an outstanding analysis of the biblical teaching against homosexuality. He also champions the biblical mandate to love other people, including homosexuals, as ourselves.

[9]The mistreatment of women in the church includes all kinds of things. One missionary couple told me, for instance, "Many conservative mission boards don't value the wife enough to provide her insurance. They don't value her time; she is to be flexible to meet the demands of her husband's schedule. She is often not given time or money to learn the language and then when the couple has to return due to the rising tension this causes, she is given the blame." (I took this quote from a personal e-mail dated July 21, 2002.)

[10]Calvin, *The Necessity of Reforming the Church*, p. i.

tury, it has become the "kind" of disease "the cure of which" can no longer be delayed.

THE WAY TO CHANGE A PARADIGM

With Bibles in hand, it is time to reevaluate the mindset evangelicals have inherited. This will not be easy. Our commonly shared mindset holds the status of a paradigm, and paradigms are not easily changed. A paradigm is a puzzle solver, a framework in which to organize a vast and complex set of data. The nature of a paradigm is such that it cannot change unless it is replaced with a new one. That is, the community will not let go of a former paradigm until people can obtain a new consensus.

In his ground-breaking book *The Structure of Scientific Revolutions* American philosopher Thomas Kuhn says, "History suggests that the road to a firm . . . consensus is extraordinarily arduous."[11] For example, Einstein's theories were not accepted by scientists until they were proven to be superior to the theories of Newton. Not only did the Einsteinian model of physics have to function as effectively as the Newtonian one, but also it had to account for certain unresolved problems that otherwise could not be explained.

If Kuhn is correct, then we can predict that the traditional Christian practice of limiting women in leadership will not be discarded until it is replaced by a paradigm that appears to be more adequate. That new paradigm will have to do more than merely function just as well as the old one. It will also have to criticize the old paradigm and then demonstrate convincingly that it answers some of the questions that the old paradigm cannot explain.

In the evangelical community, gifted Christian women are labeled as "exceptional" because they are anomalies to the paradigm. In other words, they don't fit within the framework that we're using to organize the biblical data. No matter how many times someone walks up to us Christians and says, "Your framework is inadequate because it doesn't account for the giftedness

---

[11]Thomas S. Kuhn, *The Structure of Scientific Revolutions* (Chicago: University of Chicago Press, 1962), p. 15.

of Anne Graham Lotz," the paradigm will not change unless another paradigm can effectively do three things:

1. account for the biblical data just as well or better than the last one;

2. magnify the unresolved problems of the old paradigm all the way to the extent that the community becomes able to recognize those problems as problems;

3. provide some additional solutions.

That describes the reality of our current situation because that is the nature of a paradigm.

DISCUSSION QUESTIONS

1. What is your vision for women in the church? Describe what you think is a good biblical paradigm for the church.

2. What is your view of Christian women speakers such as Anne Graham Lotz? On what basis do you believe that she should, or should not, preach God's Word to men?

3. Why is it that women are sometimes invited to speak in settings where it's usually deemed unbiblical? Have you ever seen that happen?

4. In what way, if any, has the church has been diseased in its thinking about women? In what ways has it tended to be healthy?

5

IS IT BETTER TO BE A MAN
THAN A WOMAN?

*Truly I say to you, unless you are converted and become like children, you shall
not enter the kingdom of heaven.*

MATTHEW 18:3

One of my colleagues who was teaching a class on men and women in
ministry said her students wanted to know if it is better to be a man than a
woman. I am always intrigued by the fact that that question arises. It seems
as though it wouldn't, but it does. My response was to offer her this chapter,
which had already been written. Unfortunately the need for a chapter such
as this is prevalent in the Christian community. I believe the reason this question comes up is because Christians are confused about verses in the Bible
such as I Corinthians 11:7.

First Corinthians 11:7 says, "For a man . . . is the image and glory of God;
but the woman is the glory of man." The text is plain. It says a man is the
image of God. In Greek, that word *man* means "male." Now notice, it says a
man is the image of God. Nowhere does the Bible say woman is the image of
God, not even in Genesis 1. Genesis 1:27 says, "God created man in His own
image, in the image of God He created him; male and female He created
them." The biblical wording is distinct. Two different phrases, "is the image"

and "in the image," are used. First Corinthians says a man (a male) "is the image" of God. Genesis says man, male and female, was created "in the image" of God.

It is helpful to examine I Corinthians 11:7 as it was understood by an early church father, Augustine. Augustine's interpretation is significant because of its effect on you and me. Augustine's exegesis influenced church tradition to pass down the belief that men are more like God than women are. It's true that men are more like Jesus with regard to his maleness.[1] But as I will try to show, that doesn't mean that it's better to be a man than a woman.

AUGUSTINE'S COMMENTARY

Approximately sixteen hundred years ago Augustine drew the church's attention to the distinct wording of I Corinthians 11:7 that man is the image of God. Augustine is the one who drew *my* attention to the wording of this verse. Before I read Augustine, it never occurred to me that the biblical phrase "is the image" might be understood as a biblical proof text to verify male superiority.

According to Augustine, a woman is human,[2] but she is not the image of God. To some people, this may sound like hair splitting. What is the point in imposing a distinction between being human and being the image of God? The point is to explain how the Old and New Testament reasonably fit together without logically contradicting each other. Thus Augustine said, "But we must notice how that which the apostle says, that not the woman but the man is the image of God, is not contrary to that which is written in Genesis."[3] His way of accounting for the apparent clash between I Corinthians 11:7 and Genesis 1:27 was to separate the notion of humanity from the notion of God's image. Augustine believed that a woman as a human *bears* God's

---

[1]For a more extensive discussion on the maleness of Christ, see complementarian writer Carolyn Gerber's short article, "Jesus as Male: A Stumbling Block for Women?" on the Damaris website, <www.damarisproject.com>.

[2]Augustine says, "For the human sexes are male and female."

[3]See Augustine, "On the Trinity," trans. A. W. Haddan, ed. Philip Schaff, in *Nicene and Post-Nicene Fathers* 3 (Peabody, Mass.: Hendrickson, 1994), book 12, chap. 7.

image, but a man as a man *is* God's image.

When I first read Augustine, I expected him to conclude on this basis that it is more honorable for a man to be the image of God than for a woman to be created in the image of God. But my guess was wrong.[4] To my surprise, Augustine did not reduce the distinction between women and men to a simple comparative. In other words, he did not say that men bear God's image relatively more than women do. Instead, he said man is and woman is not the image of God. To quote Augustine directly, he said "the woman herself alone" is not the image of God.[5]

To explain his view of how Genesis 1:27 (male and female created in God's image) accords with I Corinthians 11:7 (the man is the image of God), Augustine used an analogy. He compared the human mind with human nature. For him, this was the obvious comparison to make, because in Augustine's theology, the unique thing about being human is that people are rational. Men and women are categorically different from plants and animals because they alone can exercise reason. This is the point of convergence. Augustine believed that just as a man is the image of God, so the mind is too when it's focused on truth: "As we said of the nature of the human mind, that . . . when as a whole it contemplates the truth it *is* the image of God . . . but on that side whereby it is directed to the cognition of the lower things, it *is not* the image of God" (emphasis added). According to Augustine, the mind focused on the truth is the image of God. A mind distracted by lower things is not the image of God. See where his argument leads? Augustine believed that woman is not the image of God because women's minds are "directed to the cognition of lower things."[6]

Augustine was a man of his times, and men in his day automatically as-

---

[4]Had I remembered that Augustine was speaking from the perspective of one caught up in the particular theological controversies of his day, his view would not have surprised me so much. The key is to remember Augustine's context. When Augustine wrote this commentary, the challenge before him was to defend the triune nature of God, not the human nature of the female. His leaning, therefore, was more pro-Trinity than anti-women. Who knows what he would say if he were alive today?

[5]Augustine, "On the Trinity," book 12, chap. 7.

[6]This idea by no means was original to Augustine; it dates back at least to Plato.

sumed that all women are lacking. Most particularly, women were seen as lacking in rational thought. This assumption can be seen in Augustine's interpretation of Paul's teaching in 1 Corinthians 11:4-7. Consider this excerpt of the Corinthian chapter:

> Every man who *has something on his head* while praying or prophesying disgraces his head. But every woman who has her head *uncovered* while praying or prophesying disgraces her head. . . . For a man ought not to have his head covered, since he is the image and glory of God. [emphasis added]

Augustine believed from this text that women, not men, should cover their heads. But he couldn't see in the text the reason why.

Augustine wasn't satisfied simply to reason that a man has the privilege of uncovering his head by virtue of his being the image of God. Augustine wanted to know exactly what it is that makes a man the image of God. His answer? Man's mind. Augustine concluded that men are allowed to expose their heads during worship because men's minds, he believed, are more naturally inclined to contemplate higher things. Women, by contrast, should keep their heads covered since women's heads, he believed, are filled with thoughts of "lower things."[7] Thus Augustine boldly surmised that a woman is required to cover her head so as to cover her brain.[8]

> To put it more directly, Augustine believed that women have a mental disadvantage. He said that Eve had "small intelligence" and that Adam had a "spiritual mind." With that, he said it was "impossible" for Adam to have been deceived by the serpent.

---

[7] Writer Carolyn James argues that Mary of Bethany was a great theologian whose head was filled with thoughts explained by Jesus. See Carolyn James, *When Life and Beliefs Collide* (Grand Rapids, Mich.: Zondervan, 2000).

[8] Augustine may have read this text allegorically. Some scholars believe that Augustine saw men as symbols of contemplation and women as symbols of practical action. Women, he acknowledged, can contemplate the truth. But even when they do, their bodies (femaleness) still symbolize action. Action, he believed, is subordinate to contemplation because action needs to be curtailed whereas contemplation of God properly extends from now until eternity. See Tasicius, J. van Bavel, "Women as the Image of God in Augustine's De Trinitate XII," in *Signum pietatis: Festgabe für Cornelius Petrus Mayer OSA zum 60. Geburtstag*, ed. Adolar Zumkeller (Würzburg, Germany: Augustinus-Verlag, 1989), p. 272.

How could he [Adam] have believed what the serpent said? For the serpent said that God prohibited them from eating the fruit of that tree because he knew that if they did so, they would become as gods by their knowing good and evil (Gen 3:5)—as if God begrudged his creatures so great a blessing! That a man endowed with a *spiritual mind* could have believed this is astonishing. And just because it is *impossible* to believe it, woman was given to man, woman who was of *small intelligence* and who perhaps still lives more in accordance with the promptings of the inferior flesh than by the superior reason. Is this why the apostle Paul does not attribute the image of God to her? [emphasis added][9]

Augustine believed that Eve fell into deception because she lacked the image of God.[10] In other words, he believed that Eve was deceived precisely because Eve was a woman.

With that, however, Augustine believed that it's possible for a woman to become the image of God.[11] All she has to do is marry a man. A woman, he said, "is" the image of God "when joined with her husband."[12] Notice the stark contrast in what he has to say about men: "The man alone, he is the image of God as fully and completely as when the woman too is joined with him in one."[13]

Christian tradition, as informed by Augustine, says much the same thing—that a man is the image of God no matter what, and that a woman can become the image of God when she becomes a wife. Traditionally then, for a man, marriage has to do with acquiring a wife. But for a woman it has to do with acquiring a more adequate identity. If anyone thinks this tradition is gone, he or she hasn't been on the campus of a Christian university in the United States.

---

[9]See Augustine's "Literal Commentary on Genesis," *Corpus Scriptorum Ecclesiasticorum Latinorum* 28.

[10]Complementarian writer Ray Ortlund Jr. appears to be unaware of any past or present opposition to the belief that women do not bear the image of God. He ponders, "Who, I wonder, is teaching that men only bear God's image? No contributor to this volume will be found saying that." See Ray Ortlund Jr., "Male-Female Equality and Male Headship: Genesis 1—3," in *Recovering Biblical Manhood and Womanhood*, ed. John Piper and Wayne Grudem (Wheaton, Ill.: Crossway, 1991), p. 98.

[11]Analogously, Augustine said a mind can become the image of God when it contemplates the truth.

[12]Augustine, "On the Trinity," book 12, chap. 7.

[13]Ibid.

For example, many undergraduate women at Azusa Pacific University (APU) constantly worry about getting married. Despite their faith in God, they remain somewhat preoccupied throughout their college experience with the fear of being single. One resident director on campus told me that every week about four women in her dorm come to her suffering from panic attacks because they are not yet engaged. Getting married and having children define the extent of these young women's personal vision.

By contrast, the guys at APU do not limit their aspirations to getting married and having children. For some reason, young Christian men can conceive of themselves as husbands and fathers as well as active ministers in church and society. Young Christian women tend to see themselves as wives and mothers only; for them, getting married is tantamount to getting a life.[14] Very few young women at APU know what it means to ground their identity in Christ. Thus most of them are eager to establish their identity in a husband.

I wish these statements were sheer exaggerations, but I am describing something real. In the fall of 2000 the APU homecoming theme for the parade was "Describing Our Future Dreams." One women's dorm decorated their float in a wedding motif and dressed themselves as brides. To them, earning a liberal arts education meant nothing more than preparing for imminent marriage. That same year one freshman pulled her hair back and wrote on her forehead, "I want to make babies." She wore those words for two days.

For traditional women, getting married means securing a more legitimate identity. For progressive women, getting married means jeopardizing one's personal identity. I recently met some young women at Harvard who have the opposite fear of the women at APU. Harvard women feel threatened by marriage and motherhood. In the world of Harvard feminism, it takes courage to settle down and get married. In the APU community, it takes courage not to. At APU, just being called "Miss" is a prayer request in and of itself. Post-

---

[14]Early motherhood leads women to become empty nesters before the age of forty-five. Thus it is common for mothers to experience another identity crisis at that later stage of their lives.

college-aged single women can attest to the pain-producing fact that being "Miss" in the church is a visible sign that "she" has an issue, either hidden or exposed, that is keeping her off the normal "Christian track" of finding a husband (contra I Cor 7). Occasionally I wonder if the shame of being "Miss" explains in part why so many Christian women rush into marriage with unbelievers. At least it provides a way to escape the stigma.

A MAN IS THE IMAGE OF GOD

So far I have posed more questions than answers. But part of my goal is to stimulate Christians to think. And what do we think about this? What does I Corinthians 11:7, "the man is the image of God," mean? Before we answer that, it might be easier to name three things it doesn't mean.

First, it does not mean that women do not bear the image of God.[15] Genesis 1:27 affirms that male and female were created in God's image.[16] Second, it does not mean that a woman can acquire the image of God by marrying a man. Nowhere does the Bible say the image of God is conveyed from the man to the woman. True, it says the husband and wife become "one flesh," but it does not say the wife acquires a divine image from him that wasn't hers before. Third, it does not mean that women are less rational than men. The Bible knows wise and intelligent women such as Deborah, who was wise enough to exercise judgment over all the men and women of Israel;[17] Abigail, who was "intelligent" (I Sam 25:3); the woman who "opens her mouth in wisdom" (Prov 31:26); and Priscilla, who corrected an outstanding Bible teacher (Acts 18:23-28).

Furthermore, the Bible says male and female are made in the image of God. Man was made from the dust of the ground; women from the rib of the man. The man was "formed" (Gen 2:7), and the woman was "fashioned"

---

[15]Both sides of the debate agree with this. As Ortland puts it, "Man and woman are equal in the sense that they bear God's image equally." See Ortlund, "Male-Female Equality and Male Headship," p. 95.

[16]Commenting on Genesis 1:27, Ortlund says the Bible "doubtless intends to imply the equality of the sexes, for both male and female display the glory of God's image with equal brilliance." Ibid., 97.

[17]Judges 4:5 says, "She used to sit under the palm tree of Deborah . . . and the sons of Israel came up to her judgment."

(Gen 2:22) directly by the artful hand of God.[18] God breathed into their nostrils and gave each of them the breath of life.[19] As a result, both bear God's image, and both bear the image of each other. Woman reflects the man because she was taken from his rib, and the man reflects the woman because he is born of her body.

So which is better? To be a man or a woman? To be the image of God or bear the image of God?

This is not the right question to ask. I raise it only because it's the question people have. We're preoccupied with thoughts about who among us is the greatest. The New Testament tells of when the disciples asked Jesus, "Who then is the greatest in the kingdom of heaven?" (Mt 18:1). In response, Jesus called a child and set him before them. Only after that did he say, "Truly I say to you, unless you are converted and become like children, you shall not *enter* the kingdom of heaven. Whoever then humbles himself as this child, he is the greatest in the kingdom of heaven" (Mt 18:3-4, emphasis added).

Notice that Jesus didn't answer the disciples' exact question. Instead, he answered a better question, one they didn't ask. They asked him, "Who is the greatest in the kingdom of heaven?" but he answered them with instructions about how to enter the kingdom of heaven.

Jesus says, "Unless you are converted and become like children, you shall not enter the kingdom of heaven. Whoever humbles himself as this child is the greatest in the kingdom of heaven" (see Mt 18:1-6). His answer was unspecific. They asked him to tell them who. They wanted to know which exact person is the greatest. He did not engage that question. Instead of telling

---

[18]In Genesis 2, the Hebrew words that are rendered in English as "formed" and "fashioned" are different. At a marriage seminar that my husband and I attended, one of the speakers said the word *formed* indicates that man was created for work while "fashioned" indicates that woman was created for beauty. This interpretation insinuates that women are exempt from doing work, even housework. For more on this, see note 2 of chapter eight. See also Doug Sherman and William Hendricks, *Your Work Matters to God* (Colorado Springs: NavPress, 1987).

[19]Genesis 2:2 records the history of the man receiving his breath from God. We can only surmise that God did the same for the woman. Who else could have done it? Adam couldn't have; he was in a deep sleep.

them who, he told them whoever. His answer makes it sound as though more than one person can be the greatest. But if that's true, then in what sense is "the greatest" the greatest? One has to be greater to be greatest. Perhaps so, unless that worldly way of thinking is irrelevant to God.

When we ask, "Is it better to be a man or a woman?" we echo the disciples' question. And Jesus echoes the same answer: "Unless you are converted and become like children, you will not enter the kingdom of heaven. Whoever then humbles himself as this child, he is the greatest in the kingdom of heaven." The church doesn't know of any heated debate of the difference between the appropriate ministry roles for boys and girls. Perhaps that's because children have no authority or power. In the United States, a little girl can stand first in line and lead other children without anyone feeling very threatened. She can help move chairs and take a leading role in a church play. She is free to share her insights and read Scripture in front of the group. When I was a little girl, there wasn't one thing at church that the boys were allowed to do that the girls could not do also.

My intention is to not to evade the original question. Instead, I am offering a critique. I'm trying to say that it is unwise to ask if men are more like God than women are. The whole idea of saying men are and women are not the image of God leads to a genetic absurdity. Imagine the genetics of a child born of two parents, a father (made as the image of God) and a mother (made in the image of God and endowed with the potential to become the image of God.) Such a theory clashes with the first chapter of Genesis.

Genesis 1 says that plants and animals reproduce "after their kind" (Gen 1:11, 24, 25). Pear trees beget pear trees, monkeys beget monkeys, and humanity begets humanity. In other words, image-bearing parents give birth to image-bearing babies. Genesis 1 offers no hint of disparity between seed and fruit or males and females of the same kind. Unless we are prepared to concoct some kind of evolutionary marvel and say that image-being parents give birth to image-being sons and yet mere image-bearing daughters, then we have more thinking to do. Few of us in the United States are ready to say that newborn baby girls manifest God's image less than do newborn baby boys.

Augustine's theory is bizarre genetically. His theory says a father is born as the image of God and a mother *becomes* the image of God during the act of consummation. Genetically, it doesn't make sense for a baby boy to be born as the image of God unless he has a parent (or parents) who also are the image of God. Jesus was born of a virgin. If we apply Augustine's theory, Jesus was conceived in the womb of a single, unwed woman who had not yet become the image of God.[20]

Christianity is not Christianity apart from the reality of a fully human Savior who himself is the image of God (Col 1:15). Jesus Christ was "born of a woman" (Gal 4:4) apart from the seed of any man. If Jesus was fully human, then Mary was fully human. And if Mary, the virgin, was fully human, then young Christian women at APU are fully human too.

Women fully manifest the image of God. Women are so human that Jesus himself acquired his humanity from Mary. That means Mary was so human that Jesus got his male humanity from her. It means that female humanity is just as human as male humanity, even though the two are distinctive.[21] It's true that men—and not women—share maleness in common with Christ. And yet the more important point is that men do not share in Christ's divinity. A man is the image of God, but a man is nothing more than a mere human.

Every time we ask if men are better than women or more like God than women, we rupture another aspect of the bond that men and women share in Jesus Christ. The same thing occurs when we ask other wrong questions likened to it. For instance, what would happen to the church if Christian pastors and scholars seriously started asking, "Which is better? To be black or white?" Racism would only get worse. What if we started asking, "Which is better? To be the Father or the Son or the Spirit?" We would start seeing new church plants such as "The Church of the Holy Spirit" or "Disciples of the Son" or "The People of God the Father," which fortunately now do not exist. The question would drive a wedge between us because the question itself

---

[20]Jesus received his humanity from Mary and his divinity from the Holy Spirit (see Lk 1:35).
[21]John 1:14 says the Word became "flesh" (*sarx*). It does not say the Word became "male" (*anēr*).

drives a wedge between the three persons of the Trinity.

It is unwise to ask, "Which is better? To be a man or a woman?" because that question drives a wedge between men and women whom God has intended to be unified. Nevertheless, if we look at this again in a slightly different way, we can settle the question.

Which would you say is better? To be a father or a mother? Putting it this way helps me to lay the question aside, for intuitively I know it isn't better to be father than a mother, because children need both parents. It's an honor to be a father and an honor to be a mother. Even though I'm childless, I cherish my maternal instincts. I would never want to forfeit my ability to serve as a mother. Mothering is a natural part of womanhood. Likewise, fathering is a natural part of manhood.

So let's revisit the passage. Verbatim I Corinthians 11:7 says in English that man is "the image and glory of God" and that woman is "the glory of man." The textual distinction between the man and woman (contra Augustine) lies in "the glory," not in the image.[22] He is the glory of God; she is the glory of man.[23] This verse, and that distinction, is central to the thesis of this book. I will comment on it more in a later chapter. Here I want to emphasize the significant oversight in Augustine's interpretation of the verse. Augustine read I Corinthians 11:7 as if it said a man is the image of God and a woman is not.

DISCUSSION QUESTIONS

1. Review I Corinthians 11:7. What does it mean for a man to be the glory of God?

---

[22]Cf. the comments of Thomas R. Schreiner and John Frame, both of whom are contributors to *Recovering Biblical Manhood and Womanhood*, ed. John Piper and Wayne Grudem (Wheaton, Ill.: Crossway, 1991). Neither Schreiner ("Head Coverings, Prophecies and the Trinity: 1 Corinthians 11:2-16," pp. 131-35) nor Frame ("Men and Women in the Image of God," p. 225) grapples with the discrepancy in I Corinthians 11:7 discussed here. Rather, they accept it as a given that woman is made in God's image. Wayne Grudem shares the same starting point. He writes emphatically, "Men and women are made *equally in God's image*. . . . The fact that both men and women are said by Scripture to be 'in the image of God' should exclude all feelings of pride or inferiority and any idea that one sex is 'better' or 'worse' than the other." See Wayne Grudem, *Systematic Theology* (Grand Rapids, Mich.: Zondervan, 1994), p. 456.
[23]Schreiner and Frame interpret the word *glory* as meaning "honor."

2. What does it mean for a woman to be the glory of man?

3. Why might Christian women feel anxious about not being married?

4. What do you think accounts for people's tendency to ask if it's better to be a man than a woman?

6
Women and Personhood

For there is no partiality with God.
Romans 2:11

These women are going to hell," she said.

Her bluntness caught me off guard. No one else had confronted me before about the destiny of secular women.

"It's terrible," she lamented. "And the church is standing by, choosing to ignore them. I'm telling you, Christians today do not want to listen to women who are focused on social problems that people in the church don't want to face."

No one else had ever drawn my attention to the voice of the secular feminists. No one else had complained to me before about the church's unwillingness to evangelize women who see God as the ultimate chauvinist. But now Lydia[1] was doing it, and Lydia wouldn't let up. She laser beamed every sentence from the core of her being straight into the center of my heart.

Hammering the issue, she continued, "I keep wondering when God's people are going to care. When are Christians going to take action? When is the church going to formulate a response to the cries of real women who

---

[1]This is not her real name.

think our Creator is plotting maliciously against them? The secular feminists have written hundreds of books that either deny God's existence altogether, or misrepresent him as a macho male, or contrive him to be a goddess. The sad part is that the church has hardly muttered a corrective."

It took effort to endure the conversation.

"I meet so many women," she went on to say, "who refuse to go to church because women in society are more respected as leaders in the world than as participants in the Christian community."

Looking at me wistfully with eyes filled with trust, she assumed without a doubt that I felt compassion for these women. She assumed that I cared. She assumed that I cared because I was a woman who had served full time on the evangelism staff at a famous, seeker-targeted megachurch. Unfortunately she was dead wrong. I didn't feel burdened for "those women." It had never occurred to me to proclaim the gospel to secular feminists. Those women were not part of my world or part of my vision for ministry.

"You can trust Sarah—she's biblical," was my solid reputation. "You can trust me," was my unspoken message to the church. "I'm not like them. I'm not angry or political. I'm not liberal or suspicious or accusative toward men. I'm a good Christian woman who loves the Word of God. You can count on me to defend the true gospel and not distort the message by pushing some agenda for women."

I wasn't interested in clustering with other women and talking about women's rights. My goal was to travel and speak at important Christian conferences and teach in the local church. I couldn't afford to be associated with strong-willed women who rebelled against the Lord. I needed to be networked with people who would lend to my credibility.

Pensively I listened and processed my thoughts in unnoticed silence while Lydia processed out loud. She had no idea that we were on two different wavelengths.

I watched her in amazement. Driven by her conviction to champion Christ in the culture, Lydia had become a self-made, passionate expert in the interests of trend-setting women in society. She knew the writers, the books, the leaders, the spokeswomen, the history and the reasons that had led to the feminist cause. To converse with her was to take a crash course in women's studies. And as I keep saying, Lydia assumed I that was pacing with her. In a sense, I did share her passion—I fully accorded with her evangelistic agenda. But overall, I didn't want to be associated with women whom evangelical Christians don't embrace. That was my sin: I wanted to be trusted and respected by the conservative Christian community more than I wanted to serve Christ.

WOMEN AGAINST THEMSELVES

One month later I attended a national conference led by Christian women taking a hard-line approach against radical feminism. The title of the conference implied that the purpose of the gathering was to reinstitute Christian values in society. Almost everyone in the audience appeared to belong to Christ. The women I met were well versed in Scripture, unashamed of the gospel and fervent in their zeal for the Lord. Even so, something was off-center. The core committee had become more antifeminist than pro-Christian. They chose a politically conservative Jewish woman to lead an afternoon workshop in which she talked about the absurdity of forgiveness and a socially conservative atheist as the Saturday night plenary speaker. Dissension filled the room that Saturday night, and we dismissed the meeting early. The next day one of us found an opportunity to witness to the speaker, but she wasn't willing to open her heart to the Lord.

As providence would have it, I was seated that night at a table with six antifeminist evangelical women, each of whom had been educated in a conservative Christian college. After we became acquainted, I asked them to engage a question: *are women inferior to men?* The results of that conversation are worth sharing.

Only two of us, both relatively middle-aged, said that women are not inferior. Three of us, including two senior citizens, said we were unsure. Two others, both under the age of thirty, insisted that men are superior. Intrigued by the young women's responses, I began to ask them a few more questions.

"Do you think of yourself as inferior to men?"

"Yes," they replied.

"You're saying that you understand yourself as less capable than men?"

"Yes," they said again.

"Specifically, what makes you less capable?" I asked.

"Oh, I'm way too emotional," said one.

"Me too," said the other.

"And you don't account for your unrestrained emotions by calling yourself 'immature'?"

"No," they said.

"You think it's your femininity that makes you 'way too emotional'?"

"Yes," they insisted.

"Am I correct to understand, then, that you think it's your femininity that makes you inferior?"

"Yes," they agreed.

I walked away from that conversation preoccupied for hours. Only one other woman at my table said that women are not inferior to men. Five of seven said they were inclined to believe that men, by nature, are superior to women.

A few months later I told this story to a ministry leader of national stature whom I will refer to as Mary. My intention was to remind her of the prevalence of women's low expectations of themselves and prod her to use her pervasive influence to help Christian women stop underrating their worth. So there I was recounting everything, expecting my words to be received as a goading reminder of the current mentality of many dedicated conservative Christian women. But that is not what happened.

To my surprise, she physically pulled herself back from our conversation, turned her thoughts inward and unguardedly mused out loud, "I have believed the same thing." As if realizing it for the first time, she went on to say, "And I have held myself back."

I can still see her now. Eyes closed, shaking her head, pressing one hand spread upon her chest. After a pause, she finished her thought in a tone of pained confession, "I have held back because . . . *'I am woman'* . . . and I thought it was my duty to hold back."

It is one thing to self-limit due to laziness or lack of good character. It is another thing to self-limit because of a false belief acquired from people at church. When women tell themselves, "I am not supposed to be emotionally mature—because I am feminine," and "I'm not allowed to accomplish more than this—because 'I am woman,'" something is wrong. The church is missing the mark when the community of believers conditions Christian women to assume they are inferior, and if need be, prove themselves inferior to men.

WOMEN AGAINST WOMEN

A year later I saw Lydia again. Within minutes of my arrival, she bluntly asserted another Lydia-like bold declaration. "Women don't know their worth. They think it's prestigious to submit to men and degrading to submit to women. You know what I mean? It's as if they believe women are half-persons. If a woman stands behind a man, at least she can feel like a half-person. But if she stands behind a woman, what does that make her? A quarter-person?"

Internally I responded to her pointed remarks not by answering her but by posing her question to myself: *Am I less inclined to submit to women than men?* When I served in women's ministry at Willow Creek Community Church in South Barrington, Illinois, for five years, I gladly submitted to Kathy Dice, director of women's ministry. I didn't feel like a half-person. I didn't consider her to be a half-person. I never imagined myself to be a quarter-person submitting to a half-person. On the contrary, I highly esteemed her. She protected me, gave wise advice and opened doors for me. She was fabulous.

But then I asked myself additional questions. Whom do I take more seriously? Female leaders or male leaders? Female experts or male experts? The director of women's ministry or the senior pastor? It was painful to think through this. The questions were so pointed and sharp that I felt as though I had been stabbed.

Again, I was being convicted by the Spirit. I knew inside that my sensibilities were dissimilar to Lydia's. Whereas she gave men and women equal regard, I held men in higher esteem.

THE NATURE OF PREJUDICE

Until four years ago, I never seriously thought of myself as being prejudiced. In Texas, where I'm from, the rednecks were the ones who were prejudiced. My family wasn't redneck. Daddy seared into our brains the fundamental principle of valuing all people. To him, snobbery was an unconscionable cardinal sin. He said it only one time, but once was enough. Emphatically he said, "Don't you *ever* refuse to greet someone! No matter who it is, you acknowledge their presence and talk to them as a human being!"

Well, that was no tall order. Being friendly to people, and befriending them, has always been one of my strengths. Without trying, I seem to like everyone. It baffled me why my dad thought it necessary to magnify something so obvious. I wasn't a redneck, and I wasn't a snob. I guess that's why I thought I wasn't prejudiced.

A few years ago, I started getting invitations to consult with ministry leaders about the subject of Christian women in leadership. Usually I begin my presentation by posing a general question: Does the controversial subject of women's identity have anything to do with spiritual formation? In other words, Does a person's view of women somehow correlate with a person's level of Christlikeness and maturity? If so, then does a person's view of women somehow inform the way a person reads the Bible, especially the verses about women?

So far, each group has said that spiritual formation factors into a person's interpretation of the Scriptures. The reasoning goes like this. Racists are more likely to believe the Bible teaches racism. Traditionalists are more likely to believe the Bible teaches traditionalism. Chauvinists are more likely to believe the Bible teaches chauvinism. Feminists are more likely to believe the Bible teaches feminism. In every case prejudiced people produce prejudiced interpretations of God's Word.[2]

It's helpful to conceptualize the notion of prejudice in terms of an analogy to numbers. Insofar as 2 and 3 are prime numbers, and 4 and 6 are com-

---

[2]I say this not to discredit legitimate hermeneutics. It is possible for Christians to read the Bible fairly. We cannot, however, successfully do so alone. We always need to listen to a variety of views in order to be able to recognize our biases and discard them.

posite numbers, what is the best way to define prejudice? Is it a root sin or a secondary, derivative sin? In other words, is prejudice essentially a composite sin (composed of other sins more basic), or is prejudice itself a root sin?

The word *prejudice* literally means "to prejudge." I believe it's wrong to prejudge. God commands us to do "nothing in a spirit of partiality" (1 Tim 5:21). It is sinful to be partial either to men or women. None of us are to think "more highly" of ourselves or of anyone else than we ought to (Rom 12:3).

Prejudice is a sin that Christians seem afraid to talk about, for at some level we realize that our prejudice is a symptomatic sin that alerts us to something underneath. Prejudice is not a primary sin; it's a secondary sin. It derives from a basic sense of pride. Prejudice arises from the soils of fear and ignorance, though, ironically, prejudice is learned. Customarily prejudice tends to be manifest in one of two ways—either as self-superiority or self-hatred.

In a word, prejudice is narcissism. Prejudice is narcissism that discounts and discredits human beings typically in one of two ways: a self-exalting way that discounts other people because "they are not like me" or a self-rejecting way that discredits others because "they are like me."[3]

The problem with prejudice is that the person who has it typically cannot see it. It is similar to the sin of inconsideration. An inconsiderate person is blind to his or her lack of consideration. For example, an inconsiderate teenager who takes a forty-five-minute hot shower isn't trying to hurt anyone else in the family by using all the hot water. When scolded with the words, "You don't even care if the rest of the family has to suffer and take cold showers! You don't care about us at all!" the narcissistic teenager may sincerely respond, "Hey, don't take things so personally! I wasn't even thinking about anyone else in the family."

Prejudice is a sin of omission. It derives from the failure to love. Of course

---

[3]It is prideful to reject the self in this way because the self is not humble enough to self-accept. The self scorns the self for not being "better" as the self would like to be.

the worst kind of prejudice is religious prejudice that deems itself as sanctioned by God. When someone believes God sees one category of people as superior or inferior to another, then prejudice becomes blind not only to itself but also to the sinfulness of itself. It is always sinful to show partiality, "for there is no partiality with God" (Rom 2:11).

One of my favorite icebreakers is to ask women, "Why are you thankful to be a woman?" I can't tell you how often that question has the effect of making women feel slightly stunned. Typically some of the answers are sarcastic. "You want to know why I'm *thankful* to be a woman?" Others crack jokes. But then they settle down, welcome the question and answer it with thoughtful responses. When the humor subsides, some of them start to cry. I remember one woman said, "It has never occurred to me to thank God for making me a woman; I always thought being a woman was a curse." Mind you, these are Christian women. They're women from Christ-centered, Bible-based, conservative evangelical Christian churches.

I can confidently say that Christians in the United States generally agree that it is bad theology to say that poor people are inferior to rich ones or that blacks are inferior to whites. We also seem to agree that it is bad theology to think that children are inferior to adults. Unequivocally we believe it is even worse theology to say that God is inferior or that Christ became inferior to the Roman government on the day he was arrested and killed.

And yet I cannot with confidence say that Christians generally agree it is bad theology to believe that women are inferior to men. If asked point blank if women are inferior, many of us would quickly answer no. But if we trusted it was safe to speak unguardedly, some of us might answer yes. I don't think the two young women in Washington are atypical. As a matter of fact, when I told this story at a luncheon two years later, a freshman in college, perplexed, whispered to someone older, "But women *are* inferior. Those two girls in Washington were right."

Who else thinks women are inferior? Not long ago I was invited to consult a group of approximately eighty pastors at a denominational meeting. Talking to them unguardedly in a backstage kind of way, I said, "You know how sometimes you feel superior to women because . . . well . . . you can just tell that you are?" And they laughed. It struck them as funny. Do you see what that reveals about them?

When one man read this story, he nonchalantly told me that he would've laughed too. "What's the big deal?" he said. "Obviously I am not your target audience because I do not believe that men are superior to women."

So then I said to him, "Okay, consider this. Would the pastors have laughed had I said to them, 'You know how sometimes you feel superior to African Americans because . . . well . . . you can just tell that you are?' " I said to him further, "Those pastors would have known that my statement was racist. They would have been offended on the spot. They know it's wrong to think of themselves as superior to people who have black skin. But they are not yet sensitized to their prejudice against women."

Suddenly the man's face dropped. Staring at me, pained, with a very changed countenance, he softly muttered, " Oh, . . . I see what you're saying . . . "

Now it's my turn to confess. I'm not so different from those pastors. I'm not so different from that man. Although I am a woman, I have tacitly thought of myself as a special type of woman, the kind that can keep up with men. I've exercised the same pride and prejudice they exhibited that day at the conference.

Prior to my friendship with Lydia, I had no idea that I felt any kind of prejudice against women. How could I be prejudiced against women? I had spent five consecutive years leading a large Bible study and ministering to hundreds of women. For fifteen years I had spoken at women's luncheons and retreats. Besides that, I had countless women friends whom I adored. I was aware of the fact that many of my favorite women prefer to work predominantly with men. But since I was relationally connected to women with diverse backgrounds and interests, it was hard for me to recognize that I felt hesitant to identify myself fully with other women.

It wasn't a self-esteem issue. It was far deeper than that, and far more insidious and subtle. I've never for a moment wished I were a man. But I have wished in a wordless way deep inside my heart that I could somehow transcend my female self whenever I perceive that my womanhood has become a liability.

Attitudes of prejudice play out against women in many subtle ways. For some people, it means thinking women are "way too emotional" to be adequate peers of men. For others it means thinking that women should hold back so that men will appear to be superior. For someone else it might mean refusing to submit to a woman. For me, prejudice against women often plays itself out when I attempt to escape the usual stigma of being a woman by telling myself, as my professor did, that I'm exceptional, that somehow I've transcended my own being. As for men, prejudice often means not associating with women or not trusting women or dismissing them in a way that is difficult to describe, though not so difficult to discern.

WOMEN AND PERSONHOOD

Theologically, Christians are eager to say that women are made in the image of God. Socially, however, women are sometimes seen as being less dignified than men. Like the young women in Washington, there are others in the church who would openly say that women are less able to handle their emotions and face the harsh reality of life. Though this is not true of all of us, some of us have been taught that women are supposed to be inferior to men. Why else would my professor have told me to "hold back"?

In college one of my friends used to take me by the shoulders at arms' length and announce to me triumphantly, "You're a person!" I never understood why he said that to me. But I am grateful for his influence in my life. Apparently he perceived that I was subconsciously discounting myself. He saw in me what I see in other women— a hesitance to exult in the dignity of being a woman.

DISCUSSION QUESTIONS

1. Do you know any Christian women who believe it is their to duty to hold back? What is the difference between restraining oneself from sin and

holding oneself back from giving one's best to Christ?

2. What does the Bible say about women submitting to women leaders?

3. How much does a person's level of spiritual development inform her or his thinking about women?

4. Have you ever prayed for secular feminists to come to Christ? What efforts are you making to share the gospel with feminist leaders in society?

7

MEN AND MANHOOD

The gifts and callings of God are irrevocable.
ROMANS 11:29

If Christian women have a tendency to pretend they are inferior, the opposite is true for Christian men. Men in the church often feel pressured to act as though they're a little more advanced than they are. Thus the proverbial joke: the best way for a woman to promote an idea to a man is to tell him in such a way that he thinks he's the one who thought of it. Otherwise he won't be secure enough to listen deferentially to her.

Of course, there are Christian men secure enough to do this. For instance, a few years ago, a small group of men at Talbot Seminary banded around Dr. Judy TenElsof, openly acknowledging on Christian radio that the Lord had imparted a vision to her to build a retreat center for pastors. After she told her husband, they convened a few other leading men. All of them gathered in person for corporate prayer. Then they began to collaborate with her on purchasing property, developing funds, forging a plan and hiring the staff. For these men, the issue was not about who thought of the vision but rather about committing to do everything possible to make that vision a reality.

For other men, however, it is difficult to take a woman in the church that seriously. If a woman *is* taken seriously, sometimes her husband, or perhaps the senior pastor, assumes credit for her idea, especially if she says she doesn't mind. But is that honest? Granted, all the glory belongs to God, but as a matter of integrity, people in the church should be careful not to claim someone else's contribution as their own.

The temptation to take credit is particularly strong for men because in this culture it is difficult for men to feel assured that they are men. We don't have any rituals to help them. Consequently, when a man steals the credit from a woman, it might have nothing to do with his attitude toward women. It might be because he doubts himself. Like many other men, he might not understand what it means to be a man.

If we look at the big picture, many men are wondering what it means to be a man in the context of this age of technology. Indeed, technology has a way of loudly interrupting men's and women's sense of gender.

Prior to the Industrial Revolution, men and women worked on the homestead doing separate things. For instance, men hacked down trees and settled the land while women cooked and sewed and gave birth to a house full of children. But starting in the nineteenth century, the traditional distinction between men's and women's work began to blur.[1] Technology made things different. Men started riding tractors and maneuvering equipment and machinery (i.e., doing things that women can do), and men and women both worked in factories. Over time, men left the home to enter the public workplace as professionals. As a result, many families were afforded the unprecedented opportunity to have the wife stay at home while the husband went to work—without her or the kids.[2]

---

[1]As one writer explains it, "The world of work has changed. It no longer readily rewards physical strength and endurance, which had been assets that the majority of males could exploit. This affects men without higher education most directly; they fall ever further behind in economic contest, and their ability to provide support for children and wives declines as well." See Lionel Tiger, *The Decline of Males* (New York: Golden Books, 1999), p. 77.

[2]The distinction between public and private life further separated men and women. Whereas marriage and family had been connected to the homestead where preindustrial men worked, they were severed from the postindustrial workplace. As Tiger says, "A core assumption of the industrial way is that people can enjoy sex and family, but only in what is defined as private life" (ibid., p. 32).

While it's true these stay-home wives felt relieved by the luxury of technological inventions such as birth control pills, public school facilities, modern grocery stores, retail clothing stores, washing machines and other electric appliances, they were also, in a sense, robbed because modern technology rendered much of "women's work" obsolete.[3] Thus it happened about that time in the 1960s that the feminist movement exploded.[4] It was a reaction to technology.[5]

Before the 1960s, men dominated the public arena. Men were the breadwinners; men were the leaders of society.[6] Once women became professionals, men were expected to share the domain from which they drew a sense of male identity. As a result, the line of distinction between men and women was further blurred. So here we are today, still pressing the question, What is manhood?

MANHOOD IN WORLDLY TERMS

For many men, *manhood* means "to be above." It implies the idea of attempting to be higher than human. Here's the kind thing I'm talking about. A couple of years ago, a middle-aged man told me in confidence that another man in our workplace hurt his feelings. To that he added, "But I would never tell him because I don't want him to think he has any kind of power over me."

I said, "So you're just going to pretend that everything's okay?"

He nodded affirmatively. "That's the way it goes with us men."

---

[3]For a short and insightful commentary on this, see Dorothy Sayers, *Are Women Human?* (Grand Rapids, Mich.: Eerdmans, 1971).

[4]This was not the first wave of feminism in America. For a more detailed account of the history of feminism in the United States, see Sheila Tobias, *Faces of Feminism* (Boulder, Colo.: Westview Press, 1997); Bradford Miller, *Returning to Seneca Falls* (Hudson, N.Y.: Lindisfarne Press, 1995); Rebecca Merrill Groothuis, *Women Caught in the Conflict* (Grand Rapids, Mich.: Baker, 1994); see also Bernard Adeney, *Strange Virtues* (Downers Grove, Ill.: InterVarsity Press, 1995), pp. 192-219.

[5]This is an oversimplification. Many different factors led to the resurgence of the feminist movement in America. But technology, I believe, enabled women to progress the most.

[6]This is not descriptive of the lower middle class and the poor. Less wealthy women historically have always worked for pay in order to help their families survive.

I am so intrigued by men's desire to prove themselves as men. The challenge "Be a man!" doesn't rattle a woman, but it grips the very soul of a man. Even in the church, it is not a given for men to feel like men just because they are men. Yet I know it's not from God when men fall into the trap of wanting desperately to prove themselves as men on worldly terms. The male quest for identity reminds me of the time when Jesus was led into the wilderness to be tempted. The devil said to him, "If you are the Son of God, then prove it! Turn these stones to bread! Jump from the pinnacle of the temple! And don't you dare begin to show me who you are on God's terms. Show me who you are on my terms!" (Mt 4:1-11, author's paraphrase).

We all know that Jesus didn't do it. He knew who he was, the Father's Beloved, and that was enough for him.

Overall, of course, women face the same kind of temptation. The devil tempts women to question their identity and prove their personal worth by means of worldly performance. And yet, there is no special challenge looming over women that shudders them with the command "Be a woman!" Even when a woman obscures her femininity, she does not escape her womanhood. We've all heard the criticisms before. She is a woman who acts like a man. She is a woman without feelings or emotion. She is a woman who fails to represent the other women. In every complaint, she is a woman nonetheless.

That is not so for men. Men are accused of not being men. He's a little boy. He's a mama's baby. He's a jerk. He's a coward. He's a couch potato. He's gay. He's a pig. He's a beast. But the worst insult of all to slap upon a man is blatantly to call him "a woman." Indeed, the word *woman* is a loaded accusation that connotes the idea of a hopeless inability ever to become a real man. Think about it. A boy can grow up. Mama's baby can mature. A jerk or a coward can repent. A couch potato can get up. A gay can go straight. A pig and a beast can be refined. But a woman? She is forever a woman. She is forever inferior to a man. I truly believe that if women were regarded in every man's heart as God-given equals, then it wouldn't be so demeaning for a man to be labeled as a woman. Instead, it would simply be absurd.

Men need the dignity of their manhood. But they also need to know what manhood is. Otherwise they'll crater in the face of the temptation that Jesus was able to resist.

JOHN PIPER'S VIEW OF BIBLICAL MASCULINITY

What is manhood?[7] If you ask conservative Christians, some will say that mature masculinity is "a sense of benevolent responsibility to lead, provide for and protect women."[8] This definition, drafted by John Piper, is just that—a definition. In other words, it's not a quote from Scripture. Nowhere does the Bible say that God designed men to be the leaders, providers and protectors of women. Nor does the Bible say, as Piper furthermore does, that women are designed by God "to affirm, receive, and nurture the strength and leadership of worthy men."

I respect John Piper as a brother in Christ. I also recommend his other books.[9] But I do not affirm his definitions of *masculinity* and *femininity*. It's good for men to be leaders and for fathers to provide for and protect their families. It's godly for wives, as he puts it, to nurture the strength and leadership of their husbands. I benefited from having a stay-at-home mother and a father who provided for me. For a mother to be at home caring for the kids and a father to be present leading, protecting and providing for the family is a marvelous approach, if it fosters genuine love and gratitude. But it's just one

---

[7]Larry Crabb defines masculinity as "the satisfying awareness of the substance God has placed within a man's being that can make an enduring contribution to God's purposes in this world, and will be deeply valued by others . . . as a reliable source of wise, sensitive, compassionate, and decisive involvement." Crabb, moreover, says, "A man is 'manly' when he moves through life with purposeful and confident involvement, when he follows a direction that he values for reasons that are bigger than himself." See Larry Crabb, "Masculinity," in *What Makes a Man?* ed. Bill McCartney (Colorado Springs, Colo.: NavPress, 1992), p. 48. I appreciate Crabb's thoughtfulness, but I don't see how his words pertain exclusively to men. It is appropriate, not manly, for every Christian woman to move through life with purposeful and confident involvement and follow a direction that she values for reasons that are bigger than herself.

[8]See John Piper, "A Vision of Biblical Complementarity: Manhood and Womanhood Defined According to the Bible," in *Recovering Biblical Manhood and Womanhood,* ed. John Piper and Wayne Grudem (Wheaton, Ill.: Crossway, 1991), pp. 36-52.

[9]See especially John Piper, *Desiring God,* 10th anniversary ed. (Portland, Ore.: Multnomah Publishers, 1996).

model, and it's not the only way to function biblically.[10]

I don't question Piper's intentions. To me, it's evident that he's a fervent man of God who, like Wayne Grudem, truly wants nothing more than for Christians to be biblical in their relationships at home. But it concerns me, even so, that Piper's definitions guide people to think in terms of making it their goal to strive for "biblical manhood and womanhood." The Bible never commands us to strive for mature masculinity or mature femininity. Instead, the Word of God calls people to become like Christ. The right question is not "Am I fulfilling my call to become a biblical man or a biblical woman?" The right question is "Am I imitating Christ?"[11]

I'm also concerned that Piper's definition (at least of femininity) leaves it the woman to decide whether or not a man's strength and leadership is worthy enough to be affirmed. As Piper explains it, "Mature femininity . . . is discerning in what it approves."[12] Thus every man, according to Piper's plan, is subject to the test of earning a woman's approval. To me, that doesn't make sense. How can he say that men are the leaders of women, if women are endowed with the prerogative to decide if men's leadership is worthy?

The Bible includes no such prerogative for women. On the contrary, the Bible says something quite different. To begin with, it never tells the woman that it's her responsibility to "affirm the leadership" of her husband if he is "worthy." In fact, the Bible doesn't even say that the husband is her leader. There is no commandment that says, "Husbands, lead your wives." The commandment, instead, is for husbands to love their wives as themselves

---

[10]In a fascinating article on the Proverbs 31 woman, conservative scholar Bruce Waltke says, "I was aware that Al Wolters . . . argued that she is a heroic figure, but until I investigated it myself, I was not convinced." But then Waltke came, as he puts it, to the "remarkable conclusion that the poem represents the ideal wife as a heroic entrepreneur in the marketplace" (see Bruce Waltke, "The Role of the 'Valiant Wife' in the Marketplace," *Crux* 35, no. 3 [1999]: 23).

[11]As my friend Lydia puts it, "The right question for people to ask is What does Christ look like in a mother of two children? What does Christ look like in a teenage boy? What does Christ look like in all the particulars that make me *me*?"

[12]Piper, "A Vision of Biblical Complementarity," p. 48. I understand that Piper's intention is to assure women that it's not their biblical duty to submit themselves to abuse. But even so, he leaves himself open to be understood also as granting a Christian woman the prerogative to evaluate her husband's worthiness. In my opinion, this further exacerbates the problem.

(Eph 5:33). The Bible says that a wife is responsible to submit to her husband (Eph 5:24). But it also says that it is her responsibility—regardless of her husband's behavior—to see to it that she respects her husband (Eph 5:32). In other words, respect for a husband is not a feminine option. Just as Abigail in the Old Testament respected her husband Nabal, so every wife is commanded by God to respect her husband too, even if his conduct is foolish (1 Sam 25). According to the Scriptures, a wife's respect for her husband depends not on the husband but rather on the wife.

In continuing this discussion, it is helpful to consider a list of Piper's definitions, as shown in table 7.1. According to this schema, the husband leads; the wife affirms his leadership. He provides for; she receives. He protects; she nurtures.[13]

Table 7.1   Piper's view of husbands and wives

Men	Women
Lead	Affirm male leadership
Protect	Nurture
Provide for	Receive

On the surface, Piper's complementarian vision seems coherent, especially since it is neatly organized. But upon examination, it gives way to a host of unconvincing conclusions:

- When a husband nurtures his wife, he forfeits his manliness.
- When a wife provides for her husband, she offends his sense of manhood.
- When a man receives from a woman, he neglects his masculine role.
- When a woman protects a man, she disgraces him.

---

[13]Piper's view of femininity is not totally antithetical to an egalitarian point of view. In that Piper calls woman man's "assistant," he sounds traditional. But when he says that woman is man's "partner," he sounds nontraditional. Here's how Piper puts it: "She is to be his partner and assistant. She joins in the act of strength and shares in the process of leadership" (ibid., p. 49).

The most ironic thing is that although Piper sees men as women's leaders, he charges women—not men—with the final responsibility of making sure that men "feel" manly.[14] Anytime a husband starts to doubt himself as a man or feels that his manhood has been violated by a woman's expression of strength, Piper says it's her responsibility to figure out a way to adjust.[15] In other words, she is called to deal with her husband's uncertainties and manage his negative emotions.

My friend, whom I will call Mary Ellen, faithfully went to therapy, paying full price for two years, to find out later that "her baggage" belonged to her husband, whom I will refer to as Kurt. Mary Ellen experienced a tremendous sense of freedom the day she realized that it's not her responsibility to hash through her husband's unresolved issues. Kurt is a Christian, but as a man, he refused to go to counseling because the act of asking for help (receiving help) threatened his sense of manhood. Kurt told himself that

> men don't go to therapy. A real man can deal with his problems himself. A real man enters the cave alone and emerges alone with a solution. Unlike women, he doesn't need a touchy-feely process. Unlike women, he doesn't need to talk to anyone about his feelings. Men aren't bothered by feelings. Emotional issues are for women.

So when Kurt started feeling bad, Mary Ellen went to therapy.

From the time they are boys, men are challenged to attain manhood. Their

---

[14]He says, "It is simply impossible that from time to time a woman not be put in a position of influencing or guiding men. For example, a housewife in her backyard may be asked by a man how to get to the freeway. At that point she is giving a kind of leadership. She has superior knowledge that the man needs and he submits himself to her guidance. But we all know that there is a way for that housewife to direct the man that neither of them *feels* [my emphasis] their mature femininity or masculinity compromised" (Piper and Grudem, *Recovering Biblical Manhood and Womanhood*, p. 50).

[15]In "A Vision of Biblical Complementarity" Piper says, "To the degree that a woman's influence over man is personal and directive, it will generally offend a man's good, God-given sense of responsibility and leadership, and thus controvert God's created order" (ibid., 51). My question has to do with why a man's "God-given sense of responsibility and leadership" is so fragile and susceptible to offense. If it is truly God-given, then it seems that men would continue to feel like leaders, even when a woman "joins in the act of strength" and "shares in the process of leadership" (p. 49). Piper seems to be saying a man should feel offended when a woman expresses herself freely without being conscientious to protect (yes, protect) his sense of manhood.

consciences are trained by society and church and also by women such as myself. Every time I long for my husband to sweep me off my feet so that I don't have to walk on the difficult path of Christlike suffering, in essence I am asking him to prove that he is a man so that I won't have to prove that I'm a Christian.

When Jim and I were first married, I wanted him to be my Superman. I didn't like it when he felt afraid. I wanted him to rescue me from my fears and not have any fears of his own. My picture of marriage called for me to be human and for him to be superhuman. For me to be vulnerable, and for him to be invulnerable. I expected our marriage to be a comforting refuge where I would be held safe in the arms of my hero and where he would be admired by me. Jim would be Zorro, and I'd be Cinderella. And we would serve Christ in our home.

I am on a journey of repenting from my worldly view of marriage. I am letting go of my selfish expectations. I am surrendering my selfish desire to feel sorry myself when my husband doesn't save me from my fears. I am in the process of learning to accept the full responsibility for my stuff. And through it all, I am discovering a new vision of marriage, one that's based on love instead of fantasy.

That's my story. As for Piper, he does not equate manhood with being macho. His objective, I believe, is to prompt Christian men to be responsible. "At the heart of mature masculinity," he says, "is a sense of benevolent responsibility to lead, provide for and protect women."

If all men everywhere adhered to this definition, the world would be a far better place. If men were esteemed as the caretakers of women, the world would then embrace the tacit claim that women are worth being taken care of. As a result, there would no longer be any wife battering, or sex trafficking, or sexual molestation from males to females. Mothers would be assisted financially by the fathers of their children, and husbands would spend a lot more time at home. If all men would commit to following Piper's way, the cultures of the world would be renewed.

But it wouldn't solve the issue. Instead, another problem would arise. The rest of the world would face the same problem that many Christians in the United States now face. Though Piper's definition of manhood is congenial toward women, it fails women. It also inevitably fails men. Christian men are continually being taught to measure themselves against women. Instead of being trained to be macho, men at church are trained to establish their identity as men in terms of how they rank against women.

MANHOOD AS A STRUGGLE FOR IDENTITY

If men have it rough, Christian men have it rougher. Whereas a man in the world can marry a financially successful woman without catching any flack, a Christian man often is expected to match or outdo his wife's success.[16] My husband, Jim, has been openly confronted dozens of times with offhand comments about his wife being the primary breadwinner.[17] "You mean you moved to California for *her* job?" they say with incredulity. Those kinds of comments indicate something more about the church's view of men and manliness than of me.[18]

---

[16]Dan Doriani, a complementarian, says that 1 Timothy 5:8 is often misquoted as saying, "If a *man* does not provide for his family, he is worse than an unbeliever." As Doriani points out, the apostle Paul says, "If *anyone* does not provide for his *relatives*, and especially his immediate family, he has denied the faith and is worse than an unbeliever." Second, Doriani says the word translated "provide" does not mean "earn" or "acquire" but to "plan" or "look out" for something. That is, Paul does not require men to earn all the money. Rather, men must ensure that the family has all the money it needs. Thus it is fine, in his opinion, for a woman to earn money. Moreover, he says, "there is no law against a woman earning more money than her husband (although it may cause tensions)." In addition, he says a man "certainly . . . fulfills his obligations if he plans for his wife to earn most of their income for a few years while he receives training for a job that will provide for their livelihood for decades." See Daniel Doriani, *The Life of a God-made Man* (Wheaton, Ill.: Crossway, 2001), p. 41. My response to this is that Doriani seems not to have convinced himself that it is acceptable for a woman to earn more money than her husband. On the one hand, Doriani says 1 Timothy 5:8 refers to anyone, and yet he puts the onus on the man to ensure that his family has all the money that it needs. Doriani assigns no credit or responsibility to the wife. Even if she serves as the primary breadwinner, Doriani credits the man with having "ensured" that his wife take the initiative to earn enough money to provide for him, their children and any extended family who might also be in need.

[17]My husband makes less money than I do because he is the full-time children's pastor at our local church. Children's pastors tend to make less money than professors.

[18]I am here reminded of a fascinating article on the Proverbs 31 woman written by conservative scholar Bruce Waltke, who says, "I was aware that Al Wolters . . . argued that she is a heroic figure, but until I investigated it myself, I was not convinced." But then Waltke came, as he puts it, to the "remarkable

I am convinced that most Christian men are required to endure an enormous amount of extra pressure that worldly men don't face. Men in the world can shamelessly rely on their wives to protect them from sickness by helping them to eat right and stay healthy. They expect their wives to help guard their reputations and protect them from invasions by locking the door and setting the burglar alarm. They look to their wives to advise them of which people to beware of and which ones to trust. Godly men, by contrast, seem as though they're not allowed to admit that their wives protect them. For according to Piper, it is the man's role, not the woman's, to do the protecting.

A few months ago I explained to five church leaders Piper's definition of biblical manhood—that mature manhood is achieved by leading, protecting and providing for women. Intellectually all five men saw the flaws in this definition. Yet they responded to it emotionally by saying to me, "You know what? We like this definition. And you know why? Because it's a definition! It's specific, and it makes us feel secure. It feels so good to be told what it means to be a man, even if this definition isn't right."

Piper's definition of mature manhood strikes an inner cord within men. It offers men a formula by which to identify themselves as men, not boys and not women. And yet (though probably unintentionally), it teaches men to believe that manhood fundamentally is a feeling. Manhood, he says, is something a man senses within himself. If ever he doesn't sense it, he is led to believe it disappears.

Manhood is a struggle for identity. As Leon Podles puts it, "Manhood . . . is not inborn, but a great and difficult achievement." Men become men, he says, by dissociating from women psychologically. According to Podles (whose book *The Church Impotent* has been promoted by the Council on Biblical Manhood and Womanhood), manhood amounts to "separation."[19] He says, "Becoming a man begins with a break with the mother, but continues

---

conclusion that the poem represents the ideal wife as a heroic entrepreneur in the marketplace" (see Waltke, "The Role of the 'Valiant Wife' in the Marketplace," *Crux* 35, no. 3 [1999]: 23).

[19]Leon Podles, *The Church Impotent* (Dallas: Spence, 1999), p. 45.

throughout life with a rejection of the feminine."[20] More precisely, he says the key to a man's long-term success hinges upon whether or not he effectively rejects "the feminine in himself."[21] Masculinity thus requires a man to separate, isolate and alienate himself from women and children in order to be able to return "not as a recipient, but a giver."[22]

I disagree. It isn't feminine to be a recipient. It is human. Indeed, it is masculine and feminine to be able to receive. It's masculine, for instance, for a man to receive from a woman. The Bible says God created the woman for the purpose of being man's "helper" (Gen 2:18). A woman cannot help without *providing* help that is meant for him to receive. Help is a form of provision. In that sense, God created the woman to provide for the man.

With regard to the idea of defining masculinity in terms of separation, that too is contrary to the Scriptures. The Bible says that Adam identified himself with Eve from the moment he first saw her. Immediately he knew that she was likened to himself. Thus he did not perceive her as someone strangely feminine to escape from. Receptively Adam claimed her by saying, "This is now bone of my bones" (Gen 2:23). He received her because she was brought to him by God. God Not only put them together but also gave the command, "A man shall . . . be joined to his wife" (Gen 2:24)[23] because according to God, "It is not good for the man to be alone" (Gen 2:18).

To be fair, Podles doesn't tell men to dissociate entirely from women. As a father of six kids, he encourages men to join with women in order to procreate. He warns men, however, that "masculinity is always threatened by femininity" and that a man's union with a woman is a "chronic source of problems for men."[24]

This is where I see the tragedy. Podles inadvertently equates masculinity with fear. Men, he believes, should always keep their guard up against women.

---

[20]Ibid., p. 40.
[21]Ibid., p. 43.
[22]Ibid.
[23]In most cultures, the wife leaves her family and clings to her husband (contra Gen 2:24).
[24]Podles, *The Church Impotent*, p. 60.

Men should be leery. Men should live in fear. Men should be afraid that relationships with women might effectively erase a man's identity. Podles is almost
superstitious. Somehow he believes that femininity is intrinsically more powerful than manhood. Manhood is tenuous, and femininity is contagious. That's
what Podles is saying. No wonder some of his readers are so frightened.

In reality, manhood is a lot more resilient than that (Rom 11:29).

ASKING THE RIGHT QUESTIONS

Now we are getting at the root. The underlying problem is that we're asking
another wrong question. The question "What is manhood?" is not a fruitful one. Indeed, it echoes the other question, Is it better to be a man than
a woman? When the disciples asked Jesus, "Who then is the greatest in the
kingdom of heaven?" Jesus understood that his disciples were not asking
out of innocent curiosity.[25] Their real question, rather, had to do with
themselves. They wanted to know how they would be ranked and how they
might compare with other people. More important, they wanted Christ to
tell them just what it would take for them to prove themselves as men in
worldly terms.

Had the disciples asked, "Master, do you love us? Is it okay for us to be
who we are?" then I believe Jesus might have chosen to remind them of the
parable of the lost sheep (Lk 15), so that they would be assured of their
worth. But the disciples didn't ask a vulnerable question. Instead, they asked
a selfish, guarded one: "Who, then, is the greatest?"

The same could be said about the question What is manhood? It is not
from faith in God that anyone asks it. Granted, if all we want to know is
how boys emerge from childhood into adulthood, then I willingly retract
my statement.[26] But I don't think we're asking "What is adulthood?" Surely

---

[25]For further explanation of my line of reasoning, see the discussion in chapter five, "Is it Better to Be a
Man Than a Woman?"

[26]In 1 Corinthians 13:11, Paul says, "When I was a child, I used to speak as a child, think as a child,
reasons as a child; when I became a man *[aner]*, I did away with childish things." Though gender is not
the subject of 1 Corinthians 13, Paul equates becoming a man not with dismissing "the feminine" but
rather with doing away with childish things.

we are asking something else. What we want to know is how men—not women—can personally acquire a more vital and prestigious identity. That's why the question is unfruitful.

In case you're not convinced, it might be helpful to consider one more definition of manhood. One international leader put it this way. He said that manhood means "graduating from one's mother." I find this quite telling because adulthood means "graduating from one's parents." To graduate from both parents ought to be more desirable, shouldn't it, then graduating only from one's mother? But for some reason, the world's definition of manhood has more to do with dissociating with the feminine than with discovering what it means to be a man.

COMPARING MEN WITH WOMEN

I once asked a group of men, "How many of you would be embarrassed to lose a tennis match to a woman?" Every one of them said they would be, that is, if other men were watching. It's embarrassing for a man to be surpassed by a woman. But it's usually no big deal if a man is surpassed by a woman who is considered to be exceptional. The men I talked to readily agreed that it would not be bad to lose a tennis match to Steffi Graff, no matter who was on the sidelines watching.

Dr. Ted Engstrom and I have talked about this at length. One day he said to me, "I'm eighty-five years old now, so I have nothing to hide. The problem is that we men are insecure."

Stunned by his statement, I said, "Can I put that in my book?"

He laughed in reply, "Sure. We men are jealous and insecure. Back when I was president of Youth for Christ, we made a big mistake by not including women in the leadership."

A common formula for helping Christian men to feel more solid and secure is to coach Christian women to hold back. Thus many Christian women never minister to men, and thus many Christian men never are developed in the faith. Men are weakened when women hold back. Men are weakened to the point of needing all the women to hold back. Over time they become so fragile that they begin to believe that submitting to a woman is tantamount to reverting to back boyhood. Even worse, they forget to consider, much less be thrilled about, their own vast potential in Christ.

FOR MEN ONLY

When I joined the staff of Willow Creek Community Church as a leader in the evangelism department, my job was to find new believers and potential converts and make "fully devoted followers" out of them. I had no clue of how to accomplish such a task. But during prayer, God gave me the idea of pioneering a new ministry for men. For five years prior to that, I had taught in women's ministry. As a result, I knew at least fifty women whose husbands were not actively serving the Lord.

So the first thing I did was ask the wives for permission to minister weekly to their husbands. Along with that, I solicited their ongoing prayers. Their eager support heartily convinced me of God's blessing. Over the next five weeks, I targeted sixty men—a few atheists, one Jewish man, several skeptics and a handful of cynical post-churchgoers. The rest were men who needed to learn more about God. Guess how many showed up? Forty-two.

That evening we agreed to establish the class "For Men Only." We thought the name was funny since the class was going to be taught by a woman. We also established some ground rules. Number one, only men could attend; wives wouldn't be invited to join us. This was the selling point I had originally used to persuade them to attend that first night. I told them, "I'll teach you things your wife doesn't know." Then I assured them that they would not be nagged. No one would elbow them or poke them with the question, "Did ya hear that?" Nor would anybody scowl at them when the lesson coincided with their failures. The only other rule was that the men would be divided into small groups for discussion, so that they could build relationships in the process.

A few months into the class, I decided to do something different. Whereas I usually would join them at one of the tables and participate in the discussion, on this day I decided to leave the room, so the men could have their discussions without me. I divided them into groups, assigned each group a leader, gave them a couple of discussion questions, and proceeded to walk out of the room. Just as I neared the door, one of them called out to me, "Where are you going?"

I answered, "I'm leaving so that you can talk man to man without having a woman in the room." Almost all of them were looking at me.

"Ya'll don't want me to leave?" I inquired. Nope. They all wanted me to stay.

Why did they want me to be there? It wasn't because they needed theological guidance. The questions they were answering were personal. I think it's because they needed a representative, someone to fill the position of the expert in the room. As long I was there, the men could resist the temptation to establish an internal pecking order. As long as I was there, the pecking order didn't really matter. Thus the men felt free to try to make connections with each other.

Did the men in my class compromise their manhood by submitting to a woman? Were they feminized by the dynamic in our group? Podles says Christianity has been feminized by women. He blames the combined influence of Christian mothers at home, women teachers at school, and Christian women at church for the terrible lack of male participation at church.[27] With that, he accuses churchgoing men of being "less masculine" than men who don't go to church. He says, "The more masculine the man, the less likely he is to be interested in religion; the more feminine the man, the more likely he is to be interested in religion."[28] He also says, "Religion is seen as a safe field,

---

[27]The solution is for men to serve at home and school and church. Robert Hicks suggests that a man's world is a "place where he can let it all out," a place where men can be vocal and upset and yell and celebrate. See Robert Hicks, "Why Men Feel So Out of Place at Church" in *What Makes a Man?* ed. Bill McCartney (Colorado Springs: NavPress, 1992), pp. 154-55. I endorse the idea of church becoming a place where men express themselves freely in appropriate ways. Men and women need the community at church to be a place where they can talk freely without having to be "nice" all the time. The men in my men's class often expressed out loud their negative emotions. One night when I was teaching them about David and Goliath, a man with gray hair suddenly stood up and interrupted my reading of 1 Samuel. "I'm mad at you!" he said. "How come?" I replied. He was upset that I was teaching that story as if it were true. I loved that night. We had a great discussion.

[28]Podles, *The Church Impotent*, p. 8.

a refuge from the challenges of life, and therefore attracts men who are fearful of making the break with the secure world of childhood dominated by women. These are men who have problems following the path of masculine development."[29]

Podles furthermore says that evangelical Christians have assembled more committees on the place of women in the church than on the problem of the absence of men.[30]

It's true that more should be done to bring men back into church, but I disagree sharply with Podles's conclusion that men who are at church attend it because they want to be boys. The men in my class were men, not boys. They hated being less knowledgeable than their wives about the Bible. It irritated them to feel incompetent at church. I believe that's why most men would rather play golf than go to church. Most men who are bad golfers would rather go play bad golf than go to church. That's how incompetent they feel in the house of God. It would take a miracle for biblically incompetent men to feel excited about gathering with a group of biblically competent women. And yet, most men are delighted to follow a woman leader as long as she honors them as men.[31]

Someone may criticize me. But what can be said about the outcome? The wives were overjoyed when their husbands came home from class, explaining things they had learned. One wife told me her husband kept her awake at night after class for two or three hours every week—and her husband wasn't even a Christian. But a few months later, he did become a Christian. So did the Jewish man. Other men developed into leaders.

Henrietta Mears led a ministry that was far more fruitful than my men's class. She led hundreds of young men and women into relationship with

[29]Ibid., p. xiv.
[30]Ibid., p. xv. In part, Podles is right. Evangelicals have relied almost entirely upon women to rear Christian boys. Thus it's no wonder that boys in the church are subjected to the standards of women (e.g., sitting still, taking fewer physical risks during play time). Again, the solution is for Christian men to serve as leaders in youth groups and children's ministry.
[31]It helps when women do things such as give men a chance to do gentlemanly things such as open the door, acknowledge men's strength and let men speak for themselves without interrupting them.

Christ and then discipled them into maturity. Lloyd John Olgilvie, Richard
Halverson, Bill Bright and Billy Graham, to name a few, were influenced pro-
foundly in a positive way by her ministry. All four of these men, even to this
day, attribute Dr. Mears as being their primary mentor who prepared them
for a life of ministry.

THE BIBLICAL EVIDENCE

It is not unprecedented for Christian women to lead men. The Bible tells of
Miriam, Deborah, Huldah, Abigail, Priscilla, Phoebe, Junia, and others.[32]
Nor is it necessary to define masculinity in terms of leading,[33] protecting,
providing and femininity in terms of submitting, nurturing and receiving, for
none of these activities inherently are gender specific. Look at the biblical evidence.

Jesus was a man, but he received from women. His itinerant ministry was
partly funded and provided for by women (Lk 8:3). He also upheld the good
Samaritan as a model minister for nurturing the hurt man on the road (Lk
10:30-37). And what did God tell Abraham? God told him not to lead his
wife Sarah but rather to listen to her and cooperate with her wishes (Gen
21:12).[34] Moreover, God rewarded Rahab for protecting two male spies
(Josh 2; 6). God also commissioned Deborah to be the leader of the sons of
Israel, even when the people were at war. Barak so affirmed her in her leadership that he asked her to go into battle (Judg 4:6-8).

Sometimes it is wise for a man to lead and for a woman to affirm his leadership. Sometimes it is it right for a man to protect a woman and a woman
to nurture a man. Sometimes it is best for a man to provide and a woman to
receive. But at other times, God wills the reverse.

---

[32]For a more extensive list of women in the Bible, see Edith Deen, *All of the Women of the Bible* (San Francisco: Harper & Row, 1955).

[33]Author David Pawson sees leadership itself as "male" (see Pawson, *Leadership Is Male* [Nashville: Thomas Nelson, 1988]. The implication is that women are unfit, even to lead women and children.

[34]This is not to overlook the fact that Sarah submitted to Abraham. My intention is not to argue against men being leaders. My point is to confess that men are not the *only* leaders in the kingdom of God.

DISCUSSION QUESTIONS

1. What kinds of expectations do people in your church place on Christian men? What expectations do the men in your family place on themselves as men?

2. Why is it often more embarrassing for a man to go to counseling or therapy than for a woman? Weave 2 Corinthians 12:9, "My . . . power is perfected in weakness," into your discussion.

3. What do think of Leon Podles's view of masculinity?

4. How does John Piper's definition of mature masculinity compare with a mother's way of relating to her children?

8

MASCULINITY AND FEMININITY

We are all soldiers fighting battles in enemy territory.
DENNIS RAINEY

Whenever I teach the class called "Men and Women in Ministry," I ask my students to discuss their observations about the meaning of masculinity and femininity. Then I draw a chart with four different categories: the world, the Christian community, nature and the Bible (see table 8.1).

Table 8.1 The meaning of masculinity and femininity

	Men/Masculinity	Women/Femininity
The world		
The Christian community		
Nature		
The Bible		

My students typically say that the world defines masculinity as

- Being macho
- Being strong and athletic
- Being a leader
- Being autonomous and independent
- Being logical
- Being competitive
- Being tall or stout
- Being the breadwinner
- Being decisive
- Being funny
- Being in control of his emotions, except for his anger
- Being crude and vulgar (burping, etc.)
- Being a risk taker (driving fast cars, etc.)
- Being sexually potent or ready for a sexual conquest
- Being able to win a fight

The world, they say, defines femininity as

- Being emotional
- Being submissive
- Being beautiful
- Being sexy
- Being skinny (always dieting)
- Being innocent and pure
- Being soft and sensitive
- Being catty and manipulative
- Being jealous
- Being dumber than the guys
- Being ladylike
- Having babies

The Christian community, they say, defines masculinity as

- Being the Bible Answer Man
- Being the spiritual leader
- Being responsible for his family
- Being sexually moral
- Being decisive
- Being in charge
- Being gentle and strong all at once
- Being in control of his emotions, except his anger
- Being able to protect his family
- Being the breadwinner
- Being held accountable for all the above as well as his family

The Christian community, they say, defines femininity as

- Being prayerful—covering her family and church in prayer
- Taking care of her children
- Being a good mother

- Being submissive
- Being sensitive
- Having a quiet and gentle spirit
- Being a wise woman such as the Proverbs 31 woman
- Going to Bible studies

- Being dependent
- Being modest
- Being pretty and sexy in a subtle kind of way
- Being relatively slim

Here I usually pause and ask the class to compare the lists. First I ask them, "What do men give up whenever they become Christians?" Graduate and undergraduate classes typically answer, "They give up their sexual freedom. They also forfeit the attitude of being macho. They have to start submitting to God rather than being autonomous. They have to become responsible, not only for themselves but also for their family.[1] They become accountable for everything that happens at home and church. They have to become spiritual leaders. They're expected to be Bible Answer Men."

One day the president of the Azusa Pacific University student body, a young undergraduate man, blurted, "This is what makes me angry! Men are expected to be everything at church! I totally understand why so many guys hate church. It's like you can't even ask a question. My girlfriend is so lucky because she can ask all the questions she wants. If a guy like me does that, he looks stupid."

So then I ask, "What do women give up when they become Christians?"

And the students usually say, "Not as much." My students say she gains from joining the church. She finds access to God. She acquires a sense of power through prayer. She takes on the critical role of protecting her family through prayer. She doesn't have to work outside the home; she depends on her husband. She doesn't have any pressure to know everything, and yet she

---

[1]Another way to put it is that men lose their individualism. They lose their freedom to live without the "inconvenience" of having to answer to and care for other people. Of course, in today's egalitarian society, single women face the same of kind of perceived "loss." It's no surprise, then, that the national trend is for more privileged people to get married later in life.

gets to go to Bible studies to learn. Furthermore, she's allowed to reveal her sex appeal as long as she tempers her dress with a hint of modesty. About the only thing she loses is the chance to be a peer of the men.

In reality, Christian women gain nothing more from Christ than Christian men do. But culturally speaking, the losses and gains are different for women and men. According to the stereotypes, men have more to lose and women have more to gain from the Christian community. I wonder if this accounts, at least in part, for the reason why men are less likely than women to attend a local church.

MEN AND WOMEN IN THE CHRISTIAN COMMUNITY

It's interesting to note a few of the distinctions between men and women that my students say describe the Christian community. To begin with, I have found that whether I'm teaching pastors in the seminary or young Christians in college or adults in the church, one same remark is always given—that within the Christian community it's feminine to pray. Why is this? Who decided that women, and not men, should be prayer warriors? The Bible doesn't say that prayer is a woman's activity. God commands all Christians to "pray without ceasing" (1 Thess 5:17). First Timothy 2:8, of all places in the Bible, says men (males) should pray, "lifting up holy hands, without wrath and dissension." It is great that men pray at Promise Keepers events, but that is not enough. How many churches can boast of having prayer groups filled with men?

Another telling observation that comes from my classes is that while women go to Bible study, men attend accountability groups. And what is the implication? Women should know the Scriptures, and men should live the Scriptures without knowing them. Isn't that self-defeating? Men are supposed to become Bible Answer Men, and yet women are the ones at Bible study. Consequently, many Christian men remain ignorant of the Word while many Christian women remain unchallenged by the Word. And as a result, the body of Christ is weakened.

Another problem is that Christian men often feel intimidated due to their lack of knowledge of the Scriptures. Thus they don't exert themselves in church leadership or decision making because they feel too afraid that will do something unbiblical (or stupid) in the process.

Conversely, Christian women often feel intimidated due to their lack of self-confidence in the presence of Christian men. Many Christian women are afraid that they'll be hurt if they speak up around men. In their experience, men don't listen anyway, so why try? Another set of women told me they're afraid to unleash their strength. They said, "We're afraid because if we get involved in church leadership, then we're likely to go overboard and take full control of the men!"

Men are afraid, and women are afraid. Men feel overly pressured to be perfect, and women feel overly pressured to hold back. Consequently both choke under the pressure of their fears.

I could go on and on. Another observation is that while women in the Christian community are expected to be beautiful for their husbands, they're also to be modest for the Lord. But how many Christian husbands hold their wives accountable to dress modestly in public? The problem is so bad that most believers have forgotten that immodesty is sinful. In fact, from the way some preachers preach, women are led to believe that immodesty is part of being beautiful. At a national marriage conference my husband and I attended, one of the keynote speakers explicitly said that God designed men for utilitarian service (men are born to work) and women primarily for beauty (women are born to be beautiful for their husbands).[2] The moment the keynote speaker

---

[2]The speaker based his argument on the fact that the Hebrew verbs used in the Genesis account are different. He said the word *formed* in Genesis 2:7 ("the Lord God formed man of dust") implies that men were designed for usefulness since the word *yasar* can connote the idea of a potter forming "plain pottery" that lacks beauty. By contrast, he said the word *fashioned* found in Genesis 2:22 ("And the Lord God fashioned into a woman the rib") implies that women were designed for beauty since the word *banah* can connote the idea of the founding of a dazzling and sophisticated city. With that, he said the verb indicates complexity—like that of a woman—instead of the simplicity of a man. The speaker's exegesis reminds me of a comment made by Ray Ortlund Jr. In describing his vision of the creation of the man, Ortlund says nothing about Adam's physique. But in describing his vision of the creation of the woman, he says, "The Creator goes to work, opening the man's side, removing a rib, closing the wound, and building the woman. There she stands, perfectly gorgeous . . . " See Ray Ortlund Jr., "Male-Female Equality and Male Headship: Genesis 1—3" in *Recovering Biblical Manhood and Womanhood*, ed. John Piper and Wayne Grudem (Wheaton, Ill.: Crossway, 1991), pp. 100-101. Whoever says that women were made less for work and

said that, the woman next to me (whom I did not know) whispered in my ear, "My husband won't have sex with me because he says I'm too fat."[3] She groaned in discouragement, "This is the last thing I want him to hear."

Many of the norms within the Christian community are more cultural than biblical. For example, according to the Scriptures, there is nothing innately masculine about preaching. Yet how often has it been said that "men preach from the Scriptures and women share from their hearts"? If you think about it, saying that men preach and women share is like saying men sweat and women glow. Everybody knows that men and women sweat, but we don't always want to admit—for cultural reasons—that women's sweat is absolutely feminine. To be feminine means to be "of a woman." Thus women's sweat is no more masculine than women's preaching.

The next section of the chart, what nature says, further illustrates our cultural biases. Nature, my students tend to say, shows that men are

- Hunters
- Fighters
- Sexually oriented
- Sexually aroused whenever they see an attractive woman
- Competitive
- Undomestic

Nature, they say, shows that women are

- Sensitive
- Emotional
- Relational

---

more for beauty hasn't paid enough attention to Proverbs 31. Nor have they noticed that the Hebrew word *yasar* quite frequently refers to a potter making far more sophisticated things than plain pots. For example, in Isaiah 43:1, the word *yasar* is used to refer to God having formed the whole nation of Israel. In Amos 4:13, the same word refers to God having formed the mountains. In Isaiah 45:7, it refers to God having formed light.

[3]This story reminds me of a line from David Pawson, who says, "She [a wife] must not *tell* him [her husband] what she thinks he should do or be; rather, she must become more attractive to look at and more attractive to live with (both will result from a right inner attitude to the husband)." See David Pawson, *Leadership Is Male* (Nashville: Thomas Nelson, 1988), p. 63.

- Nurturing and caring
- Domestic and civil
- Maternal

Taking notice of the fact that *maternal* is listed for women while *paternal* doesn't make the list for men, I routinely ask my students, "Are women more motherly than men are fatherly? Is it more natural for a mother to be motherly than it is for a father to be fatherly? Did God design women with a greater propensity to be a good parent? Are men by design ill-suited for parenting and fatherhood?"[4]

More and more fathers are paying attention to their children, but overall, the mother is expected to be the primary caregiver of the kids. This is a cultural bias.[5] If anything, it's unnatural for children to be parented by one parent, not two. Luke 1:17 says that one of things John the Baptist was assigned to do in preparation for the coming of the Lord was to preach repentance so that "the fathers'" hearts would return to the children (Lk 1:17). The Bible says parenting is for mothers *and* fathers.[6] But within the Christian community, fathering is not always seen as a natural part of being masculine.

This brings us to another major issue. Somehow the church expects all the members in it to learn to relate to God as Father in spite of the fact that fatherhood is typically not modeled well by prominent Christian men. Father-

---

[4]Sociologist David Popenoe says, "Men are not biologically as attuned to being committed fathers as women are to being committed mothers. Left culturally unregulated, men's sexual behavior can be promiscuous, their paternity casual, their commitment to families weak." See David Popenoe, *Life Without Father* (New York: Free Press, 1996), p. 4. Is Popenoe right? Did God the Father create men with a disinclination to be fathers? Or is this another casualty of the Fall? I believe the latter—that men's propensity to dissociate from women and children is an aspect of fallenness and sin rather than of men's inherent design. I also believe that men, by grace, can be very committed husbands and fathers.

[5]Complementarian Weldon Hardenbrook says, "Over the course of 150 years, from the mid-eighteenth century to the end of the nineteenth century, American men walked out on their God-given responsibility for moral and spiritual leadership in the homes, schools, and Sunday schools of the nation." Quoting sociologist Lawrence Fuchs, Hardenbrook further notes, "The groundwork for the 20th century fatherless home was set. By the end of the 19th century for the first time it was socially and morally acceptable for men not to be involved with their families." See Weldon Hardenbrook, "Where's Dad? A Call for Fathers with the Spirit of Elijah" in *Recovering Biblical Manhood and Womanhood*, ed. John Piper and Wayne Grudem (Wheaton, Ill.: Crossway, 1991), p. 379.

[6]See Proverbs 1—4; Ephesians 6:1-4; Colossians 3:20-21; 1 Timothy 3:4.

hood isn't valued enough. Fatherhood is seen as a part-time job that requires very little from a man. Rare is the Christian father who prioritizes his kids above his work. Rare is the Christian father who exemplifies what it means to be available for his kids when they need help. Most of the time it's the mother who helps the kids, the mother who prioritizes the children. Christian fathers tend to be more absent than fatherly. Thus it's often difficult for people to conceive of God as a fatherly Father. Perhaps that helps explain why calling God "Mother" has increasingly become a growing trend.[7] These days, for most Christians in the United States, the word *mother* means "attentive and caring," while the word *father* means "busy and gone."

We're down to the last two observations. First, women are seen as prayer warriors but not warriors. This puts women at a tremendous disadvantage spiritually. The Lord is a warrior (Ex 15:3), and women, like men, are made in his warrior image. Unfortunately, however, some Christians are being taught that women are not made in the warrior image of God. Instead, they are told that God created men uniquely in God's image such they alone are designed to enter battle.[8] Women, it is said, are made in God's image too, but uniquely in the sense that they reflect God's tenderness, not his power.[9] This is not based on Scripture. The Bible does not say, "Men were made in part of the image of God while women were made in the other part." No, the Bible says male and female were created "in His own image" (Gen 1:27).

In truth, the military images in the Scriptures rightly apply to both men

---

[7]In the next chapter, I will show why I think it's wrong to call God "Mother."

[8]Writer John Eldredge, for instance, says, "The boy is a warrior; the boy is his name." See John Eldredge, *Wild at Heart* (Nashville: Thomas Nelson, 2001), pp. 11, 140ff. When Eldredge says this, he implies that the girl is *not* the warrior. Unfortunately, Eldredge sometimes argues on the basis of feeling, not Scripture. For instance, he says, "Desire reveals design, and design reveals destiny" (p. 48). Using this logic, any kind of behavior could be justified. I admire Eldredge's excellence in writing and affirm what he has to say about men needing to be healed by God, but he overuses Hollywood and classic romantic tales as a way of trying to capture men's attention. Thus some of his points are more winsome than biblically accurate.

[9]Throughout *Wild at Heart*, Eldredge contrasts men and women, claiming that men are wild like God and women are tender like God. But in doing this, he fails to say that love itself is both tender and wild (cf. Mt 22:37-39).

and women. Indeed, the Lord commands women just as much as men to do soldierly things such as "to contend earnestly for the faith" (Jude 3), "stand firm" (1 Cor 16:13) and "persevere" during hardship and tribulation (Jas 1:12). No verse in the Bible commands Christian women to be delicate or passive. Instead, the Word of God says Christian women ought to be strong.[10] The woman in Proverbs, for instance, "girds herself with strength and makes her arms strong."[11] Moreover, "strength and dignity" are her clothing. Women may be charmed by the romantic idea of being carried into the horizon by a knight in shining armor, but Jesus commands her to be donned in armor too (Eph 6:10-18). She is to walk on her own two feet, carrying her cross, following Jesus Christ (Mt 16:24).

Many Christian women do not want to be warriors. They would rather be God's little girls. To be a woman soldier in the army of the Lord sounds to them as though they have to become femi-Nazis. But that's not true. It is not unfeminine to fight "the good fight " (1 Tim 1:8; 6:12). Fighting the good fight is a Christian thing to do, not a masculine thing to do. John Piper, Dennis Rainey and Elisabeth Elliot all agree.[12] Christian women need a "wartime mentality."[13]

Recently I challenged a group of women to learn to see themselves as warriors in spiritual armor. Turning to Ephesians 6, I said, "And take . . . the sword of the Spirit, which is the word of God." One woman felt unsettled by what she heard. She said to me, "I disagree with you. I think it's best for me to keep my sword in the sheath."

---

[10]That is not to say, however, that she should be as physically strong as a man. Generally speaking, women are physically weaker than men.

[11]Scholar Bruce Waltke discovered, to his surprise, that the Hebrew of Proverbs 31 is filled with military language. See Bruce Waltke, "The Role of the 'Valiant Wife' in the Marketplace," *Crux* 35, no. 3 (September 1999).

[12] Dennis Rainey says, "We are all soldiers fighting battles in enemy territory against a fierce opponent." See Dennis Rainey, "How to Leave a Legacy in Your Home" in *Real Family Life* 4, no. 2, a publication of Family Life, a division of Campus Crusade. Elisabeth Elliot echoes the same attitude when she says, "I want to do my best to pass on to younger people those soldierly qualities and necessities that we [missionaries] have to learn." See the interview of Elisabeth Elliot by Russell Shubin, "Strength in the Face of Adversity," *Mission Frontiers: Women and Missions* (August 1999): 21.

[13]See Piper, "A Vision of Biblical Complementarity," p. 57.

Intrigued by her comment, I replied, "But if you keep it in your sheath, what's the point of having it?"

She answered, "Because I need to use it."

Perplexed by her answer, I said, "I don't understand. I thought you were planning to keep it in your sheath."

She said, "That's what I'm going to do if any men are around; that way the men will feel like men."

In light of Ephesians 6, it's unbiblical to think of war as a masculine activity. Ephesians 6 commands every Christian—young and old, male and female—to put on spiritual armor and use it every day. God doesn't consider the Bible, a two-edged sword, to be a masculine tool. Women have full access to the Word of God, and women are to handle it accurately (2 Tim 2:15). Women of God are included in the battle of the Lord. They don't sit on the sidelines watching the men. They wear the spiritual armor because they need it. They're out there too, just like the men, building the kingdom of God.

I can think of three women in Scripture who are praised for their military feats. First, Deborah is commended for leading ten thousand men into a battle against King Jabin and his army. Second, Jael is celebrated as "most blessed of all women" for killing Sisera, the commander of the enemy army. Read the story for yourself in Judges 4—5. There you will find that the Lord orchestrated the story so that women would accomplish his victory. And don't forget the woman in 2 Samuel 20. The Scriptures describe her as a "wise woman" (2 Sam 20:16) and a "mother in Israel" (2 Sam 20:19). She literally saved her city by having the head of Sheba, King David's enemy, physically chopped off and hurled over the side of the wall.[14]

It's possible to be a feminine warrior. As I mentioned in chapter one, my mother was a she-bear kind of mom who fiercely protected us children. Growing up, I felt safe because I trusted my mother implicitly to guard us. At Willow Creek, Nancy Ortberg often jokes in a serious way that as some

---

[14]I believe women can be of great service in combat, especially since intelligence is the most needed weapon in today's technological age.

women boast of being willing "to die" for their kids, so she boasts of being willing "to kill" on behalf of hers. Most Christian mothers can relate.

The last thing to mention from the chart is what I consider to be the most destructive cultural misperception of all. To claim that women by nature are "more relational" than men is to tempt men to believe that they just don't have what it takes to have a good relationship with God. This is a dangerous and demonic fallacy.[15] No wonder men don't pray. Prayer happens in the context of relationship. Contrary to popular belief, men are radically relational beings.[16] Even before the Fall, it was "not good for the man to be alone" (Gen 2:18). Male human beings, just like female human beings, are made in the image of a radically relational God. God is so relational that he's triune. Yet men have been taught to disregard this.

To compound the issue, men have been taught that friendship is another "woman thing." Thousands upon thousands of Christian men are virtually friendless. Men don't think it's manly to have close friends because friendships are relational. In the Christian culture, relating is for women. Thus I believe that Christian men are the ones most deprived by the stereotypical biases in our culture.

In the Scriptures, men enjoy deep friendships. For example, Jesus was a friend of Lazarus. In fact, Jesus cried so hard when Lazarus died that other people marveled—not at the fact that he was shedding tears in public but at the intensity of the expression of his love. "See how He loved him!" (Jn 11:36) is what they said. Another famous friendship happened between two valiant warriors, David and Jonathan. The Bible says that David proclaimed the love of Jonathan as "more wonderful than the love of women" (2 Sam 1:26). No, they weren't gay. It is not gay for a man to love another man. Loving relationships are hardly ever meant to be sexual.

---

[15]As Christians, we are not ignorant of the schemes of the devil (2 Cor 2:11).

[16]The movie *Cast Away* brilliantly depicts how the image of God causes in humanity a fundamental need to be in relationship. Tom Hanks, the protagonist in the movie, survives the ordeal in part by befriending a volleyball ("Wilson"), on which he drew a face. When Wilson is lost, Tom Hanks cries and cries. It's a gripping scene that makes the whole movie worthwhile.

When I taught third grade, I made a fully concerted effort to impress upon the children in my class the truth about love: that love is hardly ever sexual. With every drop of energy I could muster, I said to my students in the public school, "Hardly, hardly ever is love meant to be romantic. Nearly, nearly always love is meant to be for family and friends." With all my might, I told those kids, "You're going to grow up and marry only one person. There's only one person you kiss on the lips. You kiss everybody else on the cheek. Being lovey-dovey is not the norm."

In our third-grade class, it became normal for the children and me to say "I love you" to each other. I told them that I loved them every day. In our class it was acceptable for the children to say they loved one another. One parent, nevertheless, became offended when she saw on her little boy's paper that he had written to the teacher, "I love you." So I invited that mother to visit our class. Confidently I said to her, "Cory doesn't have a crush on me. Come see for yourself." She stayed in our classroom all afternoon. As soon as school ended, she came up to me and said, "Well, it was really Cory's father who had the problem. I'll tell him now that everything's okay."

For us to assume that relationships in the classroom or close friendships in the Bible were either gay or inappropriate shows that people in our culture are biased. We are so conditioned to think of sex that we hardly can conceive of genuinely wholesome affection. The love in my third-grade classroom wasn't sexual. Nor was it sexual when John the apostle reclined his head upon Jesus' breast (Jn 13:23). Nor was it sexual when Jonathan and David kissed each other and wept on the day they said goodbye (1 Sam 20:41).

It's difficult for people, especially in American Anglo culture, to accept that love doesn't have to be sexual. Though I've never heard a sermon preached on it, there is such a thing as "the affection of Christ Jesus." The apostle Paul longed for the Philippians "with the affection of Christ Jesus" (Phil 1:8). I believe he touched people tenderly and bonded with them personally without crossing sexual boundaries. Paul was so affectionate to the Thessalonian Christians that he described himself to them as having been a

gentle "nursing mother" (1 Thess 2:7). Likewise, he was so emotionally connected to the believers in Ephesus that when God called him to leave, the
Ephesian elders "wept aloud" and "embraced" and "repeatedly kissed him"
(Acts 20:37). The Bible gives ample counterevidence to the contemporary
myths that falsely say that affection has to be sexual and that men are less
relational than women.[17]

Much more could be said about the fallacies that Christians are taught to
believe about themselves. My purpose here is to challenge the church to learn
the difference between what we have been taught to think and what the Bible
says is true about men and women.

DISCUSSION QUESTIONS

1. How are masculinity and femininity undrstood within your church or
   Christian community?

2. Are women more motherly than fathers are fatherly? What is the difference between fatherhood and motherhood? How much value does fatherhood have?

3. What expectations should the Christian community place on men?

4. How much time do the men in your church spend in prayer? Do they
   know how to pray? What would help them to pray more?

---

[17]Non-Anglo men as well as men outside of the United States easily attest that this is a cultural bias.

9
The Authority of Biblical Metaphors

What comes into our minds when we think about God is the most important thing about us. The history of mankind will probably show that no people has ever risen above its religion, and man's spiritual history will positively demonstrate that no religion has ever been greater than its idea of God. . . . Always the most revealing thing about the Church is her idea about God.

A. W. TOZER, *THE KNOWLEDGE OF THE HOLY*

A. W. Tozer's famous words "What comes into our minds when we think about God is the most important thing about us" lead to the heart of the issue. Who is God? Do we believe that God is male? If so, then how can it be that women are created in his image (Gen 1:27)?

Finding Lisa

Whenever I have the chance, I like to ask Christians to close their eyes and focus on the God to whom they pray. After two or three minutes I ask them to share their impressions of God, especially with regard to what he looks like, if they imagine him visually at all. Many of them do. In fact, the two most common reports from people that I've talked to are that they see a bright light gloriously gleaming in their eyes—or that they see a vague image of a very old man with a beard.[1]

Years ago, when I taught third grade in the public schools, I asked the children one day, "Where can you always find Lisa [one of their classmates]?"

They started throwing out their guesses, "At her house!" "At her desk!" "Here in Texas!"

Shaking my head, I said, "But what if she goes on a vacation to Hawaii?" So they guessed again, "You can always find her with her family!"

I inquired, "Is she with her family *now*?" The children instantly understood the answer was no. Thus they were left feeling thoroughly stumped with no more guesses to conjecture.

Now that I had their attention, I announced to them the answer: "You can always find Lisa in Lisa's body. If you want to know where Lisa is, you've got to hunt for Lisa's body, because that's where Lisa lives." The children started giggling. I asked them further, "Wouldn't it be silly to hunt for Lisa in John's body?" They laughed even harder. "And if I ever fell asleep, would you come tap me on the shoulder and say, 'Lisa, is that you? Are you hiding in our teacher's body today?'" They thought that was hilarious.

I tell this "Finding Lisa" story because it illustrates an important point. The only way anyone can find Lisa is by locating her body. We find her by seeing her or hearing her or touching her. In other words, we find her by sensing she is there. We sense her empirically through the use of our physical senses. But that is not how we apprehend God.

The Scriptures say that "God is spirit" (Jn 4:24) and that we are not to make for ourselves "an idol" of him (Ex 20:4) in the form "of any figure, the likeness of male or female" (Deut 4:16). To quote theologian Charles Hodge, "God is immaterial. None of the properties of matter can be predicated of Him. He is not extended or divisible, or compounded, or visible, or tangible. He has neither bulk nor form."[2] In other words, God is not a creature with a body. It's heretical to assign to him a form, even the form of a male.[3]

---

[1]One influential children's book that does this is Max Lucado's *You Are Special*. I love that book; I have purchased five or six copies of it to date because its overall message is so good. The one drawback is that God is pictured in it as an old man with a beard. See Max Lucado, *You Are Special* (Wheaton, Ill.: Crossway, 2002).

[2]Charles Hodge, *Systematic Theology* (Grand Rapids, Mich.: Baker, 1988), p. 138.

[3]I refer the reader to my favorite C. S. Lewis book, *Miracles* (New York: Collier, 1947). In the chapter en-

GOD IS SPIRIT

God is invisible; we cannot see him with our eyes. Even if we could, we would die. The Bible says our bodies are too frail to behold him in person (Ex 33:20). True, we can hear God speak, not by the power of our ears, but rather by the power of our faith. We hear him speak inaudibly. His voice is so real that we don't need our ears in order to hear him. A deaf person can hear the voice of God.

Since God cannot be found, as Lisa can be, by the faculties of the senses, he must be apprehended by faith. By faith we discover him as he reveals himself. For instance, when Moses asked God to identify himself, God replied to him, "I AM WHO I AM" (Ex 3:14).

British writer Dorothy Sayers explains this very well in the following excerpt:

> The Jews, keenly alive to the perils of pictorial metaphor, forbade the representation of the Person of God in graven images. Nevertheless, human nature and the nature of human language defeated them. No legislation could prevent the making of verbal pictures; God walks in the garden, stretches out his arm. . . . To forbid the making of pictures about God would be to forbid thinking about God at all, for man is so made that he has no way to think except in pictures. But continually, throughout the history of the Jewish-Christian Church, the voice of warning has been raised against the power of the picture-makers: "God is a spirit," "without body, parts or passion"; "He is pure being." "I am that I am."[4]

I like this next one even better. Sayers writes:

---

titled "Horrid Red Things," Lewis provides a marvelous discussion about the concept and usefulness of imagery as a means for communicating divine things. For instance, he explains how impossible it is for human beings to conceive of the city of London in all its detail, and then he compares this impossibility with the even greater task of trying to gain a conception of almighty infinite God. Lewis says this is why people are inclined to do silly things such as devise in our minds, unwittingly, a picture of a God with a body, even though we know he is bodiless. Lewis thus concludes that genuine Christians tend to have traces of heresy mixed into the muddle of our thinking (see pp. 68-80). Note also, in another selection, that Lewis chides the person who holds "a shallow view of imagery" (see C. S. Lewis, "Priestesses in the Church?" *God in the Dock* [Grand Rapids, Mich.: Eerdmans, 1994], p. 237).

[4]See Dorothy Sayers, *The Whimsical Christian* (New York: Collier, Macmillan, 1987), p. 114.

It may be perilous, as it must be inadequate, to interpret God by analogy with ourselves, but we are compelled to do so; we have no other means of interpreting anything. Skeptics frequently complain that man has made God in his own image; they should in reason go further (as many of them do) and acknowledge that man has made all existence in his own image. If the tendency to anthropomorphism is a good reason for refusing to think about God, it is an equally good reason for refusing to think about light, or oysters, or battleships. It may be quite perilous, and it must be inadequate, to interpret the mind of our pet dog by analogy with ourselves; we can by no means enter directly into the nature of a dog; behind the appealing eyes and the wagging tail lies a mystery as inscrutable as the mystery of the Trinity.[5]

C. S. Lewis offers yet more helpful insight when he writes, "Events on a historical level are the sort of things we can talk about literally [for] they were perceived by the senses of men. . . . [But] the truth is that if we are going to talk at all about things which are not perceived by the senses, we are forced to use language metaphorically."[6]

No one can describe God adequately. The best we can do is speak about him in metaphors because the imagery of the natural world fails to correlate in a literal way to the supernatural being of God.[7]

THE METAPHORS ARE METAPHORS

What is a metaphor?

A metaphor is seeing one thing as something else, pretending this is that because we do not know how to think or talk about this, so we use that as a way of saying something about it.[8]

---

[5]Ibid., p. 115.

[6]Lewis, *Miracles*, pp. 72, 79, 80. Sayers echoes the same thought, "In particular, when we speak about something of which we have no direct experience, we must think by analogy or refrain from thought." See Sayers, *The Whimsical Christian*, p. 115. Note also that Thomas Aquinas likewise said all language about God must necessarily be analogical.

[7]Language such as "God is gracious" is straightforward language, not pictorial. But it is nonetheless analogical in that we can only compare his graciousness with that of a human being.

[8]See Sally McFague, *Models of God* (Philadelphia: Fortress, 1987), quoted in Alister McGrath, *Christian Theology* (Cambridge, Mass.: Blackwell, 1994), p. 139.

Biblical metaphors are statements of truth. But they are true metaphorically, not literally. For instance, it is true that God is Father. But God does not exist as a biological dad or a male parent of the Son.[9] Mysteriously, the Father is the Father, even though the Father is not a day older than the Son (Jn 1:1). By the same token, the second person of the Trinity truly *is* God's Son. But that doesn't mean he was born of a female deity. It is heretical to believe or even insinuate that the Son of God within the Trinity was ever born in the heavenlies at all. For as the Son within the Trinity, he is "begotten," not born. [10]

To keep things straight, Jesus of Nazareth had an earthly age. Jesus the Messiah was male. But Jesus the Messiah is the Son made flesh. There is nothing metaphorical about his earthly existence as a Son. He literally was conceived by the Holy Spirit and born of the virgin Mary. This is the shock of the incarnation—that the preincarnate Son became mortal flesh and walked on earth as a man.[11]

THE AUTHORITY OF BIBLICAL METAPHORS

As a professor of theology, one of my priorities is to urge my students to develop a respect for the authority of biblical metaphors. To begin with, biblical metaphors should never be mistaken for anything other than metaphors; they should always be left intact. Metaphors aren't meant to be taken literally, but neither are they meant to be ignored. It is wrong to disregard a biblical metaphor. It is wrong because the metaphors are inspired by God and therefore profitable as well as authoritative.

---

[9]In *Miracles* Lewis writes, "The assertion that God has a Son was never intended to mean that He is a being propagating his kind by sexual intercourse: and so we do not alter Christianity by rendering explicit the fact that 'sonship' is not used of Christ in exactly the same sense in which it is used of men. But the assertion that Jesus turned water into wine was meant perfectly literally, for this refers to something which . . . was well within the reach of our senses and our language" (p. 80).

[10]Referencing Athanasius's *De Incarnatione*, Lewis put it this way, "The Second Person is not only bodiless, but so unlike man that if self-revelation had been His sole purpose, He would not have chosen to be incarnate in a human form" (see Lewis, *Miracles*, p. 76).

[11]It is important to note that the apostle John says the Word became "flesh" (*sarx*), not male (*aner*). See John 1:14.

Let's take a look at one biblical metaphor. In John 10:9, Jesus said, "I am the door." Notice, there is no debate about what kind of door Jesus is. A screen door? A wooden door? A sliding glass door? People aren't squabbling about this particular metaphor, because it is obvious that Jesus isn't literally a door.

But what if people started calling him "the window"? Would that be acceptable? No, that would be unacceptable because Jesus didn't say he is the window. Jesus said, "I am the door." Indeed, the metaphor of a window communicates something different from the metaphor of a door. A window is an opening, but a door is something a person walks through. Your whole self goes through the door. Your whole self enters the kingdom of God not through a window but through one special door, Jesus Christ.

On the one hand, everybody knows that Jesus isn't literally a door. But on the other hand, some of us don't know that the fatherhood of God is metaphorical. One of my students, for example, recently said, "I can concede that Jesus isn't literally a door. But God really is our Father."

"Yes," I said. "God really is our Father. That is totally true, and it's not just a figure of speech. But we must understand that God is our Father in the very same sense that Jesus Christ really is the door. It's a literal fact that there is no other way to God but through the one door, Jesus. It is also a literal fact that God has adopted us as his children. Thus you are correct—God 'really is' our Father.

"But if you try to press the issue of God *literally* being our Father, then to be consistent, you will also have to say that the Son within the Trinity literally is God's Son. In other words, you will drive yourself into a corner by forcing yourself to say that within the Trinity, the Father is older than the Son. For if we insist on being literal, then we will have to accept the unorthodox conclusion that God as a literal father is, by definition, older than his literal son. And yet, we cannot say this and still be orthodox. Indeed, this explains why orthodox Christianity has always maintained that the fatherhood of God is *metaphorical*."[12]

---

[12]If we try to say the converse, that the Son is younger than the Father, then we accidentally suggest there was a time "when the Son was not," which is classic Arianism, an age-old heresy in the church.

Someone else may ask, "But if the fatherhood of God is metaphorical, does that mean we can just as well refer to God as Mother?" No, it doesn't. I am opposed to calling God "Mother," but not because I believe that God is male. I don't believe that at all. I am against it because to do so is to disregard the authority of the God-inspired biblical metaphor. To call God "Mother" is to tamper with the text. It changes the biblical message when God is proclaimed to be our mother.[13] If it didn't, no one would be clamoring to address him as Mother when they pray.

The Bible indicates that God indeed is motherly. Nevertheless the Scriptures do not teach us to address him or conceive of him as "mother." God is Father, and yet the Bible says that he mothered the children of Israel. In Isaiah 66:13, the Lord says, "As one whom his mother comforts, so I will comfort you, and you shall be comforted in Jerusalem."

Bearing this in mind, whenever anyone motherless asks me whether or not God can "be their mother," I say to them that he can be their God—which is better. With that, I explain that it's unbiblical to pray "Dear Mother" to God. But it's acceptable to pray, "Thank you, God, for mothering me."

GOD IS NOT MOTHER

The Bible says that God is Father and Lord and King, not Mother and Lady and Queen. Yet nothing in the Bible even hints of a description, as radical

---

[13]Regarding this, Elizabeth Achtemeier astutely says, "Many have argued that all these terms [e.g., Father, Son, King and so on] are merely metaphors and therefore can be changed at will. But these changes are not merely linguistic. They represent alterations of the understanding of God, and they form the substructure of a religion entirely different from the Christian faith. . . . Indeed, when female terminology is used for God, the birthing image becomes inevitable. Virginia Mollenkott can therefore . . . talk of 'the God with breasts,' 'the undivided One God who births and breast-feeds the universe.' " See Elizabeth Achtemeier, condensed from "Female Language for God: Should the Church Adopt It?" in *The Hermeneutical Quest: Essays in Honor of James Luther Mays on His Sixty-fifth Birthday*, ed. Donald. G. Miller. (Allison Park, Penn.: Pickwick, 1986), pp. 97-114. Roberta Hestenes criticizes Achtemeier for failing to point out that the Bible *does* use birthing imagery in the very idea of people being "born again." I can see what Hestenes means, but I am more sympathetic to Achtemeier's point of view. For when people are "born again," we are born of the Spirit in a nonfleshly way. In feminist theology, the whole creation and everyone in it is said to "born" of the goddess in such a way that human beings are considered to incarnate the divine. See Virginia Ramey Mollenkott, *The Divine Feminine: The Biblical Imagery of God as Female* (New York: Crossroad, 1983), p. 58.

feminists have accused, of a chauvinist male God who runs an ol' boys' network of male pastors and husbands and men.[14] In fact, the female imagery
that describes God in the Scriptures flies in the face of that. No chauvinist
on the planet wants to be described as a woman. And yet the God of the Bible
reveals himself comparatively as a woman who has lost a silver coin (Lk 15:8-
10).[15]

God is Father, not mother. But that doesn't mean he is male and not female, any more than Jesus is "the door" means that Jesus is wooden and not
glass. God is Father and Lord and King, and yet that doesn't mean God is
masculine. It means, rather, that God is separate from creation. This is an extremely important point. For whenever it is believed that the world is derived
from a female deity, people start confusing the biblical distinction between
God the Creator and creation.

Think of what happens if we imagine God pregnant with the world. A pregnant God strongly suggests that the world is part of God. For whenever it is believed that the world is derived from a female deity, people start supposing that
the universe emerged from the body of the deity. Within such a framework, all
of nature is imagined to have come forth from the womb of a female creator,
Mother Nature. It says all of created nature is imagined to exist with her as one.
Once that happens, Christianity collapses into pantheistic pagan religion.[16]

---

[14]Carl F. H. Henry argues persuasively against this. He writes, "The call to revise gender references to
God assumes that the scriptural precedent of masculine terms involves a doctrine of God unacceptable
to the modern mind. The biblical view is said to incorporate patriarchalist notions that need to be bal-
anced by feminist emphases. . . . But the very complaint that the Bible uses sexist language about God
rests upon mistaken assumptions. In sharp distinction from the ancient Near Eastern fertility cults and
their nature gods, the Bible studiously avoids imputing sexual organs to God even anthropomorphically"
(see Carl F. H. Henry, *God, Revelation and Authority*, 6 vols. [Dallas: Word, 1982], 5:159). Alister McGrath
puts it this way: "Neither male nor female sexuality is to be attributed to God" (McGrath, *Christian Theology*, p. 205).

[15]One of my students openly denied that the woman in the parable of the lost coin represents God. He kept
saying, "God is *not* like a woman!" The other students, however, most of whom were male, explained to
him that to be consistent, he would also have to say that the prodigal son's father does not represent God
either. For the parables go together, communicating the theme that God seeks that which is lost.

[16]Radical feminist theologian Rosemary Radford Ruether thus speaks of "the root human image of the
divine as the Primal Matrix, the great womb within which all things, Gods and humans, sky and earth,
human and nonhuman beings are generated." This God/dess, as Ruether terms her, is "the empowering

According to the Scriptures, God is physically separate from his creation. Every person bears his image. But as Father, he is separate nonetheless. Granted, the biblical metaphor is limited. After all, a father's genes are passed on to the offspring no less than are the mother's. But even so, the physical relationship of a father and child is nonetheless more separate than the physical relationship of the mother of that child, especially when she's pregnant.[17]

God is Father, not mother. But that doesn't mean that God is male. Nor does it mean that God is masculine. The metaphor is masculine, but God is not.[18] Carl F. H. Henry puts it this way, "The God of the Bible is a sexless God. When Scripture speaks of God as 'he' the pronoun is primarily personal (generic) rather than masculine (specific); it emphasizes God's personality . . . in contrast to impersonal entities."[19] The same thing is true when Scripture speaks of God in feminine terms. For instance, when Moses sings of the God who "gave [Israel] birth" (Deut 32:18), metaphorically he proclaims that God is like a mother to Israel. And yet, in that same verse, Moses sings of the Rock who "begot" them. In other words, Moses suggests that God is like a mother *and* father.[20]

Someone might argue on the basis of feminine imagery that it is biblical to refer to God as mother. My question then would be, "Is it biblical to refer to God as 'a heavenly bird'?" The Psalms, in particular, are filled with imagery of people hiding beneath "His wings"[21] and being covered by "His pinions" (Ps 91:4). But that doesn't make it proper for anyone to pray, "Dear Bird." Instead, it is better to pray as David did, "Hear my cry, O God. . . . Let me

---

Matrix; She, in whom we live and move and have our being—She comes; She is here." See Rosemary Radford Ruether, *Sexism and God-Talk: Toward a Feminist Theology* (Boston: Beacon, 1983), p. 266.

[17]The physical relationship between mother and child does not make mothers more motherly than fathers fatherly. Indeed, giving birth to children is not something fathers do.

[18]If God were masculine, then women would not be made completely in his image, contra Genesis 1:27; 9:6.

[19]See Henry, *God, Revelation and Authority*, 5:159.

[20]Cf. J. A. Thompson, *Deuteronomy: An Introduction and Commentary*, Tyndale Old Testament Commentaries (Downers Grove, Ill.: InterVarsity Press, 1974), p. 300. Thompson says, "God is here pictured both as father (*begot you*) and as mother (*gave you birth*)."

[21]See Psalms 17:8; 36:7; 57:1; 61:4; 63:7.

take refuge in the shelter of Thy wings."

Biblically we can say that God is more motherly than a nursing mother (Is 49:15). But with that, we insist that he is not to be confused with a female mother goddess physically giving birth to the world. The same principle applies whenever we call God Father. The Lord Jesus taught us to pray, "Our Father" (Mt 6:9). In fact, everywhere in Scripture that God is named, his name is rendered in masculine form. But again, that doesn't mean that God is masculine. It means, rather, that the metaphorical names for God are masculine.

God is God with a capital "G." He is not a male deity as if he were merely a god.[22] God is not a god or a goddess. The Scriptures make it clear—God is God. That means he is inscrutable, above that of being male or female. And yet it was his will to reveal himself in Scripture as Father. For regardless of anyone's culture, the metaphor of father universally reflects the biological fact that fathers on earth are physically more separate from their offspring than are mothers. Moreover, fathers are physically less vulnerable than mothers. Hence, the metaphor of Father implies something different than the metaphor of mother can convey.

DISCUSSION QUESTIONS

1. Have you ever imagined God as an old man with a beard? How do you imagine him when you pray?

2. Read and discuss the quotes from Dorothy Sayers on pages 115-16.

3. How does the masculine pronoun *he* convey that God is personal?

4. In what ways are mothers physically more vulnerable than fathers?

---

[22]The 2001 edition of *Webster's Unabridged Dictionary*, however, incorrectly says in one entry that "God" with a capital "G" is a "male deity." This is highly misleading and contrary to the Scriptures.

10
Every Passage in the Bible Means Something

All Scripture is inspired by God.
2 Timothy 3:16

The next several chapters are devoted to the task of presenting a gospel paradigm of men and women in the church. As we begin, it's important to establish the practical steps of rightly interpreting the Bible.

The first step is to acknowledge and respect the nature of Scripture, for the Bible is different from every book in the world. No other book is as reliable or authoritative as it is because no other book is God-breathed. Every line of Scripture is inspired by God and profitable for teaching, for reproof, for correction, for training in righteousness (2 Tim 3:16). I always tell my students, "I want you to be proud of every verse in the Bible. If anyone asks you about any line, any phrase, any word, then you hold your head high and claim that all of it comes from God. There is no reason to steer away from any passage. As Christians, we are to embrace the full counsel of God's Word."

The second step in interpreting Scripture is to understand the nature of human language. Language is a medium for communication. Language provides a means for people to express themselves, share ideas and connect in a personal way. Language, moreover, is used to convey specific messages. Behind every message lies an intention. The key to understanding the biblical text is to find out the author's intention. For example, what did Paul mean when he said, "The husband is the head of the wife"? The goal of the responsible reader is to answer that question correctly.

The third step in interpreting Scripture is to remember something that is easy to forget: the skills needed for interpreting the Bible are the same skills needed for interpreting any other book. Reading the Bible is no different from reading any other book. Though the Bible is unique, one has to be literate to read it. Just because a person is a believer does not mean that person is capable of reading. Believers must be educated in order to read the Scriptures. We need to know grammar, vocabulary words and basic skills of reading comprehension. It helps even more to be apprised of the historical setting of the original audience and to learn Hebrew and Greek.

The fourth step in interpreting Scripture is to rely on the Holy Spirit for help. Some of us have been told that apart from the Holy Spirit, no one can understand the Bible. Christians such as myself have occasionally been told that atheists can't understand the stories or commandments in Scripture because a veil lies over their hearts (2 Cor 3:13-15 explicitly says "a veil lies over" the hearts of unbelievers, doesn't it?).

I do not hesitate to ascribe credit to the Holy Spirit whenever someone reads the Bible with understanding. Certainly God is the only one who can reveal himself to us. The Holy Spirit enlightens the mind of every believer who comes to Christ. And yet, as I said before, the Holy Spirit does not endow every believer with excellent reading skills. Atheists can decipher the meaning of Scripture insofar as their reading skills allow. What they cannot do is interact with God in their reading.[1]

The advantage of the believer is his or her relationship with God. When Christians read the Scriptures, the Word of God written on the page reso-

---

[1]Granted, an atheist could become a Christian through reading Scripture, but that won't happen unless the atheist repents from his or her unbelief. Apart from faith, no one can interact with God.

nates with the Word of God (Jesus) in our hearts. Christ is the living Word.[2] The living Word helps us to understand the written Word. Nevertheless it is a discipline for Christians to read the Scriptures and read them rightly.

The fifth step in interpreting Scripture has to do with the way we approach our reading of the text. All too often we come to the Bible with undue assumptions, wishes and fears. To begin with, we assume things. We don't all necessarily assume the same things, but we do assume things that are foreign to the text. For instance, we might assume that God as Father means that God is like my father. For those who grew up with abusive fathers, it might seem natural to assume the God of the Bible is abusive. Likewise, for those who grew up with fathers who were passive, it might be automatic to assume the same of God. Regardless of one's upbringing, it is improper to project our private assumptions of what God must be like onto the biblical text.

Another assumption we might impose into our reading of Scripture is to assume there is no cultural gap between the first century and the twenty-first century. As a result, we may assume that it was no big deal for Jesus to teach Mary about eternal things because it's normal for women to be educated today. But indeed, it was extraordinary. Other rabbis shunned the idea of teaching a woman. Jesus was the first rabbi ever to accept a woman student.

A final assumption worth mentioning pertains to the masculine language of Scripture. Politically correct people may feel offended by the lack of feminine pronouns in the Scriptures. For instance, Proverbs 10:9 says, "He who walks in integrity walks securely." But in Hebrew and Greek, pronouns such as this are inclusive. Even so, some people might assume that the writers of the Bible were patriarchal bigots who failed to pay respect to women. But such a perspective is clouded. It cannot be true that Scripture is bigoted, because the God who inspired it is not. Romans 2:11 assures us that "there is no partiality with God." Chauvinism is utterly foreign to God's character.

As followers of Christ, many of us fail to stop to consider the assumptions we import into our reading of the text. We also often fail to recognize the

---

[2]John 1:1 conflated with John 1:14.

wishes that we bring. Unfortunately believers aren't exempt from committing these literary crimes. For instance, Christian slave owners wishing to be justified used the Scriptures as a means of defending themselves. Unmarried people longing for sex have done the same thing. I once heard a senior pastor, a single man, say in a sermon, "Folks, when the Bible says 'abstain' from sexual immorality, the Greek word means 'abstain.' I have tried and tried to find another way to translate it, but that's the only connotation for the word." Let's face it. All of us have a tendency to want to justify our wishes by citing proof texts from the Word.

We also have a tendency to read into the text our fears. If we are fearful of being condemned, for instance, we may not be willing to embrace Jesus' teaching on hell. If we're scared of being alone, we might disregard his teaching on sexual purity. If we we're afraid of losing money, we may become deaf to the biblical teaching on sharing our money with the poor. Countless examples illustrate the same idea.

In summary, the right way to approach the Scriptures is not with assumptions, wishes and fears but rather with honest questions asked in faith. The Bible ought to be read with these kinds of questions in mind:

- What is God like?
- What should I be like?
- How does God want believers to behave?
- What has God done in the past?
- What does God promise to accomplish in the future?

FINDING THE RIGHT MEANING OF THE TEXT

In the last few decades, the subject of women has effectively exposed some widespread disagreements that tend to disunite the Christian community. One of the main points of contention has to do with the fact that Christians don't all use the same method of interpretation. Complementarians and egalitarians, for example, tend to disapprove of the way each other approaches the text.

Nevertheless it seems plausible to me that most can rally around these two basic principles:

1. Every passage in the Bible means *something*.

2. And *God* knows what it means.

Indeed, Scripture attests to the fact that every passage in the Bible means something. Second Timothy 3:16 says, "All Scripture is inspired by God and profitable for teaching, for reproof, for correction, for training in righteousness." It says "all" Scripture. That is, "all" Scripture is profitable for teaching something. "All" Scripture is profitable for exposing the truth about something. "All" Scripture is profitable for correcting something. In other words, "all" Scripture is profitable for doing something very specific—that is, training the person of God in righteousness.

Accordingly, it is invalid to claim a certain passage means nothing ("Oh, this verse? It's obsolete; we can just skip over it. It doesn't teach us much of anything."). It is equally invalid to say that a passage can mean anything ("The fun thing about the Bible is that it can be twisted and contorted to mean whatever you like."). It is also invalid to say with confident omniscience, "I know" what this verse means as if "I have a corner on the truth." For no one totally understands the Bible. Together, however, as Christians, we can defer to the One who does.

In effect, these two basic principles require us to read Scripture with humility. It is true that the Spirit of God enables the human heart to hear the Word with genuine understanding. Even so, our individual opinions ought to be held humbly, as opinions. Yes, we hold strong convictions, and yes, God gives us insight into his Word. Even so, we must always remember that sometimes what appears to be a spiritual conviction turns out to be cultural bias. Thus it is vital for Christians to test our convictions against the authority of God's Word. Moreover, it is critical for believers to listen to each other with respect. But the primary key is for us continually to confess that only God knows the exact meaning of every passage in the text. As long we each believe that God—not I—is omniscient, then we can search the Scriptures in harmony together without lording our own convictions and cherished opinions over those who fail to echo our same thoughts.

Two more things regarding biblical interpretation come into play in this

book. First, every student of the Bible has to decide upon a guiding hermeneutic. In other words, each one of us is responsible to discern which verse(s)
should take priority over the others. To say the same thing in friendlier terms,
we have to find out which verse stands in charge as the boss. The "boss verse"
is preeminent.[3] Thus every other verse salutes to that verse as the chief.[4]

In an egalitarian framework, the guiding hermeneutic is Galatians 3:28,
"There is neither Jew nor Greek, there is neither slave nor free man, there is
neither male nor female; for you are all one in Christ Jesus." Thus egalitarians
say that I Timothy 2:12, "But I do not allow a woman to teach or exercise
authority over a man, but to remain quiet," should be interpreted as an aux-
iliary verse and not a major theme since oneness in Christ is more important
than the particular instructions Paul told Timothy to apply to the church in
Ephesus. From an egalitarian perspective, I Timothy 2:12 is culturally specific, whereas Galatians 3:28 is universal.

By contrast, complementarians say the guiding hermeneutic for women in
the church is I Timothy 2:12. When the Bible is read this way, it becomes
hermeneutically impossible to think that Galatians 3:28 ("there is neither
male nor female") in any way transcends the prohibition in I Timothy 2:12.
In a complementarian framework, Galatians 3:28 has nothing to do with
gender roles at church. Rather, it means that men and women alike are
equally eligible for salvation.[5]

---

[3] I coined this term.

[4] The boss verse is a guiding hermeneutic, nothing more. Metaphorically I mean that the boss verse is the
boss, not the totalitarian. In other words, it does not crowd out the rest of Scripture. One person told
me she feared that the concept of a boss verse might be misunderstood as a viable rationale to validate
a cult. Thus I want to take pains to explain that a boss verse serves as an overarching thesis. A boss verse,
therefore, stands as a general statement, not a particular one. For example, John 3:16 makes a better boss
verse than Isaiah 1:15, "So when you spread out your hands in prayer, I will hide My eyes from you. Yes,
even though you multiply your prayers, I will not listen. Your hands are covered with blood." In this case,
Isaiah 1:15 still means something, and it still counts as a God-inspired verse, but it should not be understood as a more particular statement than John 3:16. Whereas John 3:16 is a general statement, Isaiah
1:15 is not.

[5] For a complementarian commentary on Galatians 3:28, see Richard Hover, *Equality in Christ* (Wheaton,
Ill.: Crossway, 1999).

USAGE: THE KEY TO UNDERSTANDING BIBLICAL WORDS

In conjunction with identifying our guiding hermeneutic, we also have to find the correct interpretation of every word. When I was in seminary, the professors taught us students not to rely on dictionaries. If we wanted to know the meaning of a biblical word, we were taught, so to speak, "to do the work of Webster" ourselves. I remember Ray Ortlund Jr. leading us through rigorous exercises. First, he would make us look up a Bible passage in the original Hebrew, tell the English translations of it, and then explain why the translators translated it as they did. After that, we had to write our own best translation of the passage straight from the original language. If we couldn't figure out a particular word, even then we were deprived of the modern convenience of looking it up in the lexicon. Rather, our assignment was to discover how the word was used in other places in the Bible. Only after we had researched the usage of it were we ready to suggest its proper meaning.

Usage determines the meaning of a word. To illustrate the point, let's take the word *head* in English. Webster's Dictionary suggests twenty-one different definitions for the English word *head*. Just to name a few, *head* can refer to "the top part of the body in humans," or "the person who is foremost or in charge; leader, ruler, chief, director, etc.," or "the source of a flowing body of water; beginning of a stream, river, etc.," or "a position of leadership, honor, or first importance."

The only way to know what *head* means in any given context is to determine how the word is specifically used. In Genesis 3:15, the Bible says, "He shall bruise you on the head, and you shall bruise him on the heel." It's easy to discern that here "head" means "the top part of the body" since the two words being juxtaposed, "head" and "heel," are parts of the human body.

In Luke 14:21, however, the English word *head* clearly means something else. This is the passage in which Jesus tells the parable about the guests who made excuses rather than coming to the big dinner hosted by the man who invited them. Luke 14:21 says, "And the slave came back and reported this to his master. Then the head of the household became angry and said to his slave, 'Go out at once into the streets and lanes of the city and bring in here the poor and crippled and blind and lame.' " In this context, "head" means "the person who is in charge; leader, ruler."[6]

In Colossians 1:18, the word is more difficult to discern. Speaking of Christ, the Bible says, "He is also head of the body, the church, and He is also the beginning, the first-born from the dead; so that He Himself might come to have first place in everything." What does *head* mean here? Since he is the head of the body, it seems that *head* means "the top of the body." And yet, this same passage also says he is the beginning. This could thus imply that *head* means "the source, the beginning." The climax of the passage, however, says that he will come to have "first place in everything." In that sense, it appears that *head* means "a position of honor, or first importance."

Which is the right definition? It all depends on the usage of the word. Soon we will revisit this discussion. But first, we need to study 1 Peter 3:7, the verse that marks the beginning of the paradigm promoted in this book.

DISCUSSION QUESTIONS

1. What wishes, fears and assumptions do you bring to your reading of the Word?

2. What do you think "head" means in Colossians 1:18?

3. Discuss the concept of a guiding hermeneutic. Which verse in Bible do you think ought to serve as the guiding hermeneutic in this debate? Can you think of a verse more suitable than 1 Timothy 2:12 or Galatians 3:28?

4. Explain the general principle that "usage determines the meaning of a word."

---

[6]In English, the word *head* appears in Matthew 6:17 as well as Luke 14:21. In Greek, however, two different words are used. Whereas the word *kephalē* is found in Matthew 6:17 ("anoint your *kephalē*"), the word in Luke 14:21 ("Then the *oikodespotēs* . . . said to his slave") is not the same. *Oikodespotēs* refers to the master of a house rather than a physical head.

11

WHAT'S A "WEAKER VESSEL"?

You husbands in the same way, live with your wives in an understanding way,
as with a weaker vessel, since she is a woman; and grant her honor as a fellow
heir of the grace of life, so that your prayers will not be hindered.
I PETER 3:7

I will never forget the evening when I began to pray, "Abba, my Bible says I'm a 'weaker vessel.' Does that mean I'm inferior to men? I know I'm a 'fellow heir of the grace of life' and that you've secured a place for me in heaven. But I'm asking about my identity right now. Am I today as a woman on earth inferior to men? What does it mean to be a 'weaker vessel'? Please help me to understand because I'm ready to face reality, no matter what the implications. Just tell me, and I'll deal with it. I don't want to go through my life pretending to be something I am not. I want to be a woman of truth and integrity."

Suddenly in that moment it occurred to me to get up and be proactive. So I got up, reached for Webster's Dictionary and looked up the English word *weak*. Here's what I found:

Weak—I. a) lacking in strength of body or muscle; not physically strong; b) lacking vitality; feeble; infirm; 2. lacking in skill or strength in combat or competition; 3. lacking in moral strength or will power; yielding easily to temptation, the influence of others, etc.; 4. lacking in mental power or the ability to think, judge, decide, etc.; 5. lacking ruling power, or authority; 6. lacking in force or effectiveness; 7. a) lacking in strength of material or construction; unable to resist strain, pressure, etc.; easily torn, broken, bent, etc.; b) not sound or secure; unable to stand up to attack . . . 12. a) ineffective; unconvincing; b) faulty.

And under all these definitions, Webster's dictionary says:

> SYN.—weak, the broadest application of these words, basically implies a *lack*
> or *inferiority* of physical, mental, or moral strength. [emphasis added]

There it was on the printed page—the unambiguous word *inferior*. In a
flash I realized why some well-meaning Christians honestly believe that
women are inferior to men. And for the first time in my life, I thought maybe
they were right.

Silently I sat. The air in the room felt heavy and bleak. But the Lord was
there, and I knew it. Comforted by his presence, I accepted Webster's words
without argument. But I did not accept them without prayer. Breaking the
silence, I fell to my knees and began speaking to the Lord again. "So that
does mean I can't be a professor of theology anymore? Do I have to quit my
job? I've never consciously thought of myself as inferior. But it's right there
in your Word. I prayed for a plain answer, and I got it. You gave it to me
straight. I'm a woman, and that means I'm a 'weaker vessel,' and that means
I'm 'inferior.' So now what?"

Then I remembered it's a no-no in seminary to resort to the use of a dictionary. In the flash of the next moment, I was impressed with another clear
idea—or at least a new possibility to explore. I grabbed my Greek Bible,
found I Peter 3 and identified the original word used by Peter: *asthenēs*. "Oh,
Lord . . . is it the same word as I think it might be?" And it was. When I
turned to I Corinthians in the Greek, the same word sprang wildly from the
text: *asthenēs*. Except this time, it was not referring to a woman. This time
the word was referring to God: "the weakness of God is stronger than men"
(I Cor 1:25). The *asthenēs* of God? Yes, the *asthenēs* of God. I began to laugh
out loud in hilarity and assurance of the biblical fact that no woman is inferior, unless somehow God Almighty is too. It is heresy to suggest that God
could ever be inferior. The Lord God reigns supreme—above all. The very
idea of God's inferiority is preposterous.

Abounding with hope, I turned to 2 Corinthians 13:4 and found the
same word again. Except in this case, the passage is describing Jesus Christ:

"For indeed He was crucified because of weakness." That is, he was crucified because of *asthenēs*. So what shall we say? That at Calvary our Lord was inferior to the devil? That Satan was superior to him? It is unorthodox to suggest that Christ was crucified because of any inferiority. According to the Gospel of John, Jesus was crucified because he used his "initiative" and "authority" to lay down his life (Jn 10:18). Even on the cross, Jesus was superior to the devil.

That significant discovery was enough to convince me that in I Peter 3:7 *asthenēs* at least in two cases must mean something other than "inferior." It cannot mean "inferior" in I Corinthians 1:25 or 2 Corinthians 13:4; thus it's reasonable to think that it doesn't have to mean "inferior" in I Peter 3:7 in the context of describing a woman. This is how the usage serves to inform us of what a word means. In this case, the usage also tells what the word does not mean.

In saying this, I am not negating the validity of the English word *weakness*. There is no problem with the English translation "weak"; the problem lies with Webster's definition of *weak*. Since Webster says that *weak* is synonymous with *inferior*, it is helpful to find a different English word, one that reasonably fits in all three verses:

"the *asthenēs* of God is stronger than men" (I Cor 1:25)
"For indeed He was crucified because of *asthenēs*" (2 Cor 13:4)
"as with a more *asthenēs* vessel, since she is a woman" (I Pet 3:7)

Bear in mind that we can't randomly insert any English word; we have to find one that lies within the semantic range of the Greek word *asthenēs*.

What English word can be substituted for *asthenēs?* Students in every class I've taught have suggested the English words *humility* or *compassion*. Consider how this plays out: God's humility is stronger than humanity; Christ was crucified because of humility, and women are more humble than men. Wrong! The word doesn't fit. Though it may be true that God's humility is stronger than humanity (an odd thing to say) and that Christ was crucified, in part, because of his humility, it is not true that women are more humble than men. Besides that, *humility* is not a very good synonym for *weakness*. The same holds true for the word *compassion*—its meaning is not related to the word *weakness*. Though women are often perceived as more compassionate than men and though Christ was crucified, in part, because of his compassion, it's not necessarily true that women (e.g., Jezebel or Bloody Mary) are more compassionate than men. And as I said before, it doesn't make sense to say the compassion of God is stronger than humanity.

VULNERABLE AND MORE VULNERABLE

How about the English word *vulnerable?*[1]

> "the vulnerability of God is stronger than men" (1 Cor 1:25)
> "For indeed He was crucified because of vulnerability" (2 Cor 13:4)
> "as with a more vulnerable vessel, since she is a woman" (1 Pet 3:7)

Each verse now makes sense. The weakness of God is not divine inferiority; the weakness of God refers to God's willingness to be responsive.[2] God is moved by prayer and grieved by sin. And yet, God does not change.[3] The weakness of Christ refers to the fact that Christ was crucified because of vulnerability. In heaven it was impossible for him to die, but on earth Christ became vulnerable to death. The weakness of a woman is her physical vulnerability, for her body is more vulnerable than a man's.

Let's get this straight. God is vulnerable, but only in a metaphorical sense. Christ, by contrast, made himself vulnerable by becoming human flesh (Jn 1:14). Men and women are both vulnerable, and yet women are more physically vulnerable than men according to God's design.

---

[1]I understand *vulnerable* to mean: (1) that which can be wounded or physically injured; (2) open to criticism or attack; (3) affected by a specific influence.

[2]Grudem puts it this way: "God is unchangeable in His being, perfections, purposes and promises, yet He does act and feel emotions, and He acts and feels differently in response to different situations" (Wayne Grudem, *Systematic Theology* [Grand Rapids, Mich: Zondervan, 1994], p. 163).

[3]I agree with Carl Henry, "To say anything fixed about God we must abandon the notion of God as a center of change." See Carl F. H. Henry, *God, Revelation and Authority*, 6 vols. (Dallas: Word, 1982), 5:128.

The passage says "as with a more vulnerable 'vessel.'" The Greek word for "vessel" (*skeuos*) specifies physicality. The same word occurs in I Thessalonians 4:3-4, "For this is the will of God . . . that each of you know how to possess his own 'vessel' in sanctification and honor." The point is for every individual Christian to be responsible to stay sexually pure. To possess your own "vessel" means to control your own body. Thus women, as weaker vessels, are physically more vulnerable than men.

The word is a comparative—weak*er*. The implication is that husbands are *weak* and wives are *weaker*. Both are vulnerable. To be more precise, the Greek word *asthenēs* literally means "strengthless." The implication, then, is that men are strengthless and women are yet more strengthless. The difference between women and men lies in the degree of their strengthlessness, or as we said before, their vulnerability.

Now think of the worldly lie that is notoriously told to men. Falsely men are told they are invulnerable. Boys don't cry. Men are never hurt. Real men don't have feelings. It is manly to pretend that being injured doesn't hurt. It is manly to pretend to be invulnerable. Women, by contrast, are falsely told they alone are vulnerable. Crying is for women. Hurt feelings are for women. Emotions and sensitivity are for women. It is unbiblical to think that when the church becomes relational and sensitive, the church becomes impotent and "feminized."[4] Compassion, sensitivity, relational intimacy and humility are culturally associated with women. But the Bible says that men are vulnerable.

Lie: Women are vulnerable; men are invulnerable.

Truth: Men are vulnerable; women are physically more vulnerable than men.

DIFFERENT AND DIFFERENT TOO

Look at the verse again. It does not say that the wife is weak and the husband is strong. It says, "You husbands in the same way, live with your wives in an understanding way, as with someone weaker, since she is a woman." The commandment is for husbands to be mindful of the relative difference in strength

---

[4]See Leon Podles, *The Church Impotent*, pp. 113-38.

between them and their wives.[5]

Guest lecturing one day to a medium-sized group of professors and students, I said, "Women are physically more vulnerable than men. Women can be raped." A young man there responded to my statement with resentment. Openly he protested, "A man can be raped too!" Soberly I replied, "Not by a woman." You could have heard a pin drop in that room.

No doubt women can be terribly violent. In a nearby shelter 40 percent of the battered spouses are men. Even so, worldwide statistics consistently indicate that men are far more likely to be perpetrators of violence than victims of women. In some countries, for instance, it is culturally acceptable for husbands to beat their wives. Indeed, many wives have no legal recourse whenever they are battered or raped. For example, the slave trade in Sudan is mostly filled with women, not men.

It is very unpleasant to conceptualize the widespread abuse of women that happens throughout the world. In some Third World countries, women still don't have the right to open a bank account or own a place to live. Globally speaking, women are underpaid, underrecognized and tragically undervalued. The same is true for many children and men, but the physical abuse is concentrated primarily on women.[6] Indeed, men have dominated women everywhere in the world in every generation of history.

Why is this? Is it because men are more sinful than women? Of course not. It's because men are relatively less vulnerable physically. Generally speaking, women don't dominate men. Women don't because bodily women can't.

---

[5]I am saying that women are more physically vulnerable toward men than men are physically vulnerable toward women. It may be true, paradoxically, that men are more vulnerable to death. Lionel Tiger says, "From the moment of conception onward, males are the more fragile and vulnerable of the two sexes. Male fetuses die more readily than female. So do newborns. So do male infants. So do male adolescents. So do male adults. So do old men" (Lionel Tiger, *The Decline of Males* [New York: Golden Books, 1999], p. 94).

[6]It's important to note that male dominance exists also between stronger and weaker men. In prisons, for instance, stronger males become predators of weaker males. Men in prison are exploited and beaten and raped by other men just as commonly as women are outside of the prison walls. For further reading on this and other related matters, see Allan G. Johnson's *The Gender Knot* (Philadelphia: Temple University Press, 1997).

If the governments of the world ever hosted a worldwide wrestling contest between all the women and men, the women would lose. Women have less muscle fiber and relatively more body fat than men. Who can deny that God's design of the body of a woman differs physically from God's design of the body of a man?[7]

Secular feminists are keenly aware of the physical disparity that exists between women and men, but some don't like to talk about it for fear that any recognition of the difference between men's and women's strength will be used politically as an argument for male superiority. Thus they'd rather emphasize the common humanity of men and women. Evangelical feminists tend to have a similar point of view. As one Christian woman put it, "Men just so happen to be gendered as males, and women just so happen to be gendered as females. But basically, we're all just people."

Another biblical feminist told me it's "unstrategic" to talk about the difference between men and women. She said that saying the word *difference* ushers in a "death knell" to the global cause of women's concerns. She was walking ahead of me when I confronted her with the question, "Then when do we talk about the truth?" In response, she spun around to face me with her hand on her hip and her elbow jutted out to the side. Feeling slightly intimidated, I found myself dreading her reply. But to my surprise, her attitude had softened. Dropping her elbow, she looked at me and said, "Well, now you're making me think. I haven't framed the issue that way before."

I can understand this woman's determination to be cautious. It *is* unstrategic politically for women to say that women are different from men. The problem is that when women are seen as different, men are seen as normal. The rationale flows like this:

Men are normal.

Women are not men.

Women are not normal.

---

[7]For a discussion on the possibilities that technology can impose on a human body, see Anne Balsamo's *Technologies of the Gendered Body* (Durham, N.C.: Duke University Press, 1996).

Resolution to the problem comes when Christians confess the truth—that men are different too. Women are different, and men are different too. Relative to each other, women and men are distinct.

DISCUSSION QUESTIONS

1. List some practical ways that a husband can live with his wife as with "a more vulnerable vessel."

2. Discuss the paradox that husbands are "strengthless" and wives are "more strengthless" than their husbands. In what ways are husbands vulnerable to their wives? In what ways are wives even more vulnerable to their husbands?

3. Explain the rationale that says, "Men are normal; women are not men; women are not normal." How much does that reflect the values of society?

4. How do you suppose men's bodies affect men's way of thinking and men's behavior? How do you suppose women's bodies affect women's way of thinking and women's behavior?

12
NO PICTURES, PLEASE

You husbands in the same way, live with your wives in an understanding way, as with a weaker vessel [asthenesterō skeuei], *since she is a woman* [tō gynaikeiō]; *and grant honor as a fellow heir of the grace of life.*
1 PETER 3:7

First Peter 3:7 is misunderstood when people assume that women in general, more than men, need to be spiritually led. The Bible does not say for husbands to live with their wives in an understanding way, as with someone who needs to be led by a man, since she is a woman. It says for husbands to live with their wives in an understanding way as with a more vulnerable body. Almost every wife I know can remember a time when she had to tell her husband not to squeeze so hard during a playful hug. That is not to say that women aren't strong and resilient. Women's bodies are fearfully and wonderfully made (Ps 139:14). It's just that there's a difference between the body of a woman and the body of a man. Our muscle fiber, our measurements, our metabolisms, our chromosomes, our cholesterol levels, our hormone levels, our bones, and so on are not the same.

Physically women are different from men. And because men and women are physically different, we respond differently to various situations. For instance, women will tend to be more fearful then men walking alone at night. That is not to say that women are more fearful than men. Nor is it to say that women are any less capable than men of walking alone at night. It's rather to suggest that because women are physically more vulnerable to men (generally speaking, than men are to women), they are more likely to be physically attacked. It is wise for women to be more cautious than men at night. Women don't think like "reasonable men," because that which is reasonable for a man might not be reasonable for a woman. If a man is physically attacked, the most reasonable thing for him might be to launch a counterattack by striking back. But for a woman, that might be dumb. It's usually not too smart for a weaponless woman to risk fighting physically with a man.

Women don't respond to life as men—because women are women, not men. The most athletic woman in the world may run faster or jump higher or even outwrestle a man, but even so, she is vulnerable to him in a way that he can never be vulnerable to her. Their bodies are not the same. In the place where her body is physically open, his body is physically closed. Physically he cannot be invaded the same as she—"since she is a woman."

Hormones change things too. The hormones of a male body influence male behavior, just as female hormones influence women. Hormonal differences, however, vary from person to person. Men and women both have testosterone and estrogen. It's the levels of our testosterone and estrogen that differ. It is a mistake, therefore, to think women are domestic and men are not, or that men are business-minded and women are not. Beliefs such as these are uninformed.[1]

At the same time, it is evident to most parents that baby boys tend not to act the same as baby girls. Something about them is different. For instance, boys are more aggressive than girls. Girls can be rowdy, but boys engage the world in a more dramatic body-abandoning way. This has to with God's design. Because the female carries the offspring, her body is naturally more vulnerable than the male's. Even if her body never goes through puberty or pregnancy, her body is still less muscular and less loaded with testosterone. As a result, she acts in such a way that accords with her bodily experience.

In this day and age, bodily differences do not come into play as they would in a world without technology. Technology, along with wealth and democratic values, has given the world a chance to see how similar men's and

---

[1] Another misperception is that men are "more visual" than women. It might be true that men are more sexually aroused by the sight of a woman than women are by the sight of a man. But again, that is hormonal. Overall, women are just as visual as men.

women's capabilities are. When women are educated, trained and experienced, they can operate machines, perform medical surgery, defend a client in a court of law and effectively govern a nation. Technology allows for all this, and yet it does not erase, indeed cannot erase, the fact that men are still men and women are still women. No matter what, 1 Peter 3:7 is going to apply to every generation until Christ returns. For God has created men to be physically less vulnerable then women. Again, I am not saying that males are less vulnerable overall than females are. Males are just as vulnerable to bullets and drugs and car wrecks as are females. But they are not quite as vulnerable to a female body as a female body is to a male's.

In my opinion, this explains why the biblical commandment Peter gives to husbands in 1 Peter 3:7 refers to a sexual context. It is not coincidental that the commandment is not given to fathers or sons or brothers who live with women. The commandment is given to husbands. Peter says nothing to single men about honoring single women. Why not? Because they are not sexually united. They don't interact as "one flesh." The comparative vulnerability that Peter points out applies to the context of marriage. When a man and woman wed, they each uncover their vulnerability. And in that context, the husband finds out that the wife's vulnerability is relatively greater than his. Thus Peter commands him not to take advantage of the physical advantage that he has over her.

I want to emphasize this. The same verse that tells husbands to live with their wives "as with a more vulnerable body" also forbids them to dishonor their wives as if women were inferior to men. Instead of telling husbands to dissociate from their wives (contra Leon Podles), the biblical text enjoins every husband to "grant her [his wife] honor as an heir of the grace of life." It is sinful for a husband to treat his wife as an inferior. Bodily, she is more vulnerable. Bodily, he does hold an advantage over her. But that doesn't make him superior. On the contrary, it renders to him the unique responsibility of living with her in an understanding way, knowing that her body is created to give birth and to serve as a mother. To paraphrase Peter, he says, "Husbands, elevate your wife in her vulnerability, and don't use your advantage to elevate yourself instead."

Put another way, the husband is commanded not to act out what originally began as a consequence of the Fall. In Genesis 3:16—as a consequence
of the Fall—after God tells the woman that her desire will be for her husband, he also says, "and he will rule over you." Look at the verb. It says "will
rule." It does not say "shall be able to rule." It does not say, "And from now
on, he shall be able to rule over you as never before." Rather, it says that he
will start doing that which he's been able to do all along.

There was never a day in paradise when Adam lacked the ability to exploit his advantage over Eve. He was always less vulnerable bodily toward
her than she was bodily toward him. He had always been able to rule her.
The design of a man's body offers evidence of God's plan for husbands to
have a physical advantage over their wives. And yet, Scripture makes it
clear that instead of using that advantage to put their wives down, husbands are to use it as a means of lifting their wives up and granting honor
to them.

Guess what happens when a husband disobeys this commandment?

Something serious.

Something terrible.

Something devastating to a husband who wants to walk with God.

You know what happens?

His prayers are hindered.

That same verse, 1 Peter 3:7, says, "Show her honor . . . so that your
prayers will not be hindered."[2]

This is a New Testament principle. When husbands (i.e., married men
who are "heirs of the grace of life") mistreat their wives by failing to honor
them also as "heirs of the grace of life," they retard their own spiritual
progress. The moment a husband misuses the advantage that God has entrusted to him—that's when he loses God's ear.

---

[2]The Greek verb for the English word *hinder* is *enkoptō*, which means to "cut into." The word connotes
the idea of an obstacle being placed in the road, or rather, in this case, an obstacle being placed between
a husband's prayers and God.

WHAT IS HEADSHIP?

Peter's teaching on marriage is underscored in I Corinthians by the more in-depth teaching of Paul. Paul put it this way, "But I want you to understand that Christ is the head of every man, and the man is the head of a woman, and God is the head of Christ" (I Cor 11:3). He presents three different metaphors as a way of expressing how masculinity and femininity ought to interplay: "every man"[3] in relation to Christ; a man in relation to a woman;[4] and Christ in relation to God. I believe these metaphors directly correspond to the metaphor of headship in a marriage.

What is headship? Scripture doesn't tell us definitively. It tells us instead what it looks like. Thus we have a picture, not a definition. The Bible conveys a picture of the husband as the head and the wife as the body. But what does that mean? That he, as the head, is the brain? And that she, as his body, is the heart? (I have led discussions with groups of adult Christians who seriously have raised these questions.)

One woman who was brought up in a Christian home said her father taught her that the husband is the "head of the house" and that the wife is the "heart of the home." Another woman said that the husband as the head should therefore be the brain of the family. In an attempt to broaden her thinking, I asked, "Does a wife have the mind of Christ [I Cor 2:16], or does that just belong to the husband since he alone is the head?" Anticipating her thought, I expected her to say, "Of course a Christian wife has the mind of Christ!" But to my surprise, she told me her resolve was to "forfeit her intellect" and practice Christianity from a "devotional approach" because that "makes it easier" for her husband to function as the head.

---

[3]Although someone might suggest that Christ is the source of "humanity," the Greek word *anēr* cannot be translated as "humanity" here. Paul generally uses *anēr* to describe males, either men or husbands, in contrast to women or wives. The more common Greek word for "humankind" is *anthrōpos*.

[4]The Greek word for "wife" *(gynē)* used here is also the word in Greek for "woman." See it used as wife also in Matthew 1:20, 24; 5:31; 14:3; 18:25; 19:3, 5, 9, 10; 22:24, 25, 28; 27:19; Mark 6:17, 18; 10:2; 12:19, 20, 23; Luke 1:5, 3, 18, 24; 3:19; 8:3; 14:20, 26; 16:18; 17:32; 18:29; 20:28, 29, 33; Acts 5:1, 7; 18:2; 24:24; I Corinthians 5:1; 7:3, 4, 10, 11, 14, 16, 27, 33, 39; 9:5; Ephesians 5:23, 28, 31, 33; I Timothy 3:2, 11, 12; 5:9; Titus 1:6; Revelation 21:9.

In theological circles, few scholars are debating about whether or not the husband is the head of the wife. Conservative evangelicals aren't debating that at all. Within our sphere, both sides of the argument accept the biblical text as it appears. The debate for us then focuses, rather, on other specific issues such as the proper definition of the Greek word for "head." For the same word, "head" *(kephalē)*, is used in Ephesians 5:23 ("the husband is the head *[kephalē]* of the wife") as well as in 1 Corinthians 11:3 ("But I want you to understand that Christ is the head *[kephalē]* of every man, and the man is the head *[kephalē]* of a woman, and God is the head *[kephalē]* of Christ").

Broadly speaking, there is a contest going on between two definitions for "head." One definition says that "head" means "authority," and the other says that "head" means "source" (or "fountainhead"). Complementarians usually argue for the former, egalitarians for the latter. Here's how the translations commonly work out.

Complementarians say the verse should be read like this: "Now I want you to understand that Christ is the Authority *[kephalē]* of every man, and the man is the authority *[kephalē]* of a woman, and God is the Authority *[kepahlē]* of Christ."

Egalitarians, by contrast, say it should be read like this: "Now I want you to understand that Christ is the Source *[kephalē]* of every man, and the man is the source *[kephalē]* of a woman, and God is the Source *[kephalē]* of Christ."

These two readings are dissimilar. So how are we supposed to know who's right? Are the Greek words really that fluid?

Technically speaking, the Greek can be rendered in both ways. But that doesn't mean we are left in an endless guessing game, because every verse has to mean something. First Corinthians 11:3 is no exception. Thus we are obliged to discover it means. As we attempt to do so, I will explain the distinctive translations of complementarians and egalitarians and then show why I disagree with both. After that, I will propose an alternative translation that offers a more satisfying view.

AUTHORITY OR SOURCE?

As we know, complementarians look for the order of things. Thus they see 1 Corinthians 11:3 as a passage about order and authority:

God is the Authority over Christ;
Christ is the Authority over every man;
a man is the authority over a woman.

The order thus goes like this:

The Father is the Boss over   .
the Son is the Boss over
Man is the Boss over
Woman.

They don't say this without biblical backing. As they see it, Scripture reveals this as God's plan. After all, Jesus confessed, "The Father is greater than I" (Jn 14:28). Complementarians hear 1 Corinthians 11:3 as an echo of the same confession. From their point of view, it follows, moreover, that the husband ranks higher than the wife (Eph 5:23).[5]

According to egalitarians, however, this perspective is flawed. As fellow conservatives, egalitarians also acknowledge Christ's confession, "The Father is greater than I" (Jn 14:28), but they understand that it was Christ on earth, not the Son in heaven, who said it. Look again at the complementarian view:

The Father is the Boss over
the Son is the Boss over
Man is the Boss over
Woman.

The text says God is the head of Christ. It does not say that the Father is the Authority over the Son within the Trinity. And yet, complementarians

---

[5]Elisabeth Elliot, for instance, says, "The husband's 'rank' is given to him by God." See Elisabeth Elliot, *Let Me Be a Woman* (Wheaton, Ill.: Tyndale House, 1976), p. 130. She also quotes John Calvin as saying, "Let the woman be satisfied with her state of subjection. . . . Otherwise both of them throw off the yoke of God who has not without good reason appointed this distinction of ranks" (p. 139).

have concluded that it does. Indeed, complementarians have gone so far as to boldly state that the Son of God is "eternally subordinate" to the Father.[6] Soon we'll talk about that more. First we need to clarify the egalitarian argument that Christ was temporarily ranked lower than God during the time he was incarnate on earth. After that, as they see it, he rose from the grave and ascended into heaven as an equal with the Father and the Spirit.[7]

See how the debate keeps tracing back to the doctrine of the Trinity? Complementarians see a hierarchical model of complementarity among the three persons of God. Egalitarians, by contrast, see an egalitarian model of mutual equality among the three persons of God.

As egalitarian professor Gilbert Bilezikian points out, complementarians have taken the liberty to reorder the text rather than accepting it in sequence as Paul offers. (It's slightly ironic that they reorder the text in order to prove that this verse describes what they believe to be God's sovereign will for church order.) The text does not say, "Now I want you to know that God is the head of Christ, and Christ is the head of man, and man is the head of woman." Paul lists Christ first and God last. The text says, "But I want you to understand that Christ is the head of every man, and the man is the head of a woman, and God is the head of Christ." In other words, the order of the text seems jumbled. But if egalitarians are right, the text is not jumbled. In fact, it appears jumbled only to those who presume that Paul was describing a hierarchy.

This line of logic serves to explain why Christian feminists think it's more fitting to interpret I Corinthians 11:3 as precluding any notion of a hierarchy. Bilezikian, for example, argues that the verse should be read in the order by which it presents itself insofar as it conveys a chronological sequence of events.[8]

---

[6]See Steven Kovach, "Egalitarians Revamp Doctrine of the Trinity" in *CBMW News* 2, no.1 (December 1996): 3-5. A longer version of Kovach's article appears as "A Defense of the Doctrine of the Eternal Subordination of the Son," *Journal of the Evangelical Theological Society* 42 (summer 1999): 461-76.
[7]See Gilbert Bilezikian, *Beyond Sex Roles* (Grand Rapids, Mich.: Baker, 1985), p. 138.
[8]Ibid. Bilezikian strongly states his case like this: "As a careful, inspired writer, Paul knows exactly how to write an orderly sequence on a scale of gradual differentiation. Thus in I Corinthians 12:28 [when ranking spiritual gifts], he starts at the top first, then second, third, and down. But in I Corinthians 11:3, he begins with Christ/man, which in a hierarchical structure should be in second position; he goes on with

Christ is the fountainhead of every man
and man is the source a woman,
and God is the fountainhead of Christ.

Contrary to popular belief, egalitarians champion the notion of order. Not a hierarchical order but a historical order. As Bilezikian explains it, historically, it happened first that Christ became the source (or original prototype) of Adam, who represents every man. Next, Adam's rib became the source of a woman. After that, God (i.e., the Holy Spirit in Mary's womb) became the source or fountainhead of Christ.

HEADSHIP AS COVERING

So now we have two different arguments based on Scripture, two different views that clash. A third view also comes into play, one that has been popularized in conservative Christian churches, though it has no scholarly merit. This is the view of Christian women being covered by the authority of certain Christian men, usually the church elders, who give her approval to do what is otherwise forbidden.

For instance, a woman may be invited on special occasions to deliver the Sunday message to the full congregation on the notion that she is covered by the headship of a man or group of elders who in turn is covered by the headship of Christ, who in turn is covered by the headship of God. First Corinthians 11:3 is thus read like this: "Now I want you to understand that Christ is the covering *(kephalē)* of every man, and the man is the covering *(kephalē)* of a woman, and God is the covering *(kephalē)* of Christ."

The reason why scholars disregard this view is because *kephalē* doesn't mean "covering." To claim that it does is to expose one's ignorance of the Greek. I mention it here because many of us have never been taught this until now.

---

man/woman, which in a hierarchical structure should be in third position; and he ends with God/ Christ, which in a hierarchical structure should be in first position. According to this theory, Paul would have dislocated his alleged hierarchy by arranging it in this order: second, third, first. It is inconceivable that Paul would have so grievously jumbled up the sequence in a matter involving God, Christ, and humans, when he kept his hierarchy straight as he dealt with the lesser subject of spiritual gifts in 12:28."

There's another major flaw in this teaching, namely, that it offers no way to keep track of which women are covered and which ones aren't. At least one prominent Christian woman that I know of seems to be covered all of the time, though consistently she teaches other women to stay out of the limelight and not do ministry as she does. When other women proclaim the gospel publicly to groups that include Christian men, she says that it's "unbiblical" and "out of keeping with God's order," but when she does it, she says that she is "covered."

This brings us back to I Corinthians 11:3 and our need for a better translation. We're going to have to concentrate, but it's worth exerting the effort.

ENCOUNTERING A BIBLICAL PUZZLE

Remember those word puzzles we used to have to solve in grade school? You know, the ones that say something like this: "The man in the yellow house lives next to the blue house. The blue house is owned by Mr. Green. Mr. Green lives in a red house next door to a house with a dog in the backyard named Rover. Rover lives next door to the yellow house." Remember those? (This one, obviously, is incomplete. I made it up for the sake of illustration.) That's sort of what the New Testament presents in I Corinthians 11:3.

It helps to draw it out on paper. If you study table 12.1, you'll quickly surmise that the person above the line is the head of the one below. For instance, on the far left column where it says "Christ" above the line and "every man" below the line, it means that "Christ is the head of every man." Notice I have added Ephesians 5:23, "For the husband is the head of the wife, as Christ is the head of the church."

Table 12.1   Relationships in I Corinthians 11 and Ephesians 5

I Corinthians 11:3			Ephesians 5:23	
Christ	Man	God	Husband	Christ
Every man	Woman	Christ	Wife	Church

Let's take another look at the chart. We can see that Christ is the head over every man, the man is the head of a woman, God is the head of Christ, the husband is the head of the wife, and Christ is the head of the church. Our job in solving the puzzle is to figure out how all of these facts fit together, for in every case, the same Greek word *kephalē* ("head") is used.

If we start with the idea of authority—that Christ is the authority of the church, and the husband is the authority of the wife, and God is the authority of Christ, then this translation, at first blush, seems to be a fit. But the next phrase, that Christ is the "authority of every man,"[9] becomes unsuitable, if by it we mean that Christ is not the direct authority over women.[10] Indeed, this interpretation fails to square with the gospel. For the Scriptures say that all believers, men and women, can approach the throne of grace with confidence (Heb 4:16). Women are not obliged to connect with God via the authority of a man. The Bible says there is "one" mediator, the man Christ Jesus (1 Tim 2:5). No other man is the mediator.

The next phrase is problematic too. It is inappropriate to say "the man is the authority of the woman," unless we believe that all women are subject to the authority of all men.

By contrast, if we substitute the word *source*, the passage suggests something entirely different. In a way, it makes sense for Paul to say, "Christ is the source of every man, and man is the source of the woman, and God is the source of Christ." For it nicely accords with Paul's additional statement in I Corinthians 11:12: "For as the woman originates from the man, so also the man has his birth through the woman; and all things originate from God."

---

[9]Here the Greek is gender specific; it says *anēr* ("man").

[10]Unfortunately many believers have been mistaught in settings such as the Bill Gothard Seminar. Thus it is common for conservatives mistakenly to believe that while a wife is privy to a direct relationship with God, she is not directly accountable to him. This teaching is unbiblical. In fact, there is so much counterevidence in Scripture that it's hard to know where to begin. For the sake of brevity, I will say only three things: women—not just men—will stand before Christ on judgment day (Rom 3:19); the Spirit of God convicts the hearts of women directly, rather than convicting men on women's behalf (Jn 16:8-9); In the garden of Eden, Eve was directly responsible to God. God did not hold Adam responsible for Eve. Instead, God treated her individually as one who was directly accountable to him. See Bilezikian, *Beyond Sex Roles*, pp. 51-53.

Both sides agree that Paul is highlighting male and female interdependence. Nevertheless many believers, including myself, still are not persuaded that "head" means "source."

I don't see how Christ is the source of every man. In fact, I don't see how Christ is the source of any man, except in the way that he is the source of all women. If we look at the text, the Bible testifies that Adam was formed from the "dust" (Gen 2:7) and that Eve was fashioned from Adam's "rib" (Gen 2:22). It also says in I Corinthians 11 that every man other than Adam was born from the womb of his mother.[11] It is inconsistent, then, for egalitarians to say that Adam's rib was the source of Eve—which it was—and then not say that the dust was the source of Adam. Still another problem arises with the notion of God being the source of Christ. The Bible says that the Holy Spirit *and* Mary were the sources (plural) of the Christ, who was "born of a woman" (Gal 4:4). To minimize the fact that Christ came from Mary is to minimize Christ's humanity.[12]

Besides, if Wayne Grudem's research is right, the word *kephalē* never means "source" in the Greek translation of the Old Testament (called the Septuagint),[13] and it rarely means "source" in ancient literature.[14] People need to know that the major lexicons, for the most part, testify to Grudem's argu-

---

[11]In I Corinthians 11:8-12, Paul says that "man does not originate from woman, but woman from man . . . however, in the Lord, neither is the woman independent of man, nor is man independent of woman; for as the woman originates from the man, so also the man has his birth through the woman; and all things originate from God." Paul never says that man originates in Christ. Rather, he says, "All things originate from God."

[12]The mystery of the incarnation is that Christ, born of the Holy Spirit is 100 percent divine, and that Christ, born of a woman, is 100 percent human.

[13]See Wayne Grudem, "Appendix I: The Meaning of Kephale ("Head"): A Response to Recent Studies" in *Recovering Biblical Manhood and Womanhood*, ed. John Piper and Wayne Grudem (Wheaton, Ill.: Crossway, 1991), p. 428. See also Grudem's more recent article "The Meaning of Kephale ("Head"): An Evaluation of New Evidence, Real and Alleged," *The Journal of the Evangelical Society* 44, no. 1 (2001): 25-66.

[14]Grudem says there are only two examples of *kephalē* as "source" in ancient literature: Herodotus 4.91 and *Orphic Fragments* 21a, both of which come about four hundred years before the time of the New Testament. And in Grudem's opinion, neither is a convincing example. See Grudem, "Appendix I," p. 425. Grudem does consent, however, to the viability of interpreting *kephalē* as "first one, beginning," as other scholars (such as Anthony Thiselton and Judith Gundry Volf) have done.

ment.[15] Grudem researched 2,336 examples of *kephalē* from a wide range of ancient Greek literature that produced, in his judgment, no conspicuous examples of *kephalē* meaning "source."[16]

What stands out in my mind is that Grudem doesn't focus on what *kephalē* usually means in those 2,336 extrabiblical examples. Why doesn't he? Because that was not the purpose of his research. He wasn't trying to verify what is by far the most common meaning of the word. He was striving instead to prove conclusively that *kephalē* does not mean "source."[17] Grudem openly says that in the 2,336 examples, only 2 percent of them in his judgment appear to be used metaphorically to mean "person of superior authority or rank, or ruler, or ruling part."[18] I think that is telling.

What it tells me is that in 2,287 instances of the 2,336, *kephalē* clearly has a different definition.[19] In those 2,287 cases *kephalē* means the same thing that it always means either literally or metaphorically in the New Testament.[20] The word *kephalē* refers to a head. Yes, a physical head. A *caput*, as

---

[15]For a viable counterpoint to my generalized claim, see Berkeley and Alvera Mickelsen, "What Does *Kephalē* Mean in the New Testament?" in *Women, Authority and the Bible* (Downers Grove, Ill.: InterVarsity Press, 1986), pp. 97-110.

[16]In Ephesians 4:15 or Colossians 2:19, the word *head* comes across more sensibly as "source" than "authority." Even staunch complementarian James Hurley affirms that "head" means "source" in those two instances.

[17]Evidently Grudem dismisses the possibility of *kephalē* as a metaphorical term conveying a picture. Though he searched for instances in which *kephalē* was used in the context of describing the relationship of one person to another, apparently he ignored the possibility of one person relating to another as a head relates to a body. In order to be consistent, Grudem would also have to think it impossible to conceive that the members of the church should relate to one another as a hand relates to a foot or an eye relates to an ear as described in 1 Corinthians 14.

[18]Bilezikian critiques Grudem for counting "ruler" and "ruling part" as synonymous rather than as two separate definitions. See Bilezikian, *Beyond Sex Roles*, p. 220.

[19]Grudem stretches his argument beyond tenability in the forty-nine cases he presents. None of the extrabiblical examples he offers self-evidently mean "ruler." Again, see Bilezikian's critique, "A Critical Examination of Wayne Grudem's Treatment of *Kephale* in Ancient Greek Texts" in *Beyond Sex Roles*, pp. 215-52.

[20]Every biblical text (Eph 4:19; Col 2:10, 19) depicts a picture of the union of a body and head. Though someone might say Colossians 2:10, "Christ is the Head *[kephalē]* of all rule and authority" presents an exception to the rule, I don't think it does. If we read Colossians 2:10 in tandem with Ephesians 1:22, "And He put all things in subjection under His feet, and gave Him as Head over all things to the church which is His Body," we see that the union of Christ and the church stands over all things, and over all

it were, in Latin. A head, not a neck and not a foot. A head as in "the top of the body in humans."

For instance, the Bible says that the Son of man has no place to rest his *kephalē* (Mt 8:20; Lk 9:58). And that the hairs on your *kephalē* are numbered (Mt 10:30; Lk 12:7). And that when Jesus died, he bowed his *kephalē* and gave up his Spirit (Jn 19:30). And that in heaven, upon his *kephalē* are many diadems (Rev 19:12). In spite of the prominence of the arguments of both sides of the debate, I believe that "head" as it appears three times in the Greek in 1 Corinthians 11:3 and twice in Ephesians 5:23 connotes the idea of a picture of a head.

NO PICTURES, PLEASE

Sometimes evangelicals have a tendency to convert the biblical metaphors into clear-cut definitions that demystify the mysteries of God.[21] Thus we often fail to see how adequate metaphors are to communicate mysterious realities. Metaphors are powerful.[22] And yet, few of us have been taught to appreciate what a metaphor can do.

A metaphor is meant to describe a mystery. A metaphor is meant to see one thing as another and to pretend that this is that. As Sally McFague puts it, to think metaphorically means to spot "a thread of similarity between two

---

rule and authority. Imagine, if you will, Christ as the Head, the church as His body, and all things, including all rule and authority, as being "under His feet."

[21]Piper and Grudem openly say, "Paul has a picture in mind when he says that the husband is the head of the wife." They also say, "this is very important." But then they convert the picture into a verbal explanation that says the husband, therefore, is "called by God to take primary responsibility for Christ-like servant-leadership, protection, and provision *in the home* [my emphasis—notice Piper and Grudem overlook the biblical wording. They apply the husband's headship to the home, not "the wife" as is stated in Ephesians 5:23], and wives are called to honor and affirm their husbands' leadership and help carry it through according to their gifts." See John Piper and Wayne Grudem, "An Overview of Central Concerns: Questions and Answers" in *Recovering Biblical Manhood and Womanhood*, ed. John Piper and Wayne Grudem (Wheaton, Ill.: Crossway, 1991), pp. 63-64. It also worth noting that while Piper and Grudem take time to describe the implications of the picture of the husband as the head, they say nothing about this picture reflecting a "mystery."

[22]Leonard Sweet says that "metaphor" is at the "heart of spirituality" and that images "come as close as human beings can get to a universal language." See Leonard Sweet, "The Quest for Community," *Leadership* (fall 1999): 34.

dissimilar objects, events, or whatever, and [use] the better-known as a way of speaking about the lesser-known."[23] According to the Bible, marriage is a "mystery" (Eph 5:32). Indeed, headship is a mystery too. As much as we might wish to define the word *head*, it is not appropriate to do so because "head" is a metaphor, and metaphors are not meant to be defined.

One evening at church before the congregation my husband and I presented ourselves as a living picture of the biblical metaphor. Standing in the front, I bowed my head while Jim, my husband, stood on a riser behind me and then placed his head upon my neck. Immediately the people started laughing. They laughed because the picture was funny—a man's head on a woman's body. How preposterous. And yet, that is the picture we are given. According to the Scriptures, the husband is the head and the wife is the body of one person. As we turn the next chapter, we shall soon see that indeed this mystery is "great" (Eph 5:32).

DISCUSSION QUESTIONS

1. Which have you been taught? That *head* means "leadership" or "source" or "covering"?

2. What is your response to the research on the word *kephalē?* What do you think *head* means in 1 Corinthians 11:3 and Ephesians 5:23?

3. What do you think 1 Corinthians 11:3, "Christ is the head of every man," really means?

4. Explain the difference between a metaphor and a clear-cut definition.

---

[23]See Sally McFague, *Models of God* (Philadelphia: Fortress, 1987), quoted in Alister McGrath, *Christian Theology* (Cambridge, Mass.: Blackwell, 1994), p. 139.

13

The Husband *Is* the Head

For the husband is the head of the wife.

Ephesians 5:23

Most complementarians and egalitarians would probably agree that in all of Scripture, the most foundational teaching on the mystery of marriage can be found in Ephesians 5. They would argue, however, over which verse it is, Ephesians 5:21 or Ephesians 5:22, that demarcates the beginning of the paragraph that talks about marriage. This disagreement is significant because the first line of the paragraph, particularly in this case, determines the practical meaning of the passage. In other words, whichever is the first line functions hermeneutically as the boss verse.

The key to figuring this out is for us to discern when Paul's message narrows from a general audience to a more specific audience of wives and husbands.

Ephesians 5:1-21

Ephesians 5 begins by addressing a general audience of believers. Verse 1 says, "Therefore be imitators of God as beloved children." Verse 2 reads, "And walk in love, just as Christ also loved you and gave Himself up for us." Verse 3 says, "But immorality or any impurity or greed must not even be named among you, as is proper among saints." The commandment is written to saints. Verse 4 echoes something similar: "And there must be no filthiness and silly talk, or coarse jesting, which are not fitting, but rather giving of thanks." Ephesians 5:5-14 applies also to the full congregation.

Now consider the next three verses (Eph 5:15-17). "Therefore be careful how you walk, not as unwise men but as wise, making the most of your time, because the days are evil. So then do not be foolish, but understand what the will of the Lord is." In English, it may sound as if Paul is speaking specifically to men, but he's not. Though the English text says "men," the Greek *asophoi* translates in English as "unwise ones."[1] All of us are to be wise, not foolish.

Ephesians 5:18-21 form a single sentence in the Greek:

> And do not get drunk with wine, for that is dissipation, but be filled with the Spirit, speaking to one another in psalms and hymns and spiritual songs, singing and making melody with your heart to the Lord; always giving thanks for all things in the name of our Lord Jesus Christ to God, even the Father; and be subject to one another in the fear of Christ.

No one's going to argue that getting drunk is a sin for men but not for women. But someone might argue that the commandment "to be subject to" applies only to women. Unfortunately many Christians, including men and women, do not recognize that commandment is given to everyone.

But if we believe that the commandments not to get drunk with wine but to be filled with the Spirit apply to all believers, then to be consistent, we must also believe that God commands every member of the church to do four things:

1. Speak to one another psalms and hymns and spiritual songs.
2. Sing and make melody with our hearts to the Lord.
3. Give thanks to God for all things in the name of our Lord Jesus Christ.
4. Be subject to one another as a matter of fearing the Lord.

In practical terms the passage doesn't mean that "everyone should speak

---

[1] *Asophoi* is a masculine plural, but in Greek it's an inclusive term referring to men and women. In fact, the only way to say "wise ones" as a general term in Greek is to use the masculine plural. The use of the feminine applies only to women.

to everyone" and "everyone should submit to everyone" simultaneously. Otherwise, the church would experience chaos.[2] The idea, rather, is for each one of us to participate in the Christian community by speaking out loud in turn (as opposed to having only one or two spokesmen) and by submitting, not lording over, one another.[3]

How many conservatives are comfortable with the fact that God requires believers to take responsibility to submit to one another? The verse says we're commanded to submit to other Christian men and women. That means it is biblical for women to submit to other women. It is unbiblical for someone to refuse to submit just because the other person is a woman. This reminds me of the pastor's wife who unabashedly confessed, "I'd rather submit to men because I know how to work them; I can't work the women."

EPHESIANS 5:21-22

Before we go on to the next verse, I want to make a point about the current debate with regard to conservative Christians. Here we are, authentic followers of Christ, standing at odds with one another, not over a matter of orthodoxy, not over a matter of salvation, but rather because we sharply disagree on where a certain paragraph begins. (Grammatically, this is a hard conflict to resolve because the Greek text, as we know, is not arranged in paragraphs. Thus we're all doing guesswork.) Whereas egalitarians are saying the para-

---

[2]Common sense tells us that we aren't all supposed to be talking at once without anyone listening. Common sense also tells us that mutual submission does not preclude the church from having leaders. Rather, it means that all of us, including leaders, are required to defer to other people in humility.

[3]I am not convinced by the argument that "the meaning of *hypotassō* is *always one-directional*." The phrase "one another" *(allēlous)* itself connotes the idea of mutuality. Wayne Grudem, however, contends that *allēlous* commonly means "some to others" and then says it therefore means "some to others" in this passage. And yet he makes his case by referencing only two other verses. Specifically he says that *allēlous* means "some to others" in Galatians 6:2, "Bear one another's burdens," and Revelation 6:4, "it was granted . . . that men should slay one another." (See Wayne Grudem, "An Open Letter to Egalitarians," *Journal for Biblical Manhood and Womanhood* 3, no. 1 [March 1998]: 3.) I am not persuaded by this argument, however, because both verses make more sense if we understand *allēlous* as connoting the idea of mutuality. Since everyone has burdens, it's unrealistic to say that only "some" of us should bear the burdens of "others." Similarly, I believe "it was granted" in Revelation 6:4 that men literally slay one another. It's easier to imagine men killing each other than having "some" kill "others" without being killed themselves. In any battle, many of the slayers ultimately become part of the slain.

graph on marriage begins with Ephesians 5:21, complementarians are saying it begins in Ephesians 5:22.

It's important to identify where the paragraph begins. But it's much more important for us as members of Christ to respect those who contend for the opposite position than we do ourselves, especially since the answer is unknown. Rather than accusing one another or holding one another in suspicion for reading the same Bible slightly differently, we could be striving for unity. After all, it's not liberal to insist that Ephesians 5:21 informs Ephesians 5:22. Nor is it unscholarly to insist that the paragraph on marriage begins with Ephesians 5:22. And yet both accusations are constantly made from one side of the debate to the other.

I am passionate to offer my input as to how Ephesians 5 ought to be understood, but my deeper zeal is to plead with conservative Christians to give one another the benefit of the doubt. It's not worth it for local churches to divide or for relationships to be broken due to the different ways that godly people are attempting to discern the true meaning of Ephesians 5. To put things in perspective, it is not heretical to begin the paragraph with either verse.

In saying this, I want to be careful to affirm that it's important, even critical, to be accurate. It's very important to exegete the Scriptures rightly and discern the proper meaning of every principle and practice the Bible inspirationally teaches. But a minor discrepancy such as this shouldn't be so divisive. Don't forget—we all agree that Christ belongs at the center of every marriage. Isn't that the most important thing?

Dear Lord, grant us the grace to forbear with one another as we search for biblical truth and earnestly contend for the faith once delivered. May we do nothing out of selfish ambition or vain conceit but in humility, consider others better than ourselves. O God, help us to be obedient to put on love, which is the perfect bond of unity. And may our quest for truth be guided by your Spirit, so that we are Spirit-filled when we speak. In Jesus' name I pray. Amen.

In Greek, Ephesians 5:22 says verbatim, "Wives, to your own husbands, as to the Lord." In the Greek there is no verb. Wives do what? To find out, we have to refer to Ephesians 5:21. In Ephesians 5:21, the verb is to "be subject," so that's what it is in verse 22. This fact explains the reason why many scholars believe that Ephesians 5:21-22 are inseparably interconnected. For the verb in verse 22 must be supplied by verse 21. Otherwise, Ephesians 5:22 is verbless.

So then, where then does the paragraph begin? In Ephesians 5:21, from where the verb is supplied? Or in Ephesians 5:22, where Paul specifically addresses the wives?

If we start with Ephesians 5:21, it appears that a husband and wife should "be subject to one another" within the marriage. Egalitarians refer to this dynamic as "mutual submission." They say husbands are commanded to submit to their own wives, just as wives are commanded to submit to their own husbands.

If we start with Ephesians 5:22, it appears that only a wife should be subject to her own husband, since the passage doesn't tell the husband specifically to be subject to her. This reading of the text can be illustrated by the public statement issued from the Southern Baptist Convention. According to the *Baptist Faith and Message*, "A wife is to submit herself graciously to the servant leadership of her husband."[4] Most complementarians, therefore, argue that in marriage, only the wife should submit.

Notice that both sides agree that God commands the wife to be subject to her own husband. Evangelical feminists are not so feministic as to deny the biblical mandate for wives to be submissive to their husbands. Many conservative Christians, however, mistakenly believe that egalitarians dismiss Ephesians 5:22 as a culturally irrelevant verse. That is a grave misunderstanding of biblical feminism. Yet many evangelicals cling to this widespread misperception.

For example, women students, graduate and undergraduate, often call

---

[4]See *Baptist Press* (July 29, 1999) <www.sbc.net> The full statement explicitly says that "the husband and wife are of equal worth before God," that the husband "has the God-given responsibility to provide for, to protect, and to lead his family," and that the wife "is to submit herself graciously to the servant leadership of her husband" and "to serve as his helper in managing the household and nurturing the next generation."

themselves Christian feminists as a hopeful way of escaping the act of submission. They are so afraid to submit to men that they call submission "the S-word." In reality, evangelical feminism offers no escape from submission. Contrary to popular belief, the disagreement between conservatives comes not with regard to the biblical duty of the wife but with the biblical duty of the husband. The question has to do with him. Does the Bible command him to be subject to her or not?

This is a tricky question. If we say the answer is no, then the logical conclusion is that a husband is supposed to "be subject" to every believer (Eph 5:21) except his wife. That's a little difficult to imagine.[5]

At the same time, we must, at the minimum, concede that Ephesians 5:22, "Wives . . . to your own husbands, as to the Lord" means something. It is not a mere repetition of Ephesians 5:21. On the contrary, it suggests something different insofar as the verse commands the wife alone to be subject to her own husband. I think it's conspicuous that the husband is never explicitly commanded to be subject to his wife. If anyone insists that the husband must be subject to the wife in the same way that she is to be subject to him, then the onus lies with that person to explain the significance of the mandate given to wives in Ephesians 5:22. Otherwise, Ephesians 5:22 collapses into Ephesians 5:21 and ends up meaning "nothing."

EPHESIANS 5:22-33

If the truth sets us free, as Jesus said it does (Jn 8:32), then we ought to be eager to embrace every drop of truth that we can find. Though it's scary for some people to admit, the truth is that Scripture nowhere explicitly commands a husband to be subject to his own wife. It's the evangelical feminists who keep saying that husbands should submit to their wives. Evangelical feminists have little motivation to bring attention to the fact that mutual submission is not mentioned in the context of Paul's teaching on marriage found in Ephesians 5:22-

---

[5]The paradox is that while a husband is not commanded to be subject to his wife, a Christian brother is commanded to be subject to his Christian sisters.

33.[6] The truth of the matter is that when the passage narrows to the more specific audience of husbands and wives, Paul tells only wives to be submissive.

If we're going to be truthful, then there's something else we also have to say. Nowhere in Scripture is a husband told to lead his wife. This idea is very popular, but it doesn't derive directly from God's Word. Complementarians are the ones who keep saying that husbands should lead their wives. The apostle Paul never says that once in all his letters. Jesus doesn't say it either. Neither does Peter or John. No one in the New Testament ever says it. In fact, God never says it in the Old Testament, though many people like to think that it's found somewhere in Genesis 1—3. Complementarians are not interested in publicly pointing out that the words *lead, leader, servant leader* and *spiritual leader* cannot be found in any Bible passage on marriage.

One of the main reasons I don't take sides in this debate is because Ephesians 5:22-33 says something different from what I hear either side saying. Look at the text, and then I'll show you what I mean.

> Wives, be subject to your own husbands, as to the Lord. For the husband is the head of the wife, as Christ also is the head of the church, He Himself being the Savior of the body. But as the church is subject to Christ, so also the wives ought to be their husbands in everything. Husbands, love your wives, just as Christ also loved the church and gave himself up for her that He might sanctify her, having cleansed her by the washing of water with the word, that He might present to Himself the church in all her glory, having no spot or wrinkle or any such thing; but that she should be holy and blameless. So husbands ought also to love their own wives as their own bodies. He who loves his own wife loves himself; for no one ever hated his own flesh, but nourishes and cherishes it, just as Christ also does the church, because we are members of His body. For this reason a man shall leave his father and mother and shall be joined to his wife; and the two shall become one flesh. This mystery is great; but I am speaking with reference to Christ and the church. Nevertheless, let each individual among you also love his own wife even as himself, and let the wife see to it that she respect her husband.

[6]There is no "mutual submission" between Christ and the church either.

Three couplets are presented in the passage:

1. The wife is to be subject to her own husband in everything, and he is to sacrifice himself for her. The dynamic is for her to submit and him to sacrifice; thus the first couplet is submission/sacrifice.

2. The wife is the body, and the husband is the head. Together they form one flesh. The second couplet, then, is body/head.

3. The wife is commanded to respect her husband while the husband is commanded to love her. As you can see, the third couplet is respect/love.

Table 13.1 organizes the same information in a slightly different way.

Table 13.1   Responsibilities of a wife and husband

A wife	A husband
is to be subject to her own husband in everything	is to sacrifice himself for his wife
is the body of her husband	is the head of his wife
is to see to it that she respects her husband	is to love his own wife as himself

Just to make sure that everyone can see exactly where this comes from biblically, let's attach each observation directly with the words of the text. Regarding the first set, Ephesians 5:22 says the wife is to be subject to her own husband, and Ephesians 5:24 says for wives to be subject to their husbands "in everything." Correlatively, Ephesians 5:25 says husbands are to "love" their wives sacrificially, just as Christ also loved the Church and "gave Himself up for her."

Regarding the second set, two or three verses describe the wife as the body of the husband. To begin with, Ephesians 5:23 parallels the husband as the head of the wife in correlation with Christ as head of the church, he being the Savior of "the body." Implicitly, then, we see that the church is the body of Christ and the wife is the body of her husband. The same concept is reinforced in Ephesians 5:28, which says that husbands ought to love their own wives "as their own bodies." He *is* the head of his wife, and she is *as* the body of her husband. This makes sense in light of Ephesians 5:31, "The two shall become one flesh." Head and body form one flesh. It also explains the rest of Ephesians 5:28. "He who loves his own wife loves himself." As it turns out, she is not just "as" his body; she *is* "himself." Thus in Ephesians 5:33, the husband is commanded to love his own wife "even as [the body of] himself."

Regarding the third set, the wife is told in Ephesians 5:33 to see to it that she "respects" her husband. The husband's instructions, however, are repeated three times. Three times the husband is instructed to "love" his own wife (Eph 5:25, 28, 33).

MATCHING THE COLUMNS

It's time for a little quiz. Don't worry; this test is easy. After we take it, you'll see how helpful it is. There are only three questions, all given in the form of matching columns. Your assignment is to match the words on the left with the correct words on the right that form the three biblical couplets introduced in Ephesians 5:22-33. It will take only a few seconds to complete.

I. body   a. sacrifice
2. submit   b. love
3. respect   c. head

Now let's review it together. The correct answers, as you know, are I-c, 2-a, and 3-b.

The test is helpful because it shows us so simply the relational dynamics that should characterize a husband and wife. It also exposes the most popular misconceptions about marriage. The majority of Christians have been taught to believe that submission is correlative to headship.[7] Again, this is reflective

---

[7]It's true that the body submits to the head, and the head sacrifices for the body. However, it is inappropriate to connect the word *body* with *sacrifice*, because the body does not sacrifice; rather, the body submits. And yet the words *body* and *submit* belong on the side of the wife. The idea is to draw a line that crosses

of the statement issued from the Southern Baptist Convention (SBC) in 1998.[8] I remember the first moment I read it. I noticed right away that the statement says nothing about the husband's sacrifice. Instead, it says that husbands should assume the role of "provider" and "protector" and "leader." Doesn't that sound familiar?

The problem with the statement from the SBC is that it matches the word *head* with "submit."[9] Therefore it follows that nothing is said about the wife

---

from one side to the other. There are three things on the husband's side (head, sacrifice, love) and three things on the wife's (body, submit, respect). Still, someone might insist, "But we can connect *head* with *submit* and *sacrifice* with *body* by arguing that the head is submitted to and the body is sacrificed for." But here again, the attempt comes at the expense of confusing the columns. The latter argument is ill fitting because it requires us to put the words *head, body* and *love* on the same side (the head is submitted to, the body is sacrificed for, and the husband loves as the wife respects). That doesn't fit because the husband is not the body. The word *body* goes in the wife's column. The correct view instead is to say the husband is the head; the wife is the body. The husband sacrifices; the wife submits. The husband loves; the wife respects.

[8]The committee is quoted as saying that the document is "thoroughly biblical" with "every line deeply rooted in the clear teaching of Scripture " (see Carol McGraw and Hieu Tran Phan, "No Dispute for Southern Baptist: Dad Is Head of Clan," *The Orange County Register,* June 9, 1998, sec. 8, pp. 1, 8).

Without reservation, I applaud the Southern Baptist Convention for championing family values and marriage between one man and one woman. But I am grieved by the overstated claim that the statement is "thoroughly biblical." In reality, it is more reflective of the teachings of John Piper and Wayne Grudem than Scripture. Unfortunately, it omits several important aspects of Ephesians 5. To begin with, it does not say the wife is to submit to her husband "in everything." (Most Southern Baptists greatly limit her submission to times of decision making.) Nor does the statement mention the commandment for the husband to "sacrifice" himself for his wife. Furthermore, it fails to say anything about the "mystery" of marriage being reflective of Christ's union with the church. Consequently there is also nothing said about the husband and wife being made into "one flesh" as head and body. In addition to that, the statement also fails to mention the biblical commandment for the "husband" to "cleave" to "his wife."

[9]I am happy to acknowledge that the Greek word *hoti* meaning "for" in Ephesians 5:23, "For (*hoti*) the husband is the head . . ." is grammatically set such that it seems to say the wife is commanded to submit to her husband precisely because ("for") he is her leader. But that is not what the Bible says. Indeed, she is commanded to submit to him, and, indeed, he is her head. But that's just it. She is commanded to submit to her own head. She does not submit to his head as if his head alone—and not hers—is filled with answers and decisions that she is commanded to obey. The mystery is that she, as the body, is commanded to submit to her own head, which, quite mysteriously, is her husband. Similarly he is commanded to love not her body but his own body, which, quite mysteriously, turns out to be none other than his wife. The Bible says that the wife is to submit to her husband, but not because he is her leader. She is to submit to him because he is her head. When we read the word *head* as "leader," we mistake the word *kephalē* ("physical head") for *archōn* or *oikodespotēs* ("leader" or "head of the household.") We also fail to see the marvel of the three couplets in the passage. Along with that, we also miss the "mystery" of the passage (Eph 5:32). Even worse, we end up trivializing the remarkable union of Christ and the

being the husband's body. This is a significant omission. Indeed, the failure to match "head" with "body" results in the added failure to make mention in the statement that husband and wife are "one flesh." As presented in the SBC statement, the husband and wife are connected as leader and helper rather than as body and head.

Which of the two is more intimately connected? A leader and his helper? Or a body and head? The answer is obvious. It is far more profound for a wife to be the husband's own body than for her to be his functional assistant. Are you getting the picture? It really is a picture, isn't it? The Bible presents a picture of a physical body and head. Marriage is a picture of one being. A picture of a body organically connected to a head.

WHY GOD HATES DIVORCE

None of us can fully comprehend the mystery of man and woman or the mystery of husband and wife, both as head and body (1 Cor 11:3). But by virtue of the picture that the metaphor conveys, immediately we're struck by an image of unity. Man and woman are one in the sense that both were created by God. In Matthew 19, the reality of this mystery is brought out. Remember the conversation between the Lord and the Pharisees when they asked him if it is lawful to divorce? His answer to them is striking, so much so that we should analyze it here.

According to the record in the Gospel of Matthew, this is what transpired (Mt 19:1-6). The Pharisees came to Jesus, testing him and saying, "Is it lawful for a man to divorce his wife for any cause at all?" And he answered, "Have you not read that He who created them from the beginning made them male and female, and said, 'For this cause a man shall leave his father and mother and shall cleave to his wife, and the two shall become one flesh'? Consequently, they are no longer two, but one flesh. What therefore God has joined together, let no man separate."

---

church—because we fail to understand ourselves mysteriously as Christ's body. We see Jesus as Jesus; we don't see Jesus as our Head. Consequently we don't see ourselves as vitally connected to him. Thus we underestimate how much our Savior loves us. And thus we fail in our faith.

Isn't that answer strange? They asked Jesus about divorce, and he told them about creation. He told them that the man and woman were both created by God. What does creation have to do with divorce?

If we study the passage closely, we might find an answer from Jesus. So let's backtrack for a second and replay the conversation in slow motion.

The Pharisees, testing him, say, "Is it lawful to divorce?"

Jesus, being quite aware of first-century Jewish culture, in which no wife could divorce her husband and in which a husband could divorce his wife for almost any given reason,[10] responds to the Pharisees' question not by explaining the Law but rather by explaining God's intention. Look at what Jesus points out. When the Pharisees ask him about the lawfulness of a Jewish man acquiring a divorce, Jesus doesn't strictly talk about the man. Instead, he reminds them that man and woman were created by God, that male and female ultimately share the same origin (1 Cor 11:12).

Notice that he says, "For this cause."

He says, "For this cause a man shall leave his father and mother."

The reason is their maleness and femaleness. It's because God "made them male and female" that a man shall "leave his father and mother" and "be joined to his wife." In other words, male and female are designed to be together as one.[11]

This passage tells us that marriage is not only a union but also a reunion.

---

[10]According to D. A. Carson, "In mainstream Palestinian Judaism, both the school of Hillel and the school of Shammai permitted divorce (of the woman by the man: the reverse was not considered) on the grounds of *erwat dabar* ('something indecent,' Deut 24:1), but they disagreed on what 'indecent' might include. Shammai and his followers interpreted the expression to gross indecency, though not necessarily adultery; Hillel extended the meaning beyond sin to all kinds of real or imagined offenses, including an improperly cooked meal. The Hillelite R. Akiba permitted divorce in the case of a roving eye for prettier women" (*M Gittin* 9:10). See D. A. Carson, "Matthew," *The Expositor's Bible Commentary* (Grand Rapids, Mich.: Zondervan, 1984), p 411.

[11]The oneness of men and women can vaguely be seen in the fact that women in society tend inadvertently to follow the lead of the men. If men are promiscuous, then women want to be promiscuous too. If men leave home, then women want to leave home. If men have a male god, then women want a female goddess. Ironically, secular feminists notoriously take their cues from men. Man as "head" thus plays itself out in that Woman as "body" echoes the movements of him. That's why it's so important for the hearts of the fathers to return to the children (Lk 1:17). If men decide to prioritize the family, it is likely that women will decide to do the same.

It is not coincidental that the first words that Adam ever said to Eve were these: "This is now bone of my bones, and flesh of my flesh; she shall be called Woman because she was taken out of Man" (Gen 2:23). Adam did not say, "This is now flesh of my flesh; she shall be called Wife." No, he said, "This is . . . flesh of my flesh; she shall be called Woman."

I marvel at the significance of this. When Jesus tells the Pharisees about creation, his point is to remind them that man and woman already are the same flesh.[12] Because Adam and Eve, the first parents, were made of the same flesh, all people share the same flesh. Put another way, though a man and woman are two when they're unmarried, they're nonetheless two of the same flesh. Jesus, therefore, says it is doubly unthinkable for a husband and wife to divorce, for God has made them doubly into one. For when a man and woman get married, God turns *same* flesh into *one* flesh. Indeed, this is the mystery of marriage.

Let's look at the passage again. Jesus says, "For this cause a man shall leave his father and mother and cleave to his wife." Isn't that striking? Jesus tells the Pharisees that the Jewish man is supposed to "cleave to his wife," not divorce her. What a balance this brings to the biblical fact that the woman was created for the man (1 Cor 11:9). It seems as though the Scriptures would say to the woman, "Cleave to your husband since you were created from him and for him." But God gives the commandment to the man. God commands the man to cleave to the one who physically was made from him. The Bible tells him to leave and him to cleave to the one who was created for him. This really throws a wrench in the ol' boys' network. To keep the women out is not the same thing as to cleave.

What would happen in the Christian community if every husband would "cleave to his wife" (Mt 19:5)? In the Christian community, it is the wife who is told to cleave to her husband as if cleaving were synonymous to submitting. But according to the Word in the Old and New Testament, even by the mouth of Christ, the man is responsible to cleave (Gen 2:24).

---

[12]This point is echoed in 1 Corinthians 11:3, "the man is the head of the woman."

The mystery of marriage is that two become "one flesh." From the moment they are married and their bodies unite, the husband is the head and the wife is the body. This explains, at least in part, why the relationship of God and Christ cannot be reduced to a picture of a leader and a helper. God and Christ are truly one. Jesus said it plainly, "I and the Father are one" (Jn 10:30). Likewise, Christ and the church are one (Jn 17:21). Christ and the church are more closely united than just Savior and saved or Authority and subordinates. Christ and the church are married (Eph 5:32; Rev 21:2). No wonder the Bible says this is a "mystery." And no wonder it says this mystery is "great" (Eph 5:32).

Now consider what happens when the biblical metaphors are converted into more manageable definitions. When *head* is defined as "leader" and *body* is defined as "helper," the biblical mystery is lost. What is mysterious about a leader being coupled with his helper? Not very much. Nor is it particularly inspiring. But it is altogether breathtaking to see the biblical picture of body and head joined mysteriously as one.

The picture of "one flesh" communicates volumes of theology. It indicates immediately the organic unity that bonds a husband and wife. How might the divorce rate plummet among Christians if we would recognize that God joins a man and a woman into "one flesh" through the mystery of marriage? It is not so disturbing to imagine a leader breaking up with his assistant. But it is utterly disconcerting to imagine a body being amputated physically from its head. It's a horrible, bloody picture—a decapitation—too repulsive to imagine graphically. A body belongs to its head and a head belongs to its body. That's why God hates divorce (Mal 2:16). A broken marriage is a rupture of one flesh, even in a no-fault situation.

THE HUSBAND IS THE HEAD

Look again at Ephesians 5:23. Did you notice the verb? Ephesians 5:23 says the husband "is" the head of the wife. He is her head. No matter what. That means he isn't obligated to go out and kill a buffalo in order to become the head. Nor is he required to go home and be the boss so that everyone else will think of him as the head. Headship cannot be earned. Nor can it be endowed. (Unfortunately the teacher at a marriage seminar that my husband and I attended said that wives have been commissioned to "appoint" their husbands as the marital head. He said that headship is acquired only after a husband proves his worthiness to his wife.[13]) In truth, headship is a spiritual reality. Like manhood, it's a gift from God.

Granted, a man can be foolish or childish, but he cannot be stripped of his manhood. He might lack maturity, and he might be out of touch with himself. But he is man nonetheless. Men are men, no matter what the world has to say about men not being men. Manhood is an aspect of male adulthood that cannot be taken away. So too headship is an aspect of husbandhood. Manhood can be obscured,[14] and headship can be denied. But neither is elusive, and neither can be taken away. A man is a man plain and simple. And for as long as a man is married, the husband is the head of his wife.

When I was first invited to preach, I told the congregation that I am not the head of my marriage. Rather, Jim is the head of me. My participation in the kingdom of God does not interfere with my identity as Jim's body or with Jim's identity as my head. It's a biblical fact that "the husband is the head of the wife." I also explained that the text does not say that the husband is the head of the house. The Bible says, rather, that the husband is the head "of the wife." He is the head of her. That makes sense, doesn't it, in light of the biblical picture? The wife is the body the husband. His body is the wife, not the household. No husband is married to his household. No husband is "one flesh" with his children and extended family and house servants and property and pets. He is "one flesh" with his wife.

---

[13]Although this notion echoes John Piper's idea that mature femininity affirms the leadership "of worthy men," it adds a twist. Piper never says that headship is endowed upon a husband by a wife.

[14]Manhood can be obscured by a number of things, primarily by a man's attitude. If a man is worried about his identity, he is likely to deny part of himself. If he becomes a bully, he shuts down his humanity by acting like an animal, not a man. If he becomes distant, he barricades his heart by acting like a robot, not a man. If he becomes effeminate, he denies his masculinity by mimicking women, not men. But when a man *relaxes* in his God-given strength, he finds himself distinctively male. (When I say "relaxes," I don't mean that he sits around doing nothing. I mean that he walks forward in his manhood without fear.)

How might families change if parents would understand this? In many Christian homes, children are taught to look upon their mother as the lower-ranking parent whose authority can be trumped by the dad's. Thus children are not taught well to obey the fifth commandment of honoring their father *and* mother. According to the Scriptures, parental authority belongs to the mother just as much as it does to the father. Ephesians 6:1 says, "Children, obey your parents." Likewise, Proverbs 6:20 says, "My son, observe the commandment of your father and do not forsake the teaching of your mother." The matter bears repeating—the husband is the head. The father is not the head. The father is the partner of the mother. And yet, the mother, as a wife, is called by God to submit to her husband as the head.

SACRIFICE AND SUBMISSION

When a wife submits to her husband, she does not give up her will. On the contrary, she exercises her will to be guided by him. That doesn't mean she becomes a child who obeys him. It means, rather, that she conforms her will to his as a means of uniting with him. Something very similar happens when a husband takes the initiative to sacrifice himself for his wife. He doesn't become henpecked or lose his will to hers; on the contrary, he conforms his will to hers as a means of uniting with her.[15]

In Greek the word for "submit" *(hypotassō)* is used in the middle voice, which indicates grammatically that it's something one does to oneself. In

---

[15]Marriage should be characterized by a constant interplay of sacrifice and submission. The wife is commanded to be subject to the one who sacrifices himself for her. The husband is commanded to sacrifice himself for one who submits herself to him. Both are commanded to be imitators of God and walk in love and be subject to one another in the fear of Christ. And yet, because the husband is physically less vulnerable, his experience of serving his wife is most accurately described as a sacrifice. For he very well knows, in a worldly sense, that he can probably take advantage of her. By contrast, a wife's experience of serving her husband is more accurately described as submission. For though her subjection to him is sacrificial, she does not have the physique to take advantage of him in the same way that he does her. Elisabeth Elliot seems to hold a similar point of view. She writes, "Surely there are times when the Christian husband, in loving his wife as Christ loved the Church, submits to her wishes. It is impossible for love not to give, and that giving often means giving over one's own preferences. The husband is not in such a case acknowledging his wife's authority. He is laying down his life." See Elisabeth Elliot, *Let Me Be a Woman* (Wheaton, Ill.: Tyndale House, 1976), p. 139.

other words, the wife is to see to it that she submits to her husband just as she is to ensure that she respects him. It's not the husband's responsibility to get her to submit; it's hers. If he forces her to submit, then he short-circuits her submission and reduces it to something else. Submission is not submission—at least not in the middle voice—unless the one who submits actively does the submitting. The submission of a wife must be motivated by the personal will of the wife. In other words, the locus of control belongs to her. In that sense, he doesn't lead her. She leads herself into submission. She voluntarily yields herself to him.

The same thing is true with regard to the husband's sacrifice. If the wife tries to coerce him to give himself up for her, she thwarts her opportunity to be sacrificially loved and given to.

She can manipulate him—just as he can bully her—but she does not have the power to force him to love her sacrificially. That is, she can't place her grasp upon his will. Self-sacrifice, by definition, must be enacted by the self. When Jesus laid down his life, he made it clear that no one could force him to die (Jn 10:18). He died voluntarily. He was crucified voluntarily. He laid down his life voluntarily. So the godly husband lays down his life voluntarily for his bride.[16]

Once again the irony is that within the Christian community it is wives who are told to sacrifice themselves for their husbands. Not the husband but the wife is repeatedly told to give up her agenda and adjust her life to his. Rarely is the husband challenged by the church to sacrifice himself as a normal way of showing love to her. Instead, he is told to prepare himself to die for his wife, if ever her life is endangered. In other words, the commandment for him to sacrifice himself mistakenly is seen as applying only to a crisis situation. With regard to daily living, the husband is taught to see himself strictly as the loving servant leader who doesn't have to sacrifice himself.

Likewise, wives have been mistaught about submission. Most Christian

[16]I appreciate the way Grant Osborne stresses the need for husbands to sacrifice themselves for their wives (see Grant Osborne, "Hermeneutics and Women in the Church," *Journal of the Evangelical Theological Society* 20 [December 1977]: 337-52).

women think the commandment to submit applies only during times of conflict and decision. They have become convinced that when it's time to make a decision, the wife is to submit by deferring to her husband's final judgment. She can voice her opinion but must forfeit it after that, if ever the two opinions conflict.

The problem with this model of occasional submission is that it fails to meet the standards of the Bible. The Bible says that wives are be subject to their husbands "in everything," not just at decision-making points. The wife is commanded to live in a state of submission to her husband 24-7-365.[17] Submission is a relational posture. It means "coming under" her husband in order to lift him up in everything.

Conversely, the sacrifice of the husband is a full-time relational posture. For when the wife comes under the husband, thereby lifting him up, he sacrifices himself by giving up his advantage of being over her by exalting her to where he is. In other words, the husband and wife participate together in a dynamic upward spiral of lifting each other up instead of putting each other down. They don't engage in battle with each other. For example, the husband does not say, "Down, woman, I'm the boss!" Nor does the wife rebel against her husband. Instead, she lifts him up. He, in turn, lifts her up as well. As a result, they go up, up, up rather than down, down, down. There is no power struggle. On the contrary, there is genuine trust and love. In the next chapter, we will see how this trust and love dynamic traces back to the Trinity, where it is perfectly and beautifully played out.

DISCUSSION QUESTIONS

1. What have you been taught to believe about roles in marriage?

2. What do you think of the Southern Baptist Convention statement? Would you be willing to sign it? Why or why not?

3. Which is more biblical, for a wife submit to her husband merely at con-

---

[17]Twenty-four hours a day, seven days a week, three hundred sixty-five days a year.

flicting points of decision making or "in everything"? How do you think Ephesians 5:24 should be applied?

4. Discuss the dual concepts of submission and sacrifice. How is it that a wife can submit to her husband without him being her boss? How is it that a husband can sacrifice himself to his wife without being henpecked by her? (See note 15.)

14
How Does God Head Christ?

. . . that all may honor the Son, even as they honor the Father.
JOHN 5:22

One of the biggest points on which complementarians and egalitarians tend to disagree is the doctrine of the Trinity. Complementarians see God as a community of three equal persons ranked in hierarchical order.[1] As Ray Ortlund Jr. puts it, "Within the Holy Trinity, the Father leads, the Son submits to Him."[2] This view of order of the Trinity can be illustrated vertically as in figure 14.1.

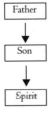

Figure 14.1   Hierarchical order within the Trinity

[1]See Jack Cottrell, *What the Bible Says About God the Redeemer* (Joplin, Mo.: College Press, 1987), p. 146.
[2]See Ray Ortlund Jr., "Male-Female Equality and Male Headship: Genesis 1—3" in Recovering *Biblical Manhood and Womanhood*, ed. John Piper and Wayne Grudem (Wheaton, Ill.: Crossway, 1991), p. 103.

Egalitarians, by contrast, see God as a community of three equal persons who are mutually reciprocal beings.[3] Any suggestion of the Son being subordinate to the Father within the Trinity is considered to be erroneous and "heretical."[4] Egalitarians see the order of the Trinity horizontally as in figure 14.2.

Father ←——————→ Son ←——————→ Spirit

Figure 14.2   Mutuality within the Trinity

In both models, the relational position of the triune persons within the Trinity is relatively static and fixed. Complementarians see the Father eternally above the Son and Spirit as the functional chief of the three. Egalitarians see the Father eternally beside the Son and Spirit as a functional equal. I agree with neither of these views.

In my assessment, neither model presented fully gives account for the biblical data. To begin with, egalitarians seem to overlook I Corinthians 15:27-28:

> For He [God] has put all things in subjection under His [Christ's] feet. But when He says, "All things are put in subjection," it is evident that He [God] is excepted who put all things in subjection to Him [Christ]. When all things are subjected to Him, then the Son Himself also will be subjected to the One who subjected all things to Him, so that God may be all in all.

To put it more succinctly, in the end God will put all things under Christ (Eph 1:22), and then Christ will put himself in subjection to God. We can sketch it as on figure 14.3.[5]

---

[3]Gilbert Bilezikian says, "God the Father reciprocated to the Son by ministering to the Son and by making Himself available to the Son. . . . and whatever the disciples would ask in Christ's name, the Father would give it to them (John 15:16; 16:23)." See Gilbert Bilezikian, *Beyond Sex Roles* (Grand Rapids, Mich.: Baker, 1985), p. 280.

[4]See Richard Clark Kroeger and Catherine Clark Kroeger, "Subordinationism" in *Evangelical Dictionary of Theology*, ed. Walter A. Elwell (Grand Rapids, Mich.: Baker, 1984). This article has been highly criticized as being unscholarly and biased in the favor of contemporary biblical feminism. For a less controversial description of the heresy of subordinationism, see Harold O. J. Brown, *Heresies* (New York: Doubleday, 1984), pp. 91-92.

[5]Christ is not the head of all things. He is above all things. See Bilezikian, *Beyond Sex Roles*, pp. 291-92.

God dynamically
puts all things
<u>under Christ</u>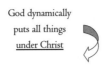

And then Christ is subjected to God.

God
⇑
<u>Christ above</u>
all things

Figure 14.3   All things in subjection

But that is not the end of the story. Something else happens in conjunction with this—Christ is seated at the right hand of God.

Very few Christians realize what it means for Christ to be seated "at the right hand of God" (Mk 14:62). Most people mistakenly believe that Christ is seated adjacent to the Father. We imagine him sitting there spatially to the right of the throne of God. That view is incorrect. The words "right hand of God" connote the idea of "the place of authority."[6] Or as Murray Harris, my former professor at Trinity, more carefully puts it, " 'God's right hand' is the place of unrivaled prestige and unparalleled authority."[7] In other words, the right of God is exactly where the Father is seated. The astounding news is that Jesus our Lord sits on the very throne of God, even the Father (Rev 4:11; 22:1).[8] Together they are seated as One.

Hence it is necessary to add another aspect, one that includes the relational dynamic of trust and love within the Trinity (see figure 14.4). Now we can see that after Christ submits himself, God, in turn, exalts him to the highest place that he could possibly be.

[6]Walter Wessel, "Mark," in *The Expositor's Bible Commentary*, ed. Frank Gaebelein (Grand Rapids, Mich.: Zondervan, 1984), 8:769.

[7]Murray J. Harris, *Colossians and Philemon* (Grand Rapids, Mich.: Eerdmans, 1991), p. 138.

[8]"The Son of Man has . . . taken His seat on the Father's throne" (Henry Barclay Swete, *The Ascended Christ* [London: Macmillan, 1916], p. 12). See also Cottrell's plain statement, "God and the Lamb have one throne," in *What the Bible Says About God the Redeemer*, p. 126.

What does this picture tell us about God? It tells us he's a God who shares. The Father delights to share his seat of power with the Son. The picture also tells us there is trust within the Trinity, not competition. Therefore Christ is not unwilling to be subject to God (1 Cor 11:3). Nor is God unwilling to share his seat of power with him. The Bible says clearly that the Father exalts the Son to the highest place (Phil 2:9-10) "so that all may honor the Son even as they honor the Father" (Jn 5:23).

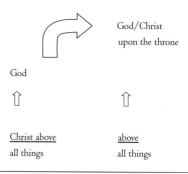

Figure 14.4   Dynamic trust and love within the Trinity

THE SUBJECTION OF CHRIST

Both sides of the debate recognize that Christ is subjected to God. And yet, once again, they sharply disagree on what that means. Egalitarians say that Christ was subjected to God temporarily on earth until he ascended into heaven to reign equally with the Father as God.[9] Complementarians say that Christ the Son is "eternally subordinate" to the Father in heaven just as he was on earth.[10] In my opinion, neither of these arguments exactly follows the text.

---

[9]See Rebecca Merrill Groothuis, *Good News for Women* (Grand Rapids, Mich.: Baker, 1997), pp. 55-60; Millard Erickson, *Christian Theology*, one-vol. ed. (Grand Rapids, Mich.: Baker, 1983), pp. 338, 735.

[10]Wayne Grudem thinks of it this way: "So we may say that the role of the Father in creation and redemption has been to plan and direct and the send the Son and Holy Spirit. This is not surprising, for it shows that the Father and the Son relate to one another as a father and son relate to one another in a human family: the father directs and has authority over the son, and the son obeys and is responsive to the directions of the father. The Holy Spirit is obedient to the directives of both the Father and the

Starting in I Corinthians 15:24 the apostle Paul says:

> Then comes the end, when He [Christ] delivers up the kingdom to the God
> and Father, when He [Christ] has abolished all rule and all authority and
> power. For He [Christ] must reign until He [God] has put all His enemies
> under His [Christ's] feet . . . for He [God] has put all things in subjection un-
> der His [Christ's] feet. But when He says, "All things are put in subjection,"
> it is evident that He [God] is excepted who put all things in subjection to
> Him [Christ]. When all things are subjected to Him [Christ], then the Son
> Himself also will be subjected to the One who subjected all things to Him,
> so that God may be all in all.

The text explicitly says that God is not subjected to the Son. The Father
and Son are not mutually submissive to each other. This verse says that "it is
evident that He [God] is excepted who put all things in subjection to Him."
Moreover, this passage says that "the Son Himself" will be subjected to
God, even after his ascension from the earth and even after all things are subjected under his feet.

And yet the Bible does not say that the Son is "eternally subordinate"[11]

'Son" (Wayne Grudem, *Systematic Theology* [Grand Rapids, Mich.: Zondervan, 1994], p. 249). The careful
reader, however, will notice that Grudem fails to take into account John 10:17-18, where Jesus says, "For
this reason the Father loves Me, because I [not the Father] lay down My life that I [not the Father] may
take it again. No one [not even the Father] has taken it away from Me, but I [as the Son] lay it down
on my own initiative. I have authority to lay it down, and I have authority to take it up again. This commandment I received from My Father [Who deferred to the Son's authority rather than, as Grudem
says, exercised authority over the Son.] If anyone argues, "See? The Father commanded the Son to exercise authority over Himself," then they are missing Grudem's point. Grudem is saying that the Son eternally assumes a submissive role rather than a role of authority. To say that the Father commands the Son
to act as though the Son has authority too is silly. It reminds me of the time when writer Jim Sire's wife,
Marj, openly disagreed with him in the presence of a man who took the initiative to rebuke her for talking back to her husband. Hearing this, Jim said, "Marj, I order you to disagree with me!"

[11]Steven Kovach asserts incorrectly that the teaching of the eternal subordination of Son is affirmed by
the ancient creeds. He says, "The doctrine of the eternal subordination of the Son has been the mainstream position in the history of the Christian church: such doctrine is clearly taught by Scripture, and
it is not limited to Jesus' time on earth." See Steven Kovach, "Egalitarians Revamp Doctrine of the Trinity: Bilezikian, Grenz, and the Kroegers Deny Eternal Subordination of the Son," *CBMW News* 2, no.1
(1996). Unfortunately, Kovach references Carl F. H. Henry as a source to confirm his conclusions.
In so doing, Kovach misunderstands Henry. Henry does not promote a doctrine of "eternal subordination" of the Son; on the contrary, Henry argues for the "eternal sonship" of the Son. He acknowledges

to the Father.[12] On the contrary, it says, "God is the head of Christ" (1 Cor 11:3) and that "the Son Himself also will be subjected to the One who subjected all things to Him, so that God may be all in all" (1 Cor 15:28).

Let's analyze this more deeply. Who delivers the kingdom to the God and Father? Christ. And who abolishes all rule and authority and power? Christ. And who puts all Christ's "enemies" under his feet? God. And who puts "all things" in subjection under Christ's feet? God. So then, to whom is Christ finally subjected? God.

Christ the Son is subject to the triune God of three persons. The Son is subjected to "the God and Father." And in that sense, the Son is subjected to himself. This is the doctrine of the Trinity. The most eminent theologian of Christendom, our familiar friend Augustine, clarified this doctrine for the church. Augustine said, "Neither may we think that Christ shall so give up the kingdom to God, even the Father, as that He shall take it away from Himself. For some vain talkers have thought even this. For when it is said, 'He shall have delivered up the kingdom to God, even the Father,' He Himself is not excluded; because He is one God together with the Father."[13]

Augustine further says, "Nor let any one, hearing what the apostle says, 'But when He saith all things are put under Him, it is manifest that He is excepted which did put all things under Him,' think the words, that He hath put all things under the Son, to be so understood of the Father, as that He should not think that the Son Himself put all things under Himself."[14]

---

the Son's subordination too, but he does not modify it with the word *eternal.* Here's how he puts it: "The biblical data put beyond doubt the subordination of the Son and the Spirit to the Father, and the eternal generation of the Son." (Notice that Henry says "eternal generation," not "eternal subordination.") But even there Henry adds a telling disclaimer: "Neither Scripture nor the ancient creeds explains these terms, however" (Carl F. H. Henry, *God, Revelation and Authority,* 6 vols. [Dallas: Word, 1982], 5:207).

[12]Henry furthermore says, "That our Lord is eternally the Son of God, and that the term Son designates not merely his office but His nature as well, and moreover designates sameness of nature and hence equality with God, was affirmed already by the Nicene Council. That is what the Bible teaches." See Henry, *God, Revelation and Authority,* 5:207.

[13]See Augustine, *On the Trinity,* trans. Arthur West Haddan in *Nicene and Post-Nicene Fathers,* ed. Philip Schaff, 14 vols. (Peabody, Mass.: Hendrickson, 1994), book 1, chap. 8.

[14]Ibid.

Hence we discover the mystery of the incarnation. Indeed, the mystery of Christ is that God the Son physically became God incarnate. Christ is at once both the Messiah and God. Christ is the Subject and the One subjected to all at once. Therefore, when Christ said, "The Father is greater than I" (Jn 14:28), he was not admitting to any lack of status within the Godhead.[15] For when God became flesh (Jn 1:14), not only did he voluntarily became less than the Father but also he also became less than the preincarnate Son (Phil 2:6).

EXALTED TO CO-REIGN

This is not irrelevant to the headship of the husband. Indeed, it relates directly. Throughout my study of the headship of the husband, I kept wondering, "How does God serve as the head of Christ?" And how does Christ serve as the head of the church?" I reasoned that however it is that God heads Christ, that must be the way that husbands are supposed to head their wives.

How does God head Christ? By exalting him to reign as Creator, Redeemer and Judge.

Think about it. The Son was involved in the creation. Orthodox theology says the Father is the Creator and the Son is the agent by whom the world was created. It's a biblical fact: "All things came into being by Him." Moreover, the Bible says that nothing was created "apart from Him" (Jn 1:3).

Is Christ, then, our Creator? Yes, in the sense that all things came into being "by Him." The nineteenth-century Princeton theologian Charles Hodge stated it boldly: "According to the Scriptures, the Father created the world, the Son created the world, and the Spirit created the world."[16] The Old Tes-

---

[15]For a more extensive commentary, see Kevin Giles, *The Trinity and Subordinationism* (Downers Grove, Ill.: InterVarsity Press, 2002).

[16]Hodge continues, "The Father preserves all things, the Son upholds all things, and the Spirit is the source of life. These facts are expressed by saying that the persons of the Trinity concur in all external acts. Nevertheless, there are some acts that are predominantly referred to the Father, others to the Son, and others to the Spirit. The Father [predominantly] creates, elects, and calls; the Son redeems [and yet Creator *is* Redeemer in Isaiah 43]; and the Spirit sanctifies [cf. 1 Cor 1:2; Heb 2:11]" (Charles Hodge, *Systematic Theology* [Grand Rapids, Mich.: Baker, 1988], pp. 167-68).

tament echoes the same thing. Indeed, Genesis 1:1 says, "In the beginning God created the heavens and the earth." And yet, Isaiah says, "Your Creator" has "redeemed you." The prophecy's surprise is that the Redeemer (the Messiah) is none other than the Creator of the world! Who is our Redeemer? It's Christ. Have you ever sung this song?

> Jesus, my Redeemer
> Name above all names,
> Precious Lamb of God, Messiah,
> Oh, for sinners slain.

Not only is Christ our Creator, he's also our Redeemer. With that, he also is the Judge. John 5:22 says, "For not even the Father judges anyone, but He has given all judgment to the Son."

Doesn't this sound like God? He is so loving, so generous, so eager to share that he exalts the Son and invites him to participate in the most exciting things. What could be more exciting than creating the world, redeeming God's people and acting as the Judge on the final day?

The same loving exaltation happens all over again as Christ serves as the head of the church. Consider what he does. He exalts us to reign with Him (2 Tim 2:12). The apostle John says, "And His bond-servants . . . will reign forever and ever" (Rev 22:3-5). Indeed, we are reigning with him now. When is the last time you heard Jesus preaching at your church? You haven't heard him directly in person because he ensures, by the power of his Spirit, that members of his church do that. The church is privileged to participate directly in the ministry of Christ because Christ does not do ministry without us. As a result, the church gets to do important things such as lead, preach, teach, wash other people's feet and give cold cups of water to those who are thirsty and in need. We get to pray for people and show mercy and offer them our help as Christ did in his ministry on earth. And in doing so, we share in the honor of Christ (Jn 12:26).

I believe something similar is supposed to happen when husbands head their wives. It's the husband's responsibility to exalt his wife as God exalts

Christ and Christ exalts the church. It's up to the husband to ensure that his wife is honored no less than he.

DISCUSSION QUESTIONS

1. Read John 5:22-23. What does it mean for "all [to] honor the Son as they honor the Father"? What do these verses imply about the Son? That he is eternally subordinate to the Father, or that God has exalted him to the highest place?

2. Read and discuss notes 11 and 12 from this chapter. How do Steven Kovach's conclusions about the Son differ from Carl Henry's point of view?

3. Review the quotes from Augustine on page 178 and then practice explaining them to someone else.

4. Name one practical way that a husband can ensure that his wife is honored no less than he.

15

THE MYSTERY OF HEADSHIP

But I want you to understand that Christ is the head of every man, and the man is the head of a woman, and God is the head of Christ.

1 CORINTHIANS 11:3

I f we want to embrace the mystery of headship, we *must* learn to think metaphorically. Metaphorically it is true that the man is the "head" of a woman (1 Cor 11:3). But it's not true in literal terms. Though humanity is united by the same flesh and blood (Gen 5:1-2), we are not male-headed female bodies. The same can be said about the mystery of marriage. The husband and wife are one metaphorically. They are not one in literal terms. So it is also with Christ. Metaphorically he is the body of God, but literally he is not. For God himself is not physical. Metaphorically, however, Christ is the body of God. Even literally speaking, Christ himself is God. Christ the living Savior *is* the living God, and yet God has no form. This is terribly abstract because the metaphors are abstract. Yet the metaphors describe something real.

I WANT YOU TO SEE

In the midst of my research on 1 Corinthians 11:3, I kept trying to crack the code, so to speak, on how the metaphors of headship fit together. I took seriously Paul's opening line, "But I want you to understand." Thus I kept praying that I would understand what these metaphors convey. Again and again, I revisited this passage. I told myself repeatedly, "This is really important. This is something that Paul wanted the Corinthians to get." I can't tell you how distracted I became in my quest to try to figure this out. For me, this was an abiding meditation. Even in my sleep, I would ponder I Corinthians 11:3. I couldn't let it go because I didn't understand what Paul said he wanted me to know.

One day when I was writing out the verse, I decided to insert the Greek word for "understand" into my sentence. But when I looked in my Greek Bible, I suddenly recognized that Paul doesn't use the Greek word for "understand." Well, he does, but he doesn't. Let me explain what I mean. The Greek word Paul uses translates into English as "understand," but that's because in English the word *understand* is a synonym for the word *see*. In Greek, the word Paul uses (*eidenai*) connotes a visual kind of knowing.

I was so unburdened to learn that Paul didn't really say that he wanted the Corinthians intellectually to comprehend these mysteries revealed by God. It relieved me to find out that we are not responsible to mentally compute exactly what it means for Christ to be the head of every man, and for the man to be head of a woman, and for God to be the head of Christ. Paul said he wanted the Corinthians to see it, to experience it, to perceive it as a picture.

COMPARING THE BIBLICAL PICTURES

I believe it is helpful to look for a connection between I Corinthians 11:3 and Ephesians 5:23. Moreover, I would like to propose that table 15.1 portrays a picture of a head and body. Christ is the head of every man, man is the head of woman, God is the head of Christ, the husband is the head of the wife, and Christ is the head of the church. Each one represents a mystery. In every case, the head and body are vitally connected as one. Is that a fair proposal?

Table 15.1   Head and body in 1 Corinthians 11 and Ephesians 5

1 Corinthians 11:3			Ephesians 5:23	
Christ	Man	God	Husband	Christ
Every man	Woman	Christ	Wife	Church

If we refer to the figure, perhaps we can evaluate it together. Instead of starting on the left, let's start on the right with Christ and the church. From there, we can proceed to discuss each metaphor and try to make some sense out of it. As we go, I'll ask specific questions to guide us along the way.

First question. Is it biblical to suggest that the church is the body of Christ? Yes, that's an easy one (Col 1:18).

The second question is similar. Is it acceptable to say the wife is the body of her husband? Yes, that is biblical too (Eph 5:28).

What about the third one? Is it orthodox to say that Christ is the body of God? Can we freely proclaim that Christ is God with skin on? After all, God doesn't have a body. "God is spirit" (Jn 4:24) and formless. That's true, and yet the Scriptures also say that "in Him [Christ] all the fullness of Deity dwells in bodily form" (Col 2:9). In Christ, God does assume a body (Jn 1:14). Indeed, the metaphor of Christ as the body of God refers to the incarnation.

Fourth, is it right to say that the woman is the body of the man? It is, if we consider the woman's origin. As we discussed, every man and woman of the same flesh since all trace back to Adam. In that sense, the woman *is* the body of the man insofar as she was fashioned from his rib.

Fifth, is it true in some sense that "every man" is the body of Christ? That's an odd thing to imagine. The Bible says that the church is the body of Christ. But the Bible also says that Christ is the head of every man (1 Cor 11:3). And yet that doesn't solve the question. It only poses it again. According to 1 Corinthians 11:3, there is something unique about Christ's relationship with men. As I explained in a prior chapter, it's not that men are the only ones directly accountable to him, and it's not that men were derived from him as their source (since Adam was created from dust). So it must be something else. In a moment, it will become apparent what that is.

I CORINTHIANS 11:3

So far we have said, on the basis of 1 Peter 3:7, that men are physically less vulnerable than women. In other words, we have established a working definition of masculinity. Masculinity is that "bodily characteristic that makes men less vulnerable women." Femininity, then, is that "bodily characteristic that makes women more vulnerable than men."

Using these definitions, we can literally say men are physically less vulnerable than women. Metaphorically we can say something else. Metaphorically we can say that while every head in the sketches is masculine (m), every body in the sketches is feminine (f). Consider figure 15.2. Now take notice of something. No woman is ever the head.

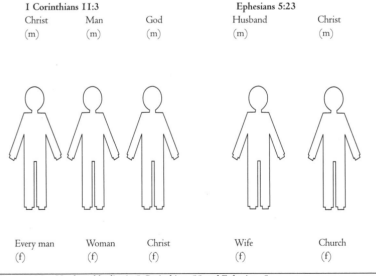

I Corinthians 11:3			Ephesians 5:23	
Christ	Man	God	Husband	Christ
(m)	(m)	(m)	(m)	(m)

Every man	Woman	Christ	Wife	Church
(f)	(f)	(f)	(f)	(f)

Figure 15.2   Heads and bodies in I Corinthians 11 and Ephesians 5

Furthermore, if you look at the figure again, you will suddenly see that in every case, the person below is physically more vulnerable than the one above. The church is physically more vulnerable than Christ (Col 3:1). The wife is physically more vulnerable than her husband, since she is a woman (1 Pet 3:7). Christ is physically more vulnerable than God (2 Cor 13:4). A woman is physically more vulnerable than a man (1 Pet 3:7). *This* is our clue to the meaning of the metaphor that Christ is the head of every man.

If femininity is defined as "being physically more vulnerable than men," then in relation to Christ, "every man" on earth is feminine. Believe it or not, none other than C. S. Lewis said the same. He said that all men are "feminine" relative to Christ.[1] That makes sense in light of the fact that the church is the bride of Christ. Indeed, the church has to be feminine. Otherwise, the church would be wed to Jesus Christ in a homosexual union.[2]

Whenever I teach class, this very moment in the discussion consistently seems to be the timeliest one in which to say—though not for the first time—that each picture in the text is a metaphor. It is not a literal reality. The metaphor of Christ as feminine toward God is not a literal reality. Christ was male, not female. But relative to God, he was "feminine" insofar as he became more physically vulnerable than God in heaven. God in heaven is not physical, nor was he beaten and killed. Christ, however, was.

Literally speaking, Christ became human and walked on earth as a man. No doubt Christ was physically masculine, not feminine. Metaphorically speaking, however, Christ is the body of God, the head (1 Cor 11:3), and in that sense, Christ is feminine.[3] I'll say it again. Insofar as Christ became "physically more vulnerable" than God, Christ took on femininity.

---

[1]See C. S. Lewis, "Priestesses in the Church?" in *God in the Dock* (Grand Rapids, Mich.: Eerdmans, 1970), p. 237.
[2]The same can be said in answer to the question of whether or not the church literally becomes "sons" of God (Gal 4:5-7). Of course, we do not. Otherwise, again, the Bride of Christ ends up being male, and the mystical union of the Christ and the church ends up being homosexual.
[3]It is critical to note that the Bible says "God" is the Head of "Christ." It does not say "the Father" is the head of "the Son." Elisabeth Elliot, however, confuses the words. Thus she mistakenly argues that the Son perpetually plays a "feminine" role within the Trinity. See Elisabeth Elliot, *Let Me Be a Woman* (Wheaton, Ill.: Tyndale House, 1976), pp. 59-60.

SOLVING THE BIBLICAL PUZZLE

We can now discern the meaning of the metaphor of Christ's headship of every man. It means that "every man"—relative to Christ—is a body, not a head.

I'll never forget what happened one night in the graduate school during theology class at Azusa Pacific University. I had posed to the students a hypothetical situation of whether or not a man and woman stranded on an island would necessarily assume that the man was the leader of the two. One student suddenly erupted out of turn and fired a heated comment straight at me.

He said, "I know for a fact that the man would be leader! If I was stranded on an island with you, I would be the leader, not you!"

I asked him, "How do you know?"

Intrepidly he answered, "Because I could beat you up!"

Then I heard myself say, "Or maybe you could be the bouncer, and I could be the brains."

The whole class responded in unison out loud with the sound that people make when someone gets publicly dogged. Though people started laughing once the heaviness had passed, that moment became a turning point for more than one pastor in the class. Almost everyone was halted by a common realization of unrealized and unspoken shared assumptions. The pastor wasn't the only one who automatically assumed that the man, being physically stronger, would therefore rule the woman. He was just more open than the rest. He felt insulted by the thought of being led on a desert island by a woman. He was biased. We could all see that. He could see it too. That's what made the moment so powerful.

I am convinced there is an underlying current of worldly competition going on between Christian men and women. And yet the whole point of the metaphors in I Corinthians 11 is to prevent us from being competitive. The whole point of what Paul was saying about men and women being interdependent in the Lord is to inspire us to cooperate, not compete.

Christ does not compete with every man. Indeed, he is not the man's competitor but his head. This is extremely significant because the same holds true

for men and women. The man is the head of a woman, not the opponent of
a woman. In other words, men and women are not designed to compete with
one another. Nor are we to wonder if it's better to be a man than a woman,
for it is not.

Here I need to make an interjection, for there is another important distinction between men and women that I have hardly mentioned until now.
As you may recall, we talked about this way in chapter five in our discussion
of Augustine. There it was said that the difference between men and women
lies not in the "image of God" that they both fully bear. Rather, it lies in the
"glory." For the man—and not the woman—is the "glory of God." It's in
I Corinthians 11:7: a man "is the image *and* glory of God; but the woman is
the glory of man" (emphasis added). Why is this? The answer is because of
his headship. A woman is not the glory of God because Christ is not her
head. According to God's plan, the head of a woman is a man (I Cor 11:3).
The man, by contrast, *is* the glory of God—not because of his maleness but
rather because his head metaphorically is Christ (I Cor 11:3; see figure
15.3).

Christ
(M)

Every man

Figure 15.3   Christ and every man

Don't forget that we're talking about headship, not leadership. Although
Christ is the Lord and Leader of women and men, he is not the head of every

woman in the exact same way that he is the head of "every man" (1 Cor 11:3). The logical implication of this is that since women are never the head, they don't need headship lessons. Men do. Men need headship lessons because men are entrusted with the unique responsibility of stewarding their headship. I believe, therefore, that Christ—as the head of "every man"—offers special lessons one-on-one to every man, so that he can learn not to take advantage of women.

Masculine Christ does not take advantage of men. He doesn't exclude or bully or patronize or deride or mock them as if he were superior. Instead, he honors men. He honors them by entrusting to them a physical advantage over women. With that, however, he requires a specific response. Men are commanded to use their relative strength not to put women down but rather to lift women up. They lift women up not as an act of leadership but rather as an act of headship. For a head can't help but want its body to be honored because the head and body are one.

THE MYSTERY OF GOD'S WILL

Without changing the subject, I want to ask an open question that has a clear answer. Ultimately, what is God's will? Do you know? The Bible clearly tells us in Ephesians 1:9-10: "He made known to us the mystery of His will, according to His kind intention which He purposed in Him with a view to an administration suitable to the fullness of the times, that is, the summing up of all things in Christ, things in the heavens and things on the earth."

What is God's will? His will is for everything to be saturated in Christ. He wants the entire creation to be "summed up" in Christ. He wants everyone on earth to emulate Christ, to be in Christ, to worship and exalt Jesus Christ.

How does that inform men and women in the church? Let's look at what the picture reveals (see figure 15.4). Women are to emulate Christ. They emulate Christ, who is feminine toward God (1 Cor 11:3). Likewise, men do the same. They emulate Christ, who is masculine toward "every man" (1 Cor 11:3).

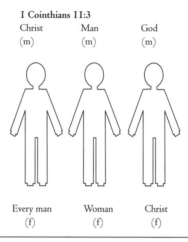

Figure 15.4   Relationships in I Corinthians 11

Isn't that something? Now we can "see" how it is that males and females are made in the image of God. Both reflect the image of Christ.[4]

DISCUSSION QUESTIONS

1. What do you think about C. S. Lewis's claim that men are "feminine" relative to Christ?

2. Is Christ feminine relative to God? If you disagree, then how do you explain the fact that women are made in the image of God?

3. Explain how it is that men can be masculine toward women yet feminine toward Christ.

4. According to Ephesians 1:9-10, what is the mystery of God's will?

---

[4]It's also important to remember that another metaphor in Scripture says that women are masculine too. Read Galatians 3:26, "For you are all sons of God through faith Jesus Christ." I say this not to get hung up or read more into the text than is there but rather to settle the record in case anyone imprudently says that women are less like God than men are since women are never the head. I will finalize the argument this way. Neither men nor women are the head of the church. In other words, the argument is moot with regard to positions in church leadership.

16

DOES MATTHEW 18 APPLY TO WIVES?

And if your brother sins, go and reprove him in private; if he listens to you, you have won your brother. But if he does not listen to you, take one or two more with you, so that by the mouth of two or three witnesses every fact may be confirmed.

MATTHEW 18:15-16

The most disturbing experience I've ever had as a professor occurred when a woman started weeping inconsolably because the theology I presented failed to offer her hope. She was grievously disappointed with my conclusions. She didn't want to submit to her husband because he wouldn't lift her up.

Thirty minutes transpired before she was able to talk.

"Is that it?" she whimpered between restrained sobs.

To her it wasn't enough to paint an ideal picture of a body and head. To her it was off-putting to be told that her duty as a Christian wife is to submit to her husband and respect him. She disrespected her husband. She resented him because he wouldn't rejoice in her giftedness or love her as Christ loves the church. He was not physically abusive. Rather, he was possessive and re-strictive. In spite of the fact that their children were grown, this husband re-fused to endorse his wife's ministry because it was outside of the home.

All her life this woman had felt called into public ministry. Even as a child trapped in the throes of unspeakable abuse, she could sense God setting her apart. Her believing husband was well aware of this. He just didn't have the faith to watch her go.

For twenty years, this woman served her family full time. During all those years the clarity of her calling never waned. On the contrary, it steadily increased. For two decades, she felt called to minister to her family primarily, but that phase of her ministry was slowly giving way to something new that connected to the calling of her childhood. Yet her husband wasn't willing to accept it. For him it felt embarrassing to be the silent husband of a Bible-teaching wife. He felt inferior to her. For all these years she had been the one to teach hundreds of adults Sunday school. She had been the one whom people praised. What was he to do while she ministered to others? Stand there with nothing to say?

Matters were made worse for this particular couple because the pastor of their church kept trying to get the husband to become a Bible teacher and the wife to hold herself back. Consequently the husband was doubly humiliated. It felt awful to be forced outside of his giftedness all for the sake of "proving his headship" publicly.

The more this woman told me her story, the more painful it became to listen. She knew what it meant to be violated. She knew what it meant to be lied to and deceived, even by top leaders in the church. But she also knew the power of forgiveness firsthand. Reconciliation wasn't just a church word for her. It was her testimony. She had forgiven her tormentors (if you could hear her story, you would know the word *tormentors* is appropriate). The Lord had restored her relationships with them. And now he was sending her out. Her passion? To help build bridges between men and women whose relationships have been breached.

And yet her husband would not agree to have her go. Her calling undermined his sense of manhood. He wasn't able within his heart to entrust his wife to the Lord. He couldn't trust God with regard to her. He didn't trust God for himself.

As a result, she felt demoralized and wronged. It was difficult for her to be invalidated by her husband. She felt robbed by him. She felt as though her life partner was stealing her blessing from God. Who would have guessed that her longstanding vision to catalyze a movement of reconciliation between men and women would be thwarted by her Christian husband?

"Is that it?" she asked with a look of desperation in her eyes.[1]

Her quiet question rang inside my ears as a siren. I went home to another sleepless night of racking my brain and praying to the Lord for further insight.

GOD'S CONTINGENCY PLAN

I don't remember how many days or weeks elapsed. But it wasn't very long before the stormy upheaval in my theology of women settled into calm and confidence. I discovered nothing new. The plan of God had been there in the Bible all along, but I hadn't seen it in this context. I had studied Matthew 18 countless times before, but never with marriage in mind.[2] I could hardly wait to tell the woman in my class what I had found.

Privately I asked her, "Have you confronted your husband in private?"

"Yes," she said with a hint of exasperation. "I have done that many, many times."

I pressed her again, "Okay, that's good. But after that, did you ever take one or two witnesses along with you and confront him in their presence?"

She said, "No, I didn't do that."

Collapsing in my chair, I threw back my head and breathed a great sigh, "Hallelujah!"

I felt great, not because this woman had neglected to follow the second step of Matthew 18 but because I knew she still had recourse. Whereas she believed that submission to her husband meant not holding him accountable, Matthew 18 said something different. Let's take a look at Matthew 18:15-17:

> If your brother sins, go and reprove him in private; if he listens to you, you have won your brother. But if he does not listen to you, take one or two more

---

[1] Much of this book was not presented in the class the woman took. At the time my theology was far less developed and clear.

[2] In perusing books on the subject later, I discovered that complementarian writer Susan Foh also believes that Matthew 18 can be properly applied within a Christian marriage. She says, "The Christian wife . . . is not to be silent when her husband sins (Matt. 18:15)" (Susan Foh, *Women and the Word of God* [Phillipsburg, N.J.: P & R, 1979], p. 186).

with you, so that by the mouth of two or three witnesses every fact may be confirmed. If he refuses to listen to them, tell it to the church; and if he refuses to listen even to the church, let him be to you a Gentile and a tax-gatherer.

The text says to go to the offender one on one and expose the nature of the offense. The idea, I believe, is to give the other person the benefit of the doubt in case there was a miscommunication. Going in private also provides the offender with a chance to repent once he or she comes to realize what has been done. But if the offender remains hardened, then it becomes necessary to select one or two people to take along with you and ask them to stand witness while you confront the offender again. In my experience, most Christians change their behavior after being reproved[3] in the presence of one or two others.

Another woman I know, however, attempted to confront her husband—not about him limiting her ministry but about him bullying her. This woman had no desire to become a vocational minister. She was a stay-at-home mom. But she also knew the Scriptures. Thus it occurred to her too to follow Matthew 18, even the part that calls for one or two witnesses. But when she did it, her effort backfired. Instead of helping her to hold her husband accountable, the two witnesses, an elder and a pastor in her church, ganged up with her husband. Furiously all three of them scolded her for questioning her husband's "God-given authority." They said he had the right as "the head of the house" to discipline his wife in whatever way that he saw fit. There was no accountability for him, only trauma and indignity for her.

Over the months, she sank into emotional depression. Her physical health also began to fade. Little by little she deteriorated, drifting into social isolation. She quit going to their church because her husband was regarded as an upstanding elder there. After church he would curse and yell, saying horrible things to attempt to keep his wife down.

By the time I met her, she had made her way into a different local church. Her prayer life was strong, and she had become friends with a godly Christian couple who eventually became her two witnesses when she attempted to

---

[3] *Reproved* does not mean scolded. To reprove means rather "to expose."

confront her husband again. For as soon as she had told me her story, I had encouraged her to redo the process, this time choosing other witnesses.[4] And the second time, it worked. This time he was caught. He broke down in tears and began to ask his wife for forgiveness.[5]

Realistically, of course, people don't usually change overnight. But they can change gradually, slowly, over time, especially if they're held accountable. I can hardly think of anything more needed in the church than systems of support that genuinely promote accountability.[6] Indeed, followers of Christ need each other to give vision to our blind spots and speak truth into the places where we're deceived. We also need the loving support that comes with authentic Christianity.

As I write, the elder-husband is slowly changing in the context of the relationships he and his wife enjoy with those who are holding them accountable. The wife is changing too. She and her husband are growing spiritually and learning how to avoid the destructive downward spiral that they used to tumble into.

As for the woman minister, she didn't have to use Matthew 18 because she and her husband joined a different church, one that affirms them in their respective giftedness. In this new setting, neither one is pressured as they were before, and that is helping their marriage.

DOES MATTHEW 18 APPLY TO WIVES?

The first weekend in February 2000, I recited the text of Matthew 18:15-17 to a group of women in a workshop at an international conference. After I read it, I posed a serious question, "Does Matthew 18 apply to wives?"

The women in the room started looking at each other as if I had said

---

[4]Though many people assume the one or two witnesses need to be positional church leaders, that is not the case. According to the Scriptures, the offender gets to choose the witnesses. It's best to choose witnesses whom the offender respects and whom the offended person trusts. Most important, it is imperative to choose witnesses who will champion God's Word and holy living.

[5]This is not a sign of being feminized. Rather, it's a sign of repentance (2 Cor 7:9-11). Jesus said, "Blessed are those who mourn" (Mt 5:4). Furthermore, as Daniel Doriani points out, "There are nearly 200 instances of people weeping and shedding tears in the Scriptures, and most of the criers were men" (Doriani, *The Life of a God-made Man* [Wheaton, Ill.: Crossway, 2001], p. 43).

[6]I plan to write a book on this subject based on my dissertation, *A Biblical Theology of Godly Human Anger*.

something revolutionary. Eyebrows were furrowed; jaws were dropped; al-most every woman shifted in her seat. The moment was amazing but uncom-fortable. You could sense a wave of hope swelling up in the room. You could also feel the ambivalence. People didn't know if it was safe to engage this type of unasked question. So I decided to pray. This is what I prayed out loud:

Dear Lord, we're confused. We've always been taught that wives are supposed to submit. So here's our big question: Does Matthew 18 apply to wives? Have you provided us a con-tingency plan that we didn't see until now? We need your wisdom. Help us to realize the truth. And give us the courage to act on it. We pray this counting on you. In Jesus' name. Amen.

So, reader, what's your answer? Does Matthew 18 apply to wives?

I think it does. I believe God has equipped all Christians with a way to hold each other accountable. It's not God's way for Christian husbands to be exempted from obeying the commandments of God. The Bible doesn't say, "Let wives be holy as I am holy, but let husbands do whatever they like." It says, "Be holy yourselves also in all your behavior; because it is written, 'You shall be holy, for I am holy' " (1 Pet 1:16).

I've never met a person, including any man, who is able to be holy apart from the help of correction. Everyone needs to be corrected. My greatest vic-tories in repentance from sin have happened in the context of my relation-ships with people who love me enough to help me follow Christ. I am much more responsive to the Spirit of God when people I'm hurting tell me they're displeased with my sin.

Especially in marriage, people need accountability. Jim can attest that many of my sins happen privately in the context of our marriage. He hears me venting in ways that I don't vent around others. He sees my selfishness. He is also there to watch me flare up with angry demands and self-serving expectations. Others can observe my lack of holiness, but not with the clarity that Jim can. God has given Jim the best seat in the house to view my sins from close up. As a result, he is my coach in holiness. God is using him more than anybody else to train me to be a loving and righteous woman. Because I am his wife, the same can be said about Jim being coached by me.

Jim and I strongly encourage Christian couples to seek counsel either from a well-trained Christian counselor or from another godly couple in the church. It's biblical to be helped by a third party. Going to a counselor (or whoever else) is the practical equivalent of obeying the second step of conflict resolution described in Matthew 18.

WIVES SHOULD WIN THEIR HUSBANDS WITHOUT A WORD

When I finished my lecture at the international conference, virtually no one stirred. They all sat there feeling satisfied and deeply affirmed. The Word of God had lifted their heads from the pit of indignity and unrelenting shame that had kept them down before. They felt validated. They felt validated to such a high degree that most of them sat there and smiled. Some of them were laughing and crying simultaneously. Others were blowing their noses. It was a glorious moment, one that I hope never to forget.

A few minutes later, someone broke the silence and said, "I have never had a thought about Matthew 18. I mean, I've thought about it before, but not within the context of marriage. I've always been taught that wives are supposed to win their husbands 'without a word' [1 Pet 3:1]. I thought I had to be silent."

Right then and there, it was seared into my mind for the thousandth time that the debate about women in ministry has far more to do with the church's view of women than with the church's view of women's ordination.[7] None of these women were crying over the issue of ordination. They were crying because this was the first time that they had been taught that God gives them a voice. They were crying because they had long believed that they were supposed to be silent, and now they knew that was wrong. The women in the

---

[7]One is hard-pressed to disagree. For if Matthew 18 does not apply wives, then neither do other verses such as 1 Timothy 5:20 and 2 Timothy 3:14-16. Nor could any wife's gift of exhortation be exercised in the context of her marriage (Rom 12:8). To be technical about it, we would also have to say that a wife cannot share any Scripture with her husband because Scripture itself will "correct" him (2 Tim 3:16). We'd also hold that a Christian wife is not allowed to tell a Christian counselor about the conflicts in her marriage because that, in effect, would be tantamount to her taking the second step prescribed by the Lord to readers of Matthew 18. The Christian counselor becomes the "one witness" who hears about the offenses from husband to wife, and wife to husband.

room honestly believed that as wives, they had no recourse other than prayer by which to hold their husbands accountable. They had it their minds that "chaste and respectful behavior" (1 Pet 3:2) precluded them from speaking the truth (Eph 4:15).

I acknowledge that the Bible says, "Wives, be submissive to your own husbands, so that even if any of them are disobedient to the word, they may be won without a word by the behavior of their wives, as they observe your chaste and respectful behavior" (1 Pet 3:1-2).[8] But being submissive does not require a wife to refrain from reproving her husband (Mt 18:15). Granted, the rules are not the same for women who are married to unbelievers.[9] But for a wife married to a Christian husband, it is appropriate to hold him accountable to biblical standards. Indeed, if her husband is wise, he will love her all the more for doing so (Prov 9:8).[10]

Conversely, when a husband understands that his wife is his body, he begins to care about her pain. It's because he is her head—because he is connected—that he feels compassion toward her. His headship ought to make him far more sensitive, not far more directive, toward her. Conversely, the bodyhood of the wife ought to make it easier for her to submit to her husband. For indeed, the paradox of their oneness means that in submitting to her husband (with whom she is one), the wife ends up submitting to herself.[11]

WHAT IF HEADSHIP IS CONFUSED WITH ENTITLEMENT?

One day Jim and I went to lunch with another couple from our church. We

---

[8]It could very well be that 1 Peter 3:1 applies to wives who are married to unbelievers. For the Greek word *kerdaino* ("to gain") is used here metaphorically to refer to the winning of souls into the kingdom of God by the gospel. See also 1 Corinthians 9:19-20.

[9]If her husband is violent, it might be best for her to call the police. If her husband is merely an unbeliever, then she should follow the guidelines in 1 Corinthians 7:13-16. The same holds true for a husband whose wife is unbelieving.

[10]A genuine Christian husband ought to praise his wife (Prov 31:28) for opening her mouth to reprove him in a spirit of wisdom (Prov 31:26). More important, a genuinely Christian husband ought to praise the Lord for using his wife to help him become a better Christian.

[11]Note the parallel between Christ's submission to himself (as God the Father, Son and Spirit) and the wife's submission to herself as the body of her husband with whom she is "one." For a reminder of Augustine's statement, see p. 178.

learned somewhere in the middle of the conversation that the husband had instructed his wife to take her bath only after he had taken his shower so that the best of the hot water would always be available to him. On hearing this, I asked him, "Does this illustrate your understanding of what it means for your wife to submit?"

Reflexively he answered, "Yes."

That conversation, along with many others like it, convinces me that many Christian men have not been taught what it means on a practical basis for a husband to lay down his life for his wife. This man sincerely believed that the husband's sacrifice was something more magnanimous such as taking a bullet for his wife. Thus he told himself—and us—that he would die for her. He did not tell himself that he would sacrifice the luxury of taking a hot shower so that she could enjoy a hot bath.

Many Christian men honestly believe that headship is the equivalent of entitlement. They feel entitled as the head because that is what they have been taught.

WHEN THE BUCK STOPS WITH THE HUSBAND

Similarly many Christian couples have not been taught to access Matthew 18. Instead, they've been told that when conflicts arise, the husband is entitled to give the final word no matter what. With that, the husband is constantly exhorted to be loving, and many Christian husbands genuinely are. But sometimes the husband confuses the verb *love* with the adverb *lovingly* and lovingly tells his wife to conform to his way of thinking. That's how the conflict is resolved.

Allow me to offer an example. There's a front-page article in the *Journal for Biblical Manhood and Womanhood* (*JBMW*) with headlines that read, "Southern Baptists Lead the Way." The article is an interview with the wife of a past president of the Southern Baptist Convention (SBC). She served on the committee that added Article XVIII, an Article on the Family, to the *Baptist Faith and Message* Statement of Faith. The purpose of the interview in the *Journal for Biblical Manhood and Womanhood* was to interview her about the process of the writing of this article.[12] I would like to highlight the portion of the interview that tells from her perspective how headship during conflict plays out in marriage. As the wife tells the story, it goes something like this.

Her husband wanted a dog, and she didn't. The reason she didn't was that she fully realized that she, not he, would be the one responsible to take care of it. She didn't want to be responsible for a big hunting dog. A big dog such as that would "require a lot exercise" and "a lot of care." She also thought that it would be difficult for her in light of their traveling schedule. To make matters worse, the dog her husband wanted had a tendency to bark whenever someone came into the house. That's why she called him "that squealer." To her, it didn't seem right for them to get this barking dog because she and her husband reside in a presidential house where she graciously hosts "four to six functions a week."

She said to her husband, "No, there's no way this is right."

After that, she "begged" him "not to bring that dog" home.

The husband listened to her reasons for making this request but ultimately used his headship to say no. Decisively he told her that "he wanted that dog" and he "felt [they] ought to get that dog." He also let her know that that she would be the one to take care of it. So they bought the dog, and the wife took care of it, and then just a year or two later, wouldn't you know, their grand-dog died. That is, their beloved "grand-dog" (as she called it) that belonged to their grown son—a different dog that lived somewhere else—died prematurely of a very unusual disease.

It's important to know that the grand-dog was of the same breed as the one that her husband had acquired (except, she says, the one that died was "obedient" and "wonderful," and the one that she has care of is "obnox-

[12]Two women served on this committee. Incidentally, this illustrates the kind of practical egalitarianism exercised by Southern Baptist leaders. In spite of their belief that women should be prohibited from exercising authority in the church, they invited two women to participate at the decision-making table to help determine the future of their denomination. Wayne Grudem was so convinced of the weightiness of the work of this committee that he used it as an example to illustrate the effectiveness and impact of the Council on Biblical Manhood and Womanhood. See Wayne Grudem, "Does the Work of CBMW Make Any Difference?" *Journal for Biblical Manhood and Womanhood* 3, no. 2 (1998): 13.

ious"). Consequently, the Southern Baptist wife reasoned to herself in retrospect that it was "somewhat comforting" for them to have the newer dog around. To quote her directly, she says, "So how do I know that God didn't put the idea into [my husband's] heart to get this other dog, because He knew what we were going to face and that this was just one way of making it a little easier?"

Why am I telling this story? I'm telling it because it exposes the mentality that many evangelicals are continually encouraged to embrace. The wife tells herself that her husband wasn't selfish but rather that her husband followed God. This is the way she manages to continue to submit without confronting him in the presence of other people (Mt 18). Call it culture, if you like. But it's not God's way. I know firsthand that the wife in this story is extremely dedicated to the Lord and to her family, but I believe this couple is naïve.

In the overall scheme of life, this story is insignificant. It's not a big deal that the wife was assigned against her will to care for her husband's dog. It's not as though he forced her to be responsible for his pet. After all, she was the one who made the decision "graciously to submit." But it *is* significant that the husband's behavior aligned more closely with the Southern Baptist statement (for the husband to be the leader and the wife to graciously submit) than with Ephesians 5:25. And it *is* a big deal that this particular story was featured as an exemplary way for complementarian Christians to live.

To be clear, I do not doubt the husband's good intentions. In fact, I imagine that he lovingly told her that they would be getting that dog. But I can't see how the husband's decision modeled any Christlike sacrifice on his part. As a matter of fact, I can't see that either spouse had any notion that it would have been more biblical (Eph 5:25) for him either to sacrifice his desire to have a dog or to assume responsibility for his pet.

In neither case do I doubt the husbands' intentions. On the contrary, I believe that the husband who used the hot water and the husband who brought home the dog truly do love their wives. What I doubt is if they or

their wives have ever been taught that it's masculine for a husband to sacrifice
himself for his wife. It's not feminine for a husband to be unselfish. It's not
womanly for him to take responsibility for something he wants for himself.
It's masculine for him to be mature. It's masculine for him to honor his wife.
It's masculine for him not to take advantage of his advantage over her. That's
what biblical headship is about.

Many Christian men mistakenly believe that it's feminine for a husband
to give in to his wife. Thus they see their own surrender as too costly. With
that, they honestly believe that the husband has the option whether to be giving or not. When a husband doesn't give, he feels entitled not to give. By virtue of his headship, he counts it a male prerogative to decide whether to be
generous or not. She, in turn, sees her surrender as required. The outcome of
this is that the wife ends up "graciously submitting" and "graciously sacrificing," while the husband remains entitled to do neither.

Of course, not all complementarians are like this. Some are far more
moderate. In fact, the research shows that most complementarians live in
egalitarian marriages.[13] For example, researchers Sally Gallagher and
Christian Smith concluded from 265 in-depth interviews in twenty-three
states that American evangelicals use "conservative rhetoric" more in
their talking than in their walking. More than 90 percent, in fact, said
"nearly all decisions were jointly made."[14] One Southern Baptist husband
and father of three put it this way: "[Decision making] should be mutual.
If the same Holy Spirit that's leading me is leading my wife, we're probably not gonna disagree, you know, we're gonna be led in the same direction. . . . If we had a big decision to make and my wife and I disagree on
it, I'd probably try to figure it out, why we disagreed, and we would defi-

---

[13]According to two different recent studies, most evangelicals operate within marriage as if they believe
in mutual submission, the sharing of household responsibilities and joint decision making. See Sally
Gallagher and Christian Smith, "Symbolic Traditionalism and Practical Egalitarianism: Contemporary
Evangelicals, Family and Gender," *Gender and Society* 13, no. 2 (1999): 211-33. See also a summary report
of a Princeton study conducted by W. Bradford Wilcox and John P. Bartkowski in a news article by Holly
Lebowitz, "Study Points Up Evangelical 'Paradox,' " *The Dallas Morning News*, August 7, 1999, p. 5G.
[14]See Gallagher and Smith, "Symbolic Traditionalism and Practical Egalitarianism," p. 221.

nitely need to sit down and talk about why."[15]

The Southern Baptist wife who was interviewed in the *Journal for Biblical Manhood and Womanhood* testified to something very similar: "99% of the time, when we finish discussing the matter, we've come to a mutual decision. We agree. And nobody's given up anything in the sense of saying, 'Oh, it's going to be your way instead of mine.' We've made a joint decision."

WHEN THE WIFE REFUSES TO SUBMIT

In pondering this, it occurs to me that it might be easier for complementarian-minded women than for egalitarian-minded women to submit. For complementarian-minded women see their husbands as their leaders, not their peers. Often times, moreover, they understand submission in terms of obedience rather than in terms of coming under. Thus they accept it as their biblical duty to love and obey their husbands in accordance with their traditional wedding vows. What they forget is that Scripture clashes with traditional wedding vows. Scripture sees the wife not as a subordinate who obeys but rather as a wife who submits.[16] It is more challenging—and more dignifying—for a wife to submit voluntarily as a peer than to submit obediently as a subordinate.[17]

By contrast, I have observed that egalitarian-minded wives have a tendency to think submission is required only when it is mutual. In other words, some egalitarians do not regard Ephesians 5:22, "Wives, be subject to your own husbands," as a discrete commandment that wives are responsible to obey. Instead, they say that Ephesians 5:21, "and be subject to one another in the fear of Christ," releases the wife from the duty of submitting unilaterally. As a result, egalitarian-minded women sometimes refuse to submit to their husbands not

---

[15]Ibid, pp. 221-22.

[16]Compare Ephesians 5:22, "Wives be subject to your own husbands, as to the Lord," with Ephesians 6:1, "Children, obey your parents in the Lord."

[17]Paradoxically, her voluntary submission to her husband is an act of obedience to the Lord. The word *voluntarily* might be somewhat misleading. For to some, it may connote the idea that submission is optional when biblically it is compulsory. When I say submission is voluntary, I mean that the wife as a peer submits herself to her husband as his equal.

because their husbands are sinning but rather because the wife is more concerned about her equality in the marriage than she is her obedience to Christ. As an egalitarian, she wants nothing less than mutual submission. Thus she demands it, and thus she refuses to come under her husband. For in her understanding, she is entitled not to submit until he submits to her too.

WHEN THE CONFLICT IS DOCTRINAL

If the conflict between a husband and wife is doctrinal, then Matthew 18 may not apply. For instance, if the husband believes that I Timothy 2 prohibits his wife from serving in pastoral leadership, then the wife is obligated to respect her husband's convictions. If the wife senses God prompting her to minister as a pastor, then respectfully she should communicate that to her husband. If the husband refuses to listen, then she follows Matthew 18 as a way of holding her husband accountable to be loving (Eph 5:28). It is not fair for a husband or wife to close a conversation just because they want their own way.

At the same, the wife is to exercise patience. As a godly wife, she should also continue to submit. That is not to say she should wait until her husband grants her permission to enter the ministry. Rather, it means that she doesn't hurry him.[18] As a dedicated wife, she pays respect to him as long as he's in the process searching the Scriptures for understanding. If her husband shuts down, she follows Matthew 18 all over again. But if her husband listens and dialogues respectfully with her—and still comes to the conclusion that his conscience is offended by her ministry to men—then the wife is advised to find a different way to serve the Lord (I Cor 8).[19]

WHEN THE WIFE AND THE HUSBAND ARE AFRAID

Finally, I would say that sometimes a wife knows no other way to protect her-

---

[18]Nor does she sin with her tongue. See James 3:5-18 and Colossians 3:8.

[19]Both can pray that God would give them oneness in heart and conviction (Phil 2:2). If God has ordained a particular woman to do a specific ministry, then he will arrange for things to fall in place, though perhaps in a new way, so that his will can be done.

self from her husband's sins or contrary beliefs than to refuse to submit to him. She refuses to follow the commandment to submit to her husband because she is too afraid to implement Matthew 18. It is not uncommon for a Christian wife to feel scared to death to nudge her Christian husband to face the raw truth about himself. She's not scared for him but for herself. Her overwhelming fear is connected to her lack of faith in God. She is afraid that God's way of proceeding won't work. She is afraid to confront her husband privately because she fears him more than she fears God. She is afraid to bring one or two others with her because she fears that other Christians might see her as rebellious and bad. Thus she submits in selfish fear rather than in marital love. And thus she forfeits her integrity in order to spare her husband an embarrassment. As a result, she enables him to avoid true repentance.

Sometimes a husband likewise knows no other way to protect his self-image than to refuse to take the risk of sacrificing himself for the sake of his wife. With that, he rejects the biblical idea of lifting her up as Christ lifts up the church. Thus he fails to support her in the thing that he perceives might jeopardize his manhood. It is not uncommon for a Christian husband to fear that his wife will upstage him. He feels afraid that if his wife takes off, mounting up with wings like an eagle (Is 40:31), then he'll be left alone waddling around feeling stupid. The husband feels threatened, but only when his feet are on the ground. As soon as he mounts up and discovers his own wings, his heart's desire will be for his wife, and everybody else, to stop holding back and start taking the chance to show the full color of their God-given, God-designed plumes.

DISCUSSION QUESTIONS

1. How does Matthew 18:15-17 apply to marriage?

2. In Matthew 18:15-17, how many witnesses does Jesus say to take with you the first time the offense is communicated to the offender? How might a person wisely go about deciding whom to ask to be a witness if one or two witnesses are needed?

3. How can the church help husbands learn the difference between headship and entitlement?

4. How can the church help wives to learn the difference between submission and obedience? (Cf. Eph 5:22 with Eph 6:1.)

17

In the Name of 1 Timothy 2

Therefore I want the men in every place to pray, lifting up holy hands, without wrath and dissension. Likewise, I want women to adorn themselves with proper clothing, modestly and discreetly, not with braided hair and gold or pearls or costly garments; but rather by means of good works, as befits women making a claim to godliness. Let a woman quietly receive instruction with entire submissiveness. But I do not allow a woman to teach or exercise authority over a man, but to remain quiet. For it was Adam who was first created, and then Eve. And it was not Adam who was deceived, but the woman being quite deceived, fell into transgression. But women shall be preserved through the bearing of children if they continue in faith and love and sanctity with self-restraint.

I TIMOTHY 2:8-15

At last we are ready to discuss I Timothy 2. Though much of the debate on women in leadership has been centered on this passage, I am convinced that the argument, at root, is not about I Timothy 2.

EXEGETING I TIMOTHY 2

First Timothy 2:8-15 is a holy message from God. The Bible says, "All Scripture is inspired by God and profitable for teaching, for reproof, for correction, for training in righteousness; so that the man [Greek *anthrōpos*= person] of God may be adequate, equipped for every good work" (2 Tim 3:16-17). By faith we confess that all Scripture, including I Timothy 2, is inspired by God. We also confess that I Timothy 2:8-15 is profitable for the people of God today. It's not an irrelevant passage. As a matter of fact, it is profitable for every believer who seeks to be equipped to live in righteousness. Just because it's profitable, however, does not mean that it's profitable whenever it is misunderstood.

The Word of God does not benefit, for instance, "the untaught and unstable" who "distort" it "to their own destruction" (2 Pet 3:16). Nor does it yield a great profit to those who misuse it. The Bible commands us to "be diligent" to present ourselves "approved [of] God . . . accurately handling the word of truth" (2 Tim 2:15). All Scripture is profitable, but only when it's rightly understood and applied. One of the most famous commandments in Scripture says, "But prove yourselves doers of the word, and not merely hearers who delude themselves" (Jas 1:22). The personal gain that Scripture yields doesn't channel automatically to everyone who reads it. The profit belongs to "doers" of the Word who read it "accurately."

I first learned the basics of hermeneutics at Baylor University. Everyone who majored in elementary education was required to take a course called "Teaching Reading." The objective of the class was for teachers to learn how to help children with their reading comprehension. I don't remember much else about the class except the most important lesson we learned—to teach kids to read for meaning. Reading isn't reading if the reader doesn't listen for the meaning. (Don't you hate it when you're reading but really you're daydreaming, and it takes you two or three pages to realize you haven't listened to a word of what you mechanically read? That happens sometimes to children when they read out loud. They recite words without really reading them.) The task in reading Scripture is to catch the proper meaning in order to apply the proper meaning, to hear for the purpose of doing what God tells us to do.

ACCEPTING THE SCRIPTURES AT FACE VALUE

Evangelical Christians believe the Bible is a book of revelation. We also agree that God reveals himself when we take the Bible literally and exercise faith by submitting to the authority of his Word. We do not see the Bible as a book of secret codes that ought to be read mystically as an allegory. When the Bible describes a miracle, we believe a miracle happened. When the Bible says God created Adam and Eve, we believe the story is true. As partakers of the gospel, we are not suspicious of the text. On the contrary, we believe that it's best to accept the plain and simple meaning of a given

Bible passage if a straightforward reading makes sense.

Granted, our interpretations of Scripture don't have to make sense to an unbelieving mind. But they should always make sense within a gospel paradigm. Here's what I mean by that. To some, it is unreasonable to believe in miracles. It doesn't make sense, they say, to believe that a donkey talked (Num 22:28), or that an axe floated in water (2 Kings 6:5-6), or that Moses really parted the Red Sea (Ex 14:21-22). As the argument goes, it's unscientific to think the sun stood still (Josh 10:12-14) or that Jesus raised Lazarus from the dead (Jn 11:43-44). But for those who place their faith in "the Everlasting God, the LORD, the Creator of the ends of the earth" (Is 40:28), it makes sense to trust in his ability to suspend the laws of nature if he wants to. By faith, we know that it's sensible to believe this because it's reasonable to believe that a supernatural God does supernatural things.

Therefore this is our method. We combine common sense with Christian faith. By faith we believe that common sense reliably leads us to read the Word of God in a straightforward way, unless for some reason, a straightforward reading conflicts with the basic gospel message.[1]

Let's run through a couple of examples. To begin with, when 1 Timothy 5:21 says to "maintain these principles without bias, doing nothing in a spirit of partiality," we believe it means that it's sinful for anything to be done with a biased attitude. As conservative evangelicals, we accept a straightforward reading of this text. In light of the fact that "there is no partiality with God" (Rom 2:11), it makes sense to believe he wants no partiality in us either. God commands his people to be unbiased and impartial, so that we will be holy as he is (1 Pet 1:16).

By way of a second example, when the Old Testament says, "Then the LORD God said, 'It is not good for the man to be alone; I will make a helper suitable for him'" (Gen 2:18), we accept the text at face value. We agree that it means what it says—that it was not good for Adam to be without Eve.

---

[1]I am not alone in thinking this. To cite one of the many theologians who agree, John Wesley said, "It is a stated rule in interpreting, never to depart from the plain, literal sense, unless it implies an absurdity." See John Wesley, *The Works of John Wesley* (Oxford: Clarendon, 1980), 25:533.

WHEN A STRAIGHTFORWARD READING IS ABSURD

A prime example of a biblical text that cannot sensibly be taken at face value is I Timothy 2:8-15. Let's examine it together.

"But women shall be preserved [saved] through the bearing of children." A straightforward reading of this line of the Bible is clearly unacceptable to the born-again Christian mind. Evangelicals don't believe that women's souls are saved by motherhood.[2] Moreover, it is counter to the gospel to insinuate that childless women are going to hell because they are childless. Therefore, theologically, this verse can't mean what it sounds like it means. The Bible says that no one can be saved by anything other than grace.[3] How is the average reader supposed to figure out that "saved through the bearing of children" means "saved through the blood of Jesus Christ"?

Consider another line of this same passage. *"But I do not allow a woman to teach or exercise authority over a man, but to remain quiet."* Here we face the same difficulty. There's no way to interpret this verse at face value unless we're ready to say that it is sinful for a man to learn about God from a woman. Of course most of us hold a more modified view. But that is the point. We hold a view that differs from a straightforward reading. We say, for example, this verse restricts women from teaching the Bible "with authority" to men "publicly at the main church service in a pulpit on Sunday morning." In other words, we add extra phrases to the biblical text in order to make sense of the verse.

Specifically, we add the part about women being limited on Sunday mornings because at any other time of the week, most of us welcome women's teaching. This explains why so many of us have heard of Elisabeth Elliot. We know who she is because she's been teaching us the Scriptures for

---

[2]Andreas Köstenberger offers this lucid comment, "Non-evangelical interpreters may claim that the author (not the apostle Paul) really believed that, for some odd reason, that women would experience spiritual salvation by fulfilling their procreative role, however that may be understood. This, of course, would introduce a contradiction into the canon, since the statement could hardly be reconciled with Paul's adamant insistence that it is 'by grace you have been saved through faith—and that not of yourselves, it is the gift of God; not as a result of works, that no one should boast.' (Eph 2:8-9)" (Andreas Köstenberger, "Saved Through Childbearing?" *CBMW News* 2, no.4 [1997]: I).

[3]See Ephesians 2:8-9, "For by grace you have been saved through faith; and that not of yourselves; it is the gift of God, not as a result of works, that no one [including mothers of many children] should boast."

decades. Over the years we've invited her to teach us whether at churches, conferences and seminaries or through magazines, radio and books.

Strikingly, John Piper and Wayne Grudem likewise celebrate her ministry.[4] Openly they believe that the biblical injunction in I Timothy 2 does not constrain all women entirely. Rather, as they see it, it constrains most women to employ "impersonal" and "indirect" communication to men whenever the gospel is proclaimed.[5]

Here again the driving point is that Piper and Grudem, like everybody else, nuance their reading of I Timothy 2. They respond to I Timothy 2:12 as if Paul had said, "I do not allow most women to teach men in person, but I *do* allow for exceptions, and I *do* allow for women to teach men through other mediums such as books and radio because that mode of communication is more impersonal and indirect."

I say this not to single out Piper and Grudem but rather to show that godly conservatives cannot read this passage without adding a caveat to their most careful interpretation. For a more straightforward reading of I Timothy 2 inevitably turns out to be impractical.

What about the next line? *"Let a woman quietly receive instruction with entire submissiveness."* Again, the verse is unpalatable to Christians if we accept it at face value. Does Paul want women to be entirely compliant as they receive instruction from men? If so, then it logically follows that Paul does not want women to be "noble-minded" (Acts 17:11) in the same way as the Bereans who examined the Scriptures to see if Paul's teaching was true. How many evangelicals believe that women should not ask questions or challenge the biblical accuracy of their teachers?[6]

Moreover, how many of us count it as sinful for a woman to wear braids, gold or pearls? And yet, the apostle Paul says, *"Likewise, I want women to adorn*

---

[4]Elisabeth Elliot has been featured in the front cover article of the *CBMW* newsletter. Moreover, she was invited to be the keynote speaker to all the women at the big CBMW conference in Dallas, March 2000.
[5]See John Piper, "A Vision of Biblical Complementarity: Manhood and Womanhood Defined According to the Bible" in *Recovering Biblical Manhood and Womanhood*, ed. John Piper and Wayne Grudem (Wheaton, Ill.: Crossway, 1991), p. 51. Although Piper wrote this chapter, Grudem publicly holds this same belief.
[6]Cults thrive on prohibiting their members to ask questions. It is dangerous to limit honest inquiry.

themselves with proper clothing, modestly and discreetly, not with braided hair and gold or pearls or costly garments, but rather by means of good works, as befits women making a claim of godliness." Contemporary evangelicals almost unanimously believe that as long as women today dress modestly, they are free to wear braids *and* costly clothes *and* gold rings. We are too pragmatic to accept a more rigid interpretation.

What about the first part of the passage? *"I want the men in every place to pray, lifting up holy hands, without wrath and dissension."* Those words, if isolated from the context and read without much thought, seem to say that God commands all Christian men ("the men in every place") to "lift up their hands" when they pray. There is probably no church in the world that follows such a rule. Why not? Because none of us consider this to be a biblical rule. Why don't we? Because that would be absurd. It's ludicrous to take seriously an interpretation that says men are commanded to "pray without ceasing" (I Thess 5:17) always with their hands up in the air. I would even venture to say that it's irreverent to interpret the Scriptures in this way because it makes God's Word sound trivial and ridiculous.

As a matter of fact, a straightforward reading of I Timothy 2:8-15 endorses several unbiblical things:

- That women are saved by the blood of childbearing rather than the blood of Christ.
- That women are to receive instruction without practicing spiritual discernment.
- That women, unlike men, are not to wear gold wedding rings.
- That men, unlike women, are to raise both hands when they pray.

It is mistaken, therefore, for anyone to say that one side of the debate accepts a straightforward reading of I Timothy 2 while the other side flatly rejects it. In truth, neither side takes the text at face value.

DISCERNMENT IN INTERPRETING THE SCRIPTURES

Every reader of the Bible is faced with the challenge of discerning which passages in the text were originally intended to apply to believers of all ages and which ones were intended to apply only to the audience the writer addressed at the time.[7]

With regard to I Timothy 2, many evangelicals say that verse 8, "Therefore I want the men in every place to pray, lifting up holy hands, without wrath and dissension," applies only to the men who were in Ephesus. The reasoning goes something like this: "Those men were angry; those men needed literally to lift up their hands when they prayed. Those men had a problem we don't have. The men at our church don't need to raise their hands because their hearts are already right with God."

A lot of evangelicals also tend to say that verse 9, "I want women to adorn themselves . . . not with braided hair and gold or pearls or costly garments," applies only to the women who were in Ephesus. "It's obvious," we say, "that Paul just wanted the women to be modest by the standards of that day. Within first-century cultural standards, wearing gold and braids and pearls and costly clothing must have been inappropriate and suggestive. But for us, it is okay."

With hardly a thought, we pass over this verse, regarding the specifics of Paul's mandate to the women in I Timothy 2 as virtually obsolete. By the time we reach verse 11, however, a lot of evangelicals have a different mindset. Suddenly we perceive that Paul is talking to us.

TESTING OUR BELIEFS AGAINST THE SCRIPTURES

This might be a good place to stop reading and take some time to pray for God's help in discerning the proper meaning of I Timothy 2. I encourage you, the reader, to try your best to suspend any borrowed theology you might have. If you're taking this much time to evaluate all this, then you might as well do it right by testing your beliefs (just as you test mine) against the Scriptures.

---

[7]The most helpful book I know on this is William Webb's *Slaves, Women and Homosexuals* (Downers Grove, Ill.: InterVarsity Press, 2001). Webb's book presents a compelling argument for using "cultural analysis" to discern which passages are culturally bound (and thus not timeless) and which are transcultural (thus communicating universal ethics that ought to be applied by all people).

Before we begin, we need to be reminded of something. I've mentioned it before, but it's important to mention it again. Neither side is saying that Paul prohibited women from teaching or exercising authority over other women and children.[8] Go back and read 1 Timothy 2:12 once again. The verse says, "I do not allow a woman to . . . over a man." It says nothing about women being limited in their leadership over women and children. Bearing that in mind, let's proceed.

WOMEN PASTORS

How many leaders of women's ministry bear the official title of "pastor"? My friend Edna has served as a leader of women's ministry for a span of twenty years. During this time, she has been assigned six different titles (coordinator of women's ministry, director of women's ministry, supervisor of women's ministry, coach of women's ministry, leader of women's ministry, and women's Sunday school superintendent). It took twenty years for her finally to be named as "pastor" of women's ministry.

In the name of 1 Timothy 2, many conservative Christians have come to believe that women are not pastors. As a result, men who lead youth groups are hired to be the youth pastor, whereas women leaders are hired as youth directors. Likewise, men who oversee the church's children's ministry are hired as the children's pastor. Women, by contrast, are hired as the children's director.

Where in the Bible does it say that no one but a man can be pastor? First Timothy 2 doesn't even mention the word *pastor*. But in Ephesians 4:11, Paul proclaims that God has given "some as apostles, and some as prophets, and some as evangelists, and some as *pastors* [emphasis added] and teachers." It doesn't say God has given some men as pastors. It says he has given some people as pastors.

---

[8]When I say "neither side," I mean none of the prominent evangelicals in this debate. Certain anti-intellectual fundamentalists might be saying it. In fact, some churches do not allow women to lead women's ministry or even meet with other women to study the Bible quietly in their homes. One woman, Amy, who lives in Florida and has attended seminary, was told that the only way she could continue to lead her small women's prayer group was to have a male elder present there with them at all times. See J. Lee Grady, *Ten Lies the Church Tells Women* (Lake Mary, Fla.: Charisma House, 2000), p. 4.

I am aware that certain evangelicals think the word *pastor* necessarily refers to an office. Likewise, I understand that that explains why they disapprove of having a woman be called the "women's pastor." But this only serves to illustrate the point, not negate it. The point is that apostles, prophets, evangelists, pastors and teachers are selected by God. They are not elected by members of the church. Nor are they appointed by the bishop or denominational leader. It is not the church's prerogative to decide who will be "given" by the Spirit as a pastor or an evangelist. God makes those decisions. We don't have a say in the matter. Furthermore, it is inconsistent to claim that the word *pastor* in this context uniquely refers to an office while none of the other words—*apostles, prophets, evangelists* and *teachers*—do the same.[9]

WOMEN PREACHERS

According to the Scriptures, the Holy Spirit has the divine prerogative to distribute spiritual gifts to whomever he wills: "But to each one is given the manifestation of the Spirit for the common good . . . one and the same Spirit works all these things, distributing to each one individually just as He wills" (1 Cor 12:7, 11).

I believe the Spirit has gifted Anne Graham Lotz to be a preacher. In the name of 1 Timothy 2, however, many followers of Christ are unwilling to recognize Christian women speakers as preachers. Many women preachers, such as Elisabeth Elliot, have been socially constrained to learn to feel comfortable with the title "Christian speaker." When Elisabeth came to Azusa, I approached her husband Lars with the question, "Would you agree that your wife Elisabeth and Anne Graham Lotz, relatively speaking, are sort of gifted the same? They're different in style, but both of them travel and write books and speak."

He nodded his head. "Yes, I see what you're saying."

I said, "But Billy Graham says his daughter Anne Graham Lotz is the 'best

---

[9]The implications here are considerable. For many complementarians see the word *pastor* as synonymous with the word *elder*. As a result, they are loath to confess that pastors are given by God (Eph 4:11; 1 Cor 12:18) rather than selected by members of the church (or ordained clergy) as elders typically are.

preacher in the family.' If Anne is a preacher, what does that make Elisabeth?"

Lars replied, "Now wait a minute. Elisabeth doesn't claim to be a preacher."

I assured him, "Yes, sir, I know that."

It's upsetting to some of us in conservative Christian culture to recognize a woman as a preacher. The very idea of a woman being a preacher arouses our suspicion, causing us to wonder if someone might be pushing feminism. I tried to be careful when I spoke to Elisabeth Elliot's husband Lars. Thus I emphasized to him, "I think it's possible for Elisabeth to preach without ever having to become a feminist." He said, "Well, of course she doesn't have to become a feminist."

I think that bears repeating. "Well, of course she doesn't have to become a feminist." Is Lars right? Is it possible for Elisabeth Elliot to preach the Word of God? Can we, as conservative believers who champion the doctrine of inerrancy, separate the act of preaching from the act of promoting feminism? If so, then we ought to have a theological category for all the godly women who go around preaching God's Word. The church needs a category for nonfeminist women preachers because these women exist. Anne Graham Lotz is not a feminist. Anne Graham Lotz is a preacher. Elisabeth Elliot is not a women's libber. Elisabeth Elliot is a teacher of God's Word.

The open truth is that Elisabeth Elliot's ministry has blessed the "common good" for many years. When Elisabeth came to Azusa Pacific University, more than three thousand people were riveted by her message. She minced no words and allowed for no excuses. She was funny and courageous and clear. Boldly she declared the Word of God to a mixed crowd of adults, including college students, their parents, faculty, staff and university administrators. And though someone said she "shared from her heart," everybody there heard her share from her heart straight from the Gospel of Matthew.

The Bible has a category for women pastors and preachers. We need to have one too. The apostle Paul never warned anybody to guard against the women whom God has given to be pastors and preachers. In Philippians 4:2-3, he urged Euodia and Syntyche to "live in harmony," but he didn't tell them to stop sharing in his struggle to publicize the gospel.[10] Paul was not worried about godly women preachers promoting feminism in lieu of their commitment to Christ.

In the name of 1 Timothy 2, however, a lot of evangelicals have mistakenly equated women's preaching as a blatant violation of scriptural teaching. No verse in the Bible says that women are prohibited to preach. But in evangelical circles, the idea of a woman preaching a sermon is commonly taboo.

A year or two ago, at a certain women's conference, I asked approximately four hundred Christian women to open their Bibles to 2 Timothy 3:16-17. Before I read it, I explained that the chapter and verse markings in Scripture were not inserted until the thirteenth century. In other words, I told them that if Paul were alive today, he wouldn't know what was meant by "1 Timothy 2:12" because he never did see any chapters and verses superimposed upon his letters. Paul wrote and sent the letters as letters. In other words, his intention was for the letters to be read all at once. My intention at the conference was for the women to see what happens when we read 2 Timothy 3:16-17 with that in mind. As we already know, this text says, "All Scripture is inspired by God and profitable for teaching, for reproof, for correction, for training in righteousness that the man [Greek *anthrōpos*, "person"] of God may be adequate, equipped for every good work."

At the conference, I asked the women, "Is everyone convinced that these two verses apply to all of us here today?" There were many nods of heads.

I posed the question again, "Everyone here is totally convinced that these two verses apply to you? You're *sure* the Bible is profitable to equip you, a woman, for every work?" The answer again was yes.

I repeated myself again, "None of you are doubtful that these two verses speak directly to you as women?"

The answer was so obvious that people were beginning to wonder what I had up my sleeve. I repeated again for a fourth time, and again for a fifth. I

---

[10]For a more detailed study, see A. Boyd Luter Jr., "Partnership in the Gospel: The Role of Women in the Church at Philippi," *Journal of the Evangelical Theological Society* (September 1996): 411-20.

said, "Okay, this is the last call. Is there *anyone* in this room who believes that 2 Timothy 3:16-17 was not intended to apply to us?"

They all held their ground.

Then my eyes fell to the text where I begin to read the next two verses (2 Tim 4:1-2), which explicitly say, "I solemnly charge you in the presence of God and of Christ Jesus, who is to judge the living and the dead, and by His appearing and His kingdom: preach the Word; be ready in season and out of season; reprove, rebuke, exhort, with great patience and instruction."

I looked up and paused for about one or two seconds. Then quietly I said, "Do these two verses *also* apply to you?"[11]

Silence.

After a few more seconds, the room began to stir. There were nudgings and whispers and feelings of uncertainty and excitement. Everyone's interest was piqued.

But some of the women were disturbed. After the session one woman talked openly with me about some of her negative reactions. Carefully broaching the subject, she said, "You took the passage in 2 Timothy out of context. That whole book was written for the headship of the church."[12]

She said this in a cordial tone. There wasn't any tension between us. I was so glad to be able to listen to her so that I could understand why that part of the session was unsettling. She went on to say, "You made it sound as though women are free to just go out and preach. I felt like you unleashed us."

As we visited a little more, I learned that she is a speaker. She told me that someday she would like to speak at a church on a Sunday morning. Then she told about how she "loved it" when Elisabeth Elliot gave (she said "gave")

---

[11]I understand that the letter was written privately from Paul to Timothy. But if we are going to say that 2 Timothy 4:2 applies to no one but Timothy, then we must also say that 2 Timothy 1:7, "For God has not given us a spirit of timidity, but of power and love and discipline," applies only to Paul and Timothy as well. In other words, if we insist that only Timothy was admonished to "preach," then in order to be consistent, we would also have to say that God gave a spirit of love, power and discipline to Paul and Timothy but not to us.

[12]Biblically there is no such thing as "the headship of the church" apart from Christ. Christ is the head of the church (Eph 5:23).

the Sunday morning sermon (she said "sermon") once in a Presbyterian church in Jackson, Mississippi.

This intrigued me all the more. So I asked her again about her view of women preaching, especially in light of 2 Timothy 4:2.

After thinking it through further, she said, "A woman can't preach because that would make her a preacher, so these verses *can't* apply to women."

I became confused. So I asked her, "Is it sinful for a woman to preach the Bible?"

She answered, "I suppose that all depends on what you mean by the word *preach*."

Gladly I told her that in Greek, the word *kēryssō* means to "herald" or "proclaim."

She said, "Of course it isn't wrong for women to proclaim the Word of God."

I said, "Then don't you think it's biblical for a woman to go out and preach?"

She answered, "Well, in the way that you're saying it, she can. But in our culture, we can't freely say that a woman preaches because people might start calling her a preacher."

I asked, "What's so bad about that?"

She said, "It's not that a woman can't speak. It's that women aren't supposed to be, well you know, senior pastors. Culturally, the word *preacher* connotes the idea of a local church senior pastor."

I said, "Thank you for telling me this. But before we go, I want to make sure I understand what you are saying. I still need a little more clarity. If you don't mind me asking, I'm really curious if both of us remember that one portion of the conference the same. As I recall, I presented the question [about the Scriptures applying to women] to everyone five times, even offering a last call in a kind of dramatic way, challenging anyone to speak up if they don't believe that 2 Timothy 3:16-17 fully applies to them. Do you remember it being like that too?"

"Yes."

I continued, "All I did after that was to read the next two verses that follow in the text and then ask them a similar question, 'Do these two verses also apply to you?'"

She interrupted, "Yes, I remember that too. But that's just it. You left the question open. You never did answer it." She said, "By asking that question, you made it sound as though women are supposed to go out and preach."

I didn't know what to say, so I said nothing. But I had a thought in mind: *Am I the one who makes it sound as though women are supposed to preach? Or does the Bible do that?*

Discussion Questions

1. Does 2 Timothy 4:2 apply to every Christian, or only to senior pastors? Does it also apply to missionaries? Or perhaps to students in seminary? Does this verse apply to you?

2. What is your view of women preaching? Discuss your answer in light of 1 Timothy 2:12 and other passages from Scripture that come to mind.

3. What does 1 Timothy 2:12 have to say about women preaching to and pastoring women and children? Do you think it's biblical for a woman to baptize a child who has come into the faith?

4. What misunderstandings about women's identity have you had in the name of 1 Timothy 2?

18
The Order of Creation

Let Us make man in Our image.
GENESIS 1:26

H ave you ever tried to convince someone Jewish that the God of Israel is triune? It's not a very easy thing to do. Orthodox Jews have a preset mindset that the Lord is "One" (Deut 6:4) and that there is no way for the Messiah to be God because that would make God into two. You can show a Jewish person Genesis 1:26, where God says, "Let Us make man in Our image," and Psalm 110:1 where David says, "The LORD says to my Lord: 'Sit at My right hand,' " all to no avail, even though both verses indicate plurality in the Godhead.

To a Christian it is obvious that God is three in one. It's obvious because Christians today presuppose that the doctrine of the Trinity is true. We presuppose it because we were told about it before we ever read a word from the Bible. It's no surprise, therefore, that whenever we do read the Scriptures, we see evidence in the text of that which we were told to expect. I was told as a little child that Jesus of Nazareth is God. God sounded like One to me. For God to be God, and Jesus to be God, and the Holy Spirit to be God, was acceptable to me because I was taught from the get-go that that's just how God is.

But what if I had been raised Jewish? Would I still believe that God is tri-une? What would it have taken to convince me that he is? If you were Jewish, would you be willing to reconsider the way you had always understood Gen-esis 1:26 and Psalm 110:1?[1] Would you open your mind enough to question your upbringing and risk being converted to Christianity?

It's hard to face the truth. It's hard because truth exposes the things we have believed that are not true. For Jewish people, it's difficult to come to terms with the fact that Jesus is the Messiah. Likewise, it's hard for some con-servatives to admit that godly women can preach God's Word as Christians, not feminists.

Another hard truth for Christians to face is that Eve was created in the image of God just as much as Adam. It's hard for believers to accept the fact that Eve was equal to Adam. It's hard because most of us have been trained to believe that Eve was deceived because Eve was a woman, and women are the weaker sex. With that, we've been taught that Eve was designed to be Adam's subordinate.

What have you been taught? Did anyone ever tell you that Eve led Adam when she handed him the piece of forbidden fruit?[2] Or that she stepped out of line by taking the initiative to make a decision for herself? Has anyone ever told you that Adam should have been the one to guide Eve's decisions but that he passively allowed her to think independently apart from his mascu-line guidance?

What does the Bible say? Does it say anywhere that Eve was supposed to follow Adam? Does it say anywhere that Adam was smarter than she was? These are legitimate questions. Did God design Eve with a mind that could reason and discern as well as Adam's mind was able to do? Or did God give Eve a mind that was disinclined to make wise decisions?

---

[1]For a detailed survey of Jewish interpretations of Psalm 110, see David Hay, *Glory at the Right Hand: Psalm 110 in Early Christianity* (New York: Abingdon, 1973), pp. 21-33.

[2]I don't see how handing him a piece of fruit can be counted as "leading" him, and yet I have heard that said many times.

REVISITING AUGUSTINE

As you may recall from a previous chapter, Augustine believed a mind focused on the truth is the image of God, and a mind distracted by lower things is not the image of God.[3] Remember what Augustine concluded? He said that a woman is not the image of God because women's minds are "directed to the cognition of lower things." With that, he said that a woman should "cover her head" (I Cor 11:6) during worship because female heads are naturally filled with thoughts of "lower things."

Augustine openly assumed that men have a mental advantage over women.[4] He said that Eve had "small intelligence" and that Adam had a "spiritual mind." With that, he said it was "impossible" for Adam to have been deceived by the serpent. Remember these few lines?

> How could he [Adam] have believed what the serpent said? For the serpent said that God prohibited them from eating the fruit of that tree because he knew that if they did so, they would become as gods by their knowing good and evil (Gen 3:5)—as if God begrudged his creatures so great a blessing! That a man endowed with a *spiritual mind* could have believed this is astonishing. And just because it is *impossible* to believe it, woman was given to man, woman who was of small intelligence and who perhaps still lives more in accordance with the promptings of the inferior flesh than by the superior reason.

In other words, Augustine believed that Adam was not deceived because Adam, unlike Eve, was not deceivable.

RETURNING TO I TIMOTHY 2

Paul says in I Timothy 2:12-14, "But I do not allow a woman to teach or exercise authority over a man, but to remain quiet. For it was Adam who was first created, and then Eve. And it was not Adam who was deceived, but the

---

[3]See previous discussion of Augustine, pp. 59-62.
[4]David Pawson echoes the same conclusion. He writes, "This . . . probably means that Eve was more vulnerable to being seduced in mind . . . [Paul] seems to be saying that Eve, as a typical woman, was more liable to be misled and therefore more likely to mislead" (David Pawson, *Leadership Is Male* [Nashville: Thomas Nelson, 1988], p. 34).

woman being quite deceived, fell into transgression."

It is typical for Christians in the past *and* present to read this passage unknowingly with the eyes of Augustine. Almost all of us have been taught to
see in this text an "obvious fact" that women are not allowed to teach men
at church because Eve was deceived and fell into transgression. Our eyes have
been trained to see in the text that women, by design, are not as reliable as
men. And yet we haven't realized that our presuppositions echo a tradition
that overtly claims that women are inferior to men.

Augustine, among others, has influenced us to wonder about Eve's intelligence.[5] We aren't too sure if Eve was very smart, but we seem to be convinced that Eve was beautiful in face and form. Tradition doesn't doubt her
physical beauty. In fact, throughout church history, her body has been regarded
as exquisite. Her mind, by contrast, has traditionally been criticized as having
been inherently flawed.

What does that say about church tradition? More importantly, what does
that say about God? That God made a goof when he designed Eve's mind?
Or rather that God intended to create a "helper" for Adam who wasn't actually bright enough to help him?[6] Is it fair to say this of God? [7] If so, then
how do we account for Eve's constitution? That is, how do we explain the
biblical fact that she was "wonderfully" handmade by the art and thought of
God (Ps 139)? And that she, like Adam, bore God's image?

---

[5]For instance, Epiphanius (A.D. 365-403) says, "The female sex is easily mistaken, fallible, and poor in
intelligence" (Epiphanius, *Medicine Box* 79 in *Maenads, Martyrs, Matrons, Monastics: A Sourcebook on Women's Re-
ligions in the Greco-Roman World*, ed. Ross S. Kraemer [Philadelphia: Fortress, 1988], p. 51).

[6]In Hebrew the word "helper" (*ezer*) does not mean "lower-ranked assistant." In fact, the word *ezer* commonly refers to God. See Exodus 18:4; Deuteronomy 33:7, 29; Psalms 20:2; 33:20; 70:5; 89:19; 115:9,
10, 11; 121:1; 124:8; 146:5; Hosea 13:9. When *ezer* refers to human help, it is never of a woman, except
in the Genesis passage. Otherwise, it refers to the help of foreign armies. See Isaiah 30:5; Ezekiel 12:14;
Daniel 11:34.

[7]Traditionally theologians such as Augustine and Luther have said yes. God made her dull-witted so that
she would be satisfied by the lower form of her work. For instance, Luther says, "Since, therefore, God
... added to the man an *inferior aid* [emphasis added], the Apostle justly reminds us of the order of creation in which the eternal and inviolable appointment of God is strikingly displayed" (Martin Luther,
"The First Epistle to Timothy" in *Luther's Works*, ed. Jaroslav Pelikan, 55 vols. [St. Louis: Concordia,
1973], 28:278).

We can tell ourselves that we're long past the practice of limiting women on the basis of Eve's unforgettable offense. But when we read the Bible, it does seem to some of us that 1 Timothy 2 offers causal reasons for Paul's prohibition on women. It does seem to us that Adam truly was Eve's superior. We might as well say it out loud. Many of us have been taught to believe that Eve was vulnerable and Adam was not.[8] That she was gullible, and he was not. As much as we prefer not to say it, the truth is that many conservative Christians traditionally have been taught that women should be limited precisely on the basis that women are not designed to make leadership decisions on behalf of Christian men.

How many times have we heard it said that it violates God's order when women take the initiative with men?[9] For according to church tradition, Adam is the one who should have led her in the garden because God created him first, and Adam wasn't gullible like Eve.

REREADING 1 TIMOTHY 2

I think it might be helpful to run an experiment. It's a reading experiment, a simple kind of test to discover what might happen if we read 1 Timothy 2:12-14 in two dissimilar ways. It's sort of like trying on clothes, if you will. First we'll read the passage while wearing one set of assumptions. Then we'll read it again, wearing a different attire. In order to start, we're going to say, for the sake of making a point, that women really are designed to be led by men.[10] We will also assume that Adam was Eve's leader even before the fall. Moreover, we will also begin by expecting the Bible to say that men, not women, are leaders. With this mindset, let's read through the passage again: "But I do not allow a woman to teach or exercise authority over a man, but to remain quiet. For it was Adam who was first created, and then Eve. And

---

[8]I do believe Eve was more vulnerable physically toward Adam than he was toward her. But this does not make Eve inferior. To say that a man's greater strength makes him physically superior is just as foolish as saying that a woman's ability to have a baby makes her physically superior to a man.

[9]I believe more order is established when a woman takes the initiative to lead a man to Christ.

[10]See Pawson, *Leadership Is Male*, and the foreword by Elisabeth Elliot.

it was not Adam who was deceived, but the woman being deceived, fell into transgression."

When we read it this way, it sounds like a straightforward message. Moreover, it sounds as though Paul is saying that women are prohibited from leading and teaching men for two specific reasons:

1. Eve was created second, not first (meaning that the second should not have authority over the first).

2. Eve, unlike Adam, was deceived (meaning that women aren't supposed to exercise authority over men because women are more gullible).

When I was growing up, this was pretty much my perspective, even though it didn't make sense. Back then, it didn't have to make sense to me. I received it as a given. My mindset had been trained to "just believe it no matter what." I was like a Jewish person who takes it for granted that God cannot be triune, even though he said, "Let Us make man in Our image" (Gen 1:26).

There's something I haven't said until now. About eight or ten years ago, when I was still in seminary, I came to a point of surrendering to the Lord on this issue. Having heard the feminist argument—and disagreed with it— I concluded, by default, that I must somehow agree that women should be limited in ministry.[11] I decided to prepare myself to live as a traditional Christian woman. And because I tend to be a crusader, I decided to prepare

---

[11]The best way I can explain it is to parallel it with the crisis I experienced twenty years ago when I seriously contended with the difficult question of whether or not God truly exists. To be honest, I never did become a true atheist. I *tried* to suspend my belief in God, so that I could genuinely test the validity of my faith. But I accidentally prayed all through the test. "Lord, please help me not to be duped by the idea of you if there's really no such thing as God. I don't want to be foolish or gullible. Nor do I desire to be involved in a false religion. Please show me the truth of Christianity." By analogy, the same thing happened again when I seriously contended with the difficult question of whether or not God had truly called me into ministry. My prayers sounded something like this, "Lord, if I'm sinning when I teach the Bible to men, and if it's from the devil when men look to me as their pastor, and if it's wrong for men to draw closer to you on account of my ministry to them, will you please help me to sense your displeasure? Why do I feel close to you whenever I minister to men? Why do I sense your Spirit working in me when I lead men to Christ? Am I being unbiblical?"

myself to do it gung-ho by publicly defending that stance. And I would have done that had it not been for the fact that in trying to defend it, I realized that it's illogical.

I tried to believe that it's wrong for women to teach men the Bible because Eve was created second, but I couldn't. For if it's wrong for a woman to teach a man on the basis of the order of creation, then it has to be wrong for a woman to teach a man piano lessons. If her teaching him per se upsets the order of creation, then her teaching him anything must also be regarded as wrong. In other words, if it's wrong in principle for the second to teach the first, then it's wrong for a woman to teach a man.

I understand that Christians say it's wrong for a woman to teach a man the Bible (as opposed to the piano). This is assumed on the basis of I Timothy 3:15, where the apostle Paul says, "I write so that you may know how one ought to conduct himself in the household of God, which is the church of the living God, the pillar and support of the truth."

It's illogical to believe that it's wrong to defy the order of creation only in "the household of God." That's tantamount to saying it's wrong to commit adultery on Sunday morning at church, but it's perfectly acceptable at any other place and during any other time of the week. The Bible says adultery is immoral and unrighteous (Ex 20; Mt 5). Therefore adulterous activity is wrong anytime and anywhere. It's wrong because it's unholy. It's wrong because it's wrong in principle.

My argument against the claim that women shouldn't teach men the Bible is that *that* claim does not arise from a general principle. It is said that women are prohibited on the basis of the general principle of the order of creation. But the words of this claim fail to correlate with the way this general principle can practically be applied. If the order of creation is a general principle, then it ought to be applied across the board. Instead, it's applied inconsistently and selectively as if it were specific, not general.

HONORING MALE HEADSHIP

As mentioned before, most complementarians fully approve of women teaching men "indirectly" and "from a distance" through mediums such as books or radio. Piper and Grudem openly quote women writers and even include women writers in their book.[12] For them, the fundamental issue is not per se about "a woman" being either prohibited or allowed to teach "a man."[13] Instead, the issue has to do with the context, something specific, not general.

According to Piper and Grudem, a woman can give "occasional" or "periodic," as they put it, "lectureships" or "addresses." She cannot, however, serve as a seminary professor or "recognized Bible teacher of the church."[14] Nor can she serve as a pastor or preacher "of a fellowship of women and men,"[15] because that would give her "recognized" authority. The implication is that when people *recognize* authority in a woman, the order of creation is breached. Her authority is not the concern. The concern, rather, is to prevent other people from recognizing it.[16]

By now it should be clear that Piper and Grudem indeed are not tied to a literal understanding of I Timothy 2. If they were, then they would have to say that it's wrong for a woman to teach or have authority over a man. But they don't. They don't say it because they do not believe that it's wrong, in general, for the second to teach the first. (They do think it's possible that women may be more gullible than men, but even so, they say they're "attracted" to a different understanding of the text.[17])

---

[12]Dee Jepsen ("Women in Society: The Challenge and the Call," pp. 388-93) and Elisabeth Elliot ("The Essence of Femininity: A Personal Perspective," pp. 394-99) contribute chapters to *Recovering Biblical Manhood and Womanhood*, ed. John Piper and Wayne Grudem (Wheaton, Ill.: Crossway, 1991).

[13]Piper and Grudem say a woman (or rather a wife with her husband) may "teach" a man privately as Priscilla (and Aquila) did Apollos (John Piper and Wayne Grudem, "An Overview of Central Concerns: Questions and Answers" in *Recovering Biblical Manhood and Womanhood*, ed. John Piper and Wayne Grudem [Wheaton, Ill.: Crossway, 1991], pp. 68-69).

[14]Ibid., p. 85.

[15] Ibid.

[16]This explains why prominent women speakers tend to resist the idea of referring to themselves as pastors or preachers.

[17]Explicitly they say, "First Timothy 2:14 says, 'Adam was not the one deceived; it was the woman who was deceived and became a sinner.' Paul gives this as one of the reasons he does not permit women 'to teach or have authority over a man.' Historically, this has usually been taken to mean that women are more gullible or deceivable than men and therefore less fit for the doctrinal oversight of the church. This

Here again, I am further convinced that 1 Timothy 2 does not lie at the heart of this debate. The issue for conservatives is male headship. Piper and Grudem continually uphold the thematic idea of men being honored in their headship.[18] For example, they say, "Our understanding of what is fitting for men and women . . . is not an oversimplified or artificial list of rules for what the woman and man can say and do. It is rather a call for the delicate and sensitive preservation of personal dynamics that honor the headship of [men] without squelching the wisdom and insight of [women]."[19]

At least for Piper and Grudem,[20] the underlying principle in 1 Timothy 2 is not for a woman to refrain in all times and all places from teaching a man the Bible and sound doctrine, but rather for women to refrain in all times and all places from "offending" a man's "sense of" masculinity.[21] To quote Piper

---

may be true. However, we are attracted to another understanding of Paul's argument." In addition, they say, "Even if 1 Timothy 2:14 meant that in some circumstances women are characteristically more vulnerable to deception, that would not settle anything about the equality or worth of manhood and womanhood" (ibid., p. 73).

[18]For example, in their explanation of women leaders in the Old Testament, they say, "First, we keep in mind that God has no antipathy toward revealing His will to women. Nor does He pronounce them unreliable messengers. The differentiation of roles for men and women in ministry is rooted not in women's incompetence to receive or transmit truth, but in the primary responsibility of men in God's order to lead and teach. The instances of women who prophesied and led do not call this into question. Rather, there are pointers in each case that the women followed their unusual paths in a way that *endorsed and honored* [emphasis added] the usual leadership of men, or indicted their failures to lead" (ibid., p. 72).

[19]Ibid., p. 69. In the context, they are talking about Priscilla and Aquila, but if I understand Piper and Grudem correctly, they believe "the call for delicate and sensitive preservation" applies generally.

[20]Douglas Moo may or may not agree. It seems that Moo's view is notably more restrictive than Piper's and Grudem's, for Moo makes the dramatic proclamation, "We think 1 Timothy 2:8-15 imposes two restrictions on the ministry of women: they are not to teach Christian doctrine to men and they are not to exercise authority *directly* [emphasis added] over men in the church. These restrictions are permanent, authoritative for the church in all times and places and circumstances as long as men and women are descended from Adam and Eve" (Douglas Moo, "What Does It Mean Not to Teach or Have Authority over Men? 1 Timothy 2:11-15," in *Recovering Biblical Manhood and Womanhood*, ed. John Piper and Wayne Grudem [Wheaton, Ill.: Crossway, 1991], p.180).

[21]I agree that it is good and loving for women to honor men as well as to acknowledge the God-given complementarity of the sexes. I think it's spiritually dangerous, however, for men to understand headship as a means of exempting themselves from being held accountable by women. Men can't hold themselves accountable to be loving to women apart from the help of women any more than women can hold themselves accountable to be loving to men apart from the help of men. It takes a woman to explain how his actions are hurtful to her. Conversely, it takes a man to explain how her actions are hurtful to him. Sometimes, moreover, it takes a prophet or a prophetess to help Christians understand that our actions are

and Grudem again, they say, "We recognize that these [women's] lectures and addresses *could* be delivered in a spirit and demeanor that would assault the principle of male leadership."[22]

When I was in seminary, one of my professors told me face to face that if I ever wrote a good Bible commentary, he might use it as a textbook in his class. He said my teaching would be welcome although I would not personally be welcomed to teach his class. Upon hearing this, I asked him, "So you're saying that the class might be 'contaminated' by my femininity?" Nodding his head, he said, "Yes."

By this, I believe my professor was trying to tell me that the men in his class would not "feel like men" if I were to stand as their teacher. More specifically, I believe he was saying that *he* would not feel like a man if I were to teach his class. Following Piper and Grudem, it would be more respectful for me as a woman to guest lecture outside of official class time as a way of honoring male headship.

I like the idea of honoring men in their headship. But I'm not sure that having women be unofficial is the best way to go about doing that. Nor do I think it's wise to read 1 Timothy 2 with what Piper and Grudem call the "principle of male leadership" in mind. For when we do this, we come to the text with an assumption. We come to the text assuming that it says, "But I do not allow a woman to teach or have authority over a man . . . because it violates the principle of male leadership."

Once we do this, we exchange Paul's statements about Adam and Eve (that Adam was created first and that Eve was deceived) with church tradition's claim that endorsing women in leadership violates the order of creation.[23]

---

displeasing to God. Thus I strongly disagree with Piper's and Grudem's statement for Christian women to "avoid the kind of teaching that by its very nature calls for strong, forceful pressing of men's consciences on the basis of divine authority." To say that headship is offended by the corrective words of Scripture—if uttered publicly from the mouth of a godly woman—is to misunderstand not only headship but also Christian fellowship. See Piper and Grudem, "An Overview of Central Concerns," p. 70. If you look up the reference, you will also see that when Piper and Grudem say this, they offer no biblical support.

[22]Ibid., p. 85.

[23]See John Chrysostom (347-407), who says, "'Neither was the man created for the woman, but the

WOMEN BEFORE GOD

Perhaps it might helpful to focus our attention on God. For centuries, God has used women to minister directly in person as leaders over men.[24] God chose Deborah to lead and judge Israel in person (Judg 4—5). I have heard the arguments that Deborah was exceptional, and that was a bad time in the history of Israel, and that was the Old Testament, so it doesn't count since the church had not yet been established. But if the principle of the order of creation truly is a universal principle, then it has to apply to the time of the Judges in order to apply to us today.

Consider the example of Jesus. Jesus commanded Mary to "go" and tell the gospel to men (Jn 20:17). He also prepared the Samaritan woman with enough theology to go back to her town, serving as the first evangelist (Jn 4). In spite of the fact that Eve was "deceived," Jesus entrusted the gospel to women.

Hence I believe that God himself defies the general principle of the order of creation even more than we do. Though it's true that God chose twelve men to lead the twelve tribes of Israel and that Christ chose twelve male apostles, it's also true that God providentially chose Elisabeth Elliot, not her husband Jim, to be the one to evangelize and disciple the Auca Indians.[25] I believe Elisabeth was sent to South America by the Spirit of the Lord, who gifted her to lead a family ministry (1 Cor 12:11).

The same thing could be said of the woman I mentioned earlier who started three hundred churches in China. Eager to visit with her, I asked her to tell me how she ever got the impulse to plant and pastor churches. As if she were whispering a secret, she quietly said, "God does not see me as a

---

woman for the man.' (1 Cor. Xi.9). Why then does he say this? He wishes *the man to have the preeminence* in every way; both for the reason above [i.e., Adam formed first], he means to let him have precedence, and on account of what occurred later" (Chrysostom, "Homilies on Timothy (Homilies 8-9)," in *A Select Library of the Nicene and Post-Nicene Fathers of the Christian Church*, first series, ed. Philip Schaff [1886-1890; reprint, Grand Rapids, Mich.: Eerdmans, 1976], 13:435).

[24]For instance, God has used women missionaries such as Elisabeth Elliot and Amy Carmichael to oversee whole people groups in their spiritual development and learning.

[25]See the full story in Elisabeth Elliot's *The Savage My Kinsman* (Ann Arbor, Mich.: Servant, 1996).

woman." Of course she said this in Chinese. Thus I had no idea of what she said. Consequently I stared blankly at her interpreter.

Her interpreter smiled demurely. "She said, 'God does not see me as a woman.' "

I said back to the interpreter, "Tell her that God does *too* see her as a woman."[26]

Isn't that sad? This very gifted woman is telling herself that God doesn't see her as a woman. And yet she serves today as senior pastor of a church she planted that runs about twenty-five hundred people in attendance. Who is going to argue that this particular woman is not gifted and anointed by the Spirit?[27]

If you ask me, God did it again. He defied the so-called general principle of the order of creation. For some reason or another, he lifted up the second to serve as a leader of the first.[28]

I do not believe that Paul had any intention of leading the Christian community to come to the conclusion that 1 Timothy 2 is grounded in a principle. For the order of creation is not a principle. It's a historical fact. It's a matter of history that God created Adam before Eve. Tradition, how-ever, has showcased this historical fact as if it were a principle that says "men have higher status than women in the church" because Adam was older than Eve.

---

[26]It pained me to hear her deny her femininity and hear her prejudice against herself. The interpreter re-sumed the dialogue in first person on behalf of the Chinese woman pastor. She said, "For two years I wrestled with God about this. At first, I kept telling him that I would be a businesswoman and finance the full salary of a pastor. But God said to me, 'No, I want *you* to be the pastor of the church.' So I prayed to God again, 'Okay, I will be a businesswoman and finance the full salary of *three* pastors.' But again, God answered, 'I want *you* to be the pastor.' And then I told him, 'But God, I am a woman.'" Then more quietly she added, "But God did not understand because God doesn't see me as a woman." Does that sound strange? It's not unprecedented. Desert ascetic Amma Sarah said, "According to nature I am a woman, but not according to my thoughts" (see Thomas C. Oden, *The Living God* [San Francisco: Harper, 1987], p. 8).

[27]In China it is dangerous to lead churches since leaders are often martyred. Both the uncle and grandfa-ther of the Chinese woman pastor I met were murdered for the sake of the gospel. This woman realizes that her life is being jeopardized too.

[28]Likewise, God chose Isaac, not Ishmael, and Jacob, not Esau.

DISCUSSION QUESTIONS

1. What were you taught to believe about Adam and Eve? That Adam should have been Eve's leader? Or that Adam and Eve were equals?

2. Discuss the meaning of the statement "But if the principle of the order of creation truly is a general principle, then it has to apply to the time of the Judges in order to apply to us today."

3. What is the significance of the statement on page 230, "Once we do this, we exchange Paul's statements about Adam and Eve (that Adam was created first and that Eve was deceived) with church tradition's claim that endorsing women in leadership violates the order of creation"?

4. Did it bother you to hear the Chinese woman say, "God does not see me as a woman"? What does that statement reveal about her theology? What does it say about her view of God? If God *does* see her as a woman, then what does that say about God?

19

IT WAS ADAM, AND NOT ADAM

For it was Adam . . . and not Adam.
I TIMOTHY 2:13

When the early church fathers read I Timothy 2, they assumed that women are inferior to men. Because of their mindset, no verse in the Bible swayed them to believe that men and women are spiritually equal. Unlike us (on both sides of the debate), the vast majority of the fathers of the faith counted Christian women as being spiritually inferior to Christian men.

Some did recognize that woman was created as an equal to man. But with that, they believed she lost her equality in the moment that she used it, as John Chrysostom put it, to "ruin everything" at the Fall.[1] To quote Chrysostom, bishop of Constantinople (A.D. 398-404), from his "Homilies on Timothy," he says:

> God said in effect to Eve, "I made you equal in honor. You did not use your authority well, so consign yourself to a state of subordination. You have not borne your liberty, so accept servitude. Since you do not know how to rule—as you showed in your experiment with the business of life—henceforth be among the governed and acknowledge your husband as lord.

---

[1]See Chrysostom, "Homily 26 on I Corinthians" in *Nicene and Post-Nicene Fathers,* ed. Philip Schaff, 14 vols. (Peabody, Mass.: Hendrickson, 1995), 12:151.

Does the bishop's interpretation reflect the biblical text? Let's study the passage again.

> But I do not allow a woman to teach or exercise authority over a man, but to remain quiet. For it was Adam who was first created, and then Eve. And it was not Adam who was deceived, but the woman being quite deceived, fell into transgression.

Chrysostom said Eve "ruined everything" at the Fall. Moreover, Tertullian cast the guilt of Eden upon women. It's worthwhile to reiterate what Tertullian said (to a group of "beloved women"):

> You are the devil's gateway; you are the unsealer of that tree; you are the first forsaker of the divine law; you are the one who persuaded him whom the Devil was not brave enough to approach; you so lightly crushed the image of God, the man Adam; because of your punishment, that is, death, even the Son of God had to die.

The apostle Paul, by contrast, doesn't blame the woman. Nor does he start any sentence with the indicting word *you*. There is no accusation. In all of his writings, the only thing Paul does is to remind other Christians as he does in 1 Timothy 2 that Adam was not deceived. In 2 Corinthians 11:3, Paul says that he fears the Corinthian Christians may have strayed from simplicity and devotion to Christ. More specifically, he admits his fear that their minds might be "deceived" by the devil in the same way that Eve's was by the serpent (2 Cor 11:3). He does not point a finger at Eve.[2]

In 1 Timothy 2, Paul recounts the facts. He lays out the truth, reminding Timothy that it was Adam whom God created first, and it was not Adam

---

[2]I do not believe (contra countless commentators) that Paul prohibited women on account of any belief that women are more susceptible to transgression. In Romans 16:4, Paul said Priscilla was so trustworthy that she and her husband had "risked their own necks" for his life. Paul thanked Priscilla. He and "all the churches of the Gentiles" thanked Priscilla. That's how far he was from labeling Priscilla as an Eve. In truth, Paul warned Timothy to "flee" from temptations because Paul believed that Timothy was susceptible to transgression (1 Tim 6:11). Paul confessed to the Romans that his own susceptibility to transgression was so constantly overwhelming that Christ alone could set him "free" from his "body of death" (Rom 7:24).

who was deceived. The difference in the quotes is conspicuous, isn't it? Whereas Paul put the emphasis on "Adam" and "not Adam," Chrysostom glared the spotlight on Eve.

Perhaps it is due to the influence of church tradition that Christians today continue to read 1 Timothy 2 as if the focus of the passage is on Eve. The focus of the passage is on Adam. If the focus were on Eve, it would say, "I do not allow a woman to teach or exercise authority over a man, but to remain quiet. For it was Eve who was created second, and Adam first. And it was Eve, not Adam, who was quite deceived and fell into transgression."

Paul does not say, "For it was Eve . . . and it was Eve." On the contrary, he writes, "For it was Adam . . . and not Adam."

THE FOCUS IS ON THE GENTILES

When I was in seminary, one of my favorite professors, John Sailhamer, programmed into our heads that Scripture itself contains the most important clues to inform us today of the historical situation in which the books of the Bible were written. He told us that he spent eight years formally studying ancient Near Eastern history at the University of Southern California only to find out that he didn't need such an exotic education in order to read the Scriptures with understanding. It was mainly under his influence that I began to read the Bible anew, paying close attention to the clues that are there in the text.[3]

Almost every line of Scripture gives us hints about the historical situation. Sometimes it tells us what the people needed to be reminded of, and sometimes it tells us what they needed to be taught for the first time. In many cases, it tells us specifically what the recipients of the text were thinking or doing. For instance, in Galatians, when Paul said to the churches, "Let us not become boastful, challenging one another, envying one another" (Gal 5:26), we

---

[3]That is not to discount the importance of acknowledging the historical situation. Rather, I mean to be magnifying the importance of the words of the text.

can safely guess that Christians in Galatia were competing, not cooperating, with each other. Likewise, when Paul told the Corinthians, "For as in Adam all die, so also in Christ all shall be made alive" (1 Cor 15:22), we can accurately surmise that the Corinthian Christians didn't fully realize their dual connection with Adam *and* Christ.

Thus when we read 1 Timothy 2 we can reasonably guess from Paul's statement, "I was appointed a preacher and an apostle (I am telling the truth; I am not lying) as a teacher of the Gentiles in faith and truth" (1 Tim 2:7), that Paul must have been concerned that someone might doubt his apostleship. People had doubted it before (1 Cor 9:1-2). After all, it was quite an odd thing for a "Hebrew of Hebrews" who did not walk with Jesus during his time on earth to call himself a preacher, apostle and teacher "of the Gentiles." One would be more likely to think that Paul was a teacher of the Jews. Thus it makes sense for Paul to explain that he was set apart not just for the Jews but also "for the Gentiles."

CHANGING OUR ATTIRE

As some readers may have noticed, we never did finish our experiment. Let's do that now, assuming this time—for the sake our test—that Paul did not believe that women are unfit to lead men. In other words, I'm asking everyone to read 1 Timothy 2 with the expectation that Paul was saying something very different.[4]

Starting over, let's look at the passage, but this time beginning in 1 Timothy 2:7:

> And for this I was appointed a preacher and an apostle (I am telling the truth; I am not lying) as a teacher of the Gentiles in faith and truth. Therefore I want the men in every place to pray, lifting up holy hands, without wrath and dissension. Likewise, I want women to adorn themselves with proper clothing,

---

[4]I agree with Douglas Moo when he says, "We must be very careful about allowing any specific reconstruction—tentative and uncertain as it must be—to play too large a role in our exegesis" (Douglas Moo, "What Does It Mean Not to Teach or Have Authority over Men? 1 Timothy 2:11-15" in *Recovering Biblical Manhood and Womanhood*, ed. John Piper and Wayne Grudem [Wheaton, Ill.: Crossway, 1991], p. 181).

modestly and discreetly, not with braided hair and gold or pearls or costly garments, but rather by means of good works, as befits women making a claim to
godliness. Let a woman quietly receive instruction with entire submissiveness.
But I do not allow a woman to teach or exercise authority over a man, but to
remain quiet. For it was Adam who was first created, and then Eve. And it was
not Adam who was deceived, but the woman being quite deceived, fell into
transgression. But women will be preserved through the bearing of children if
they continue in faith and love and sanctity with self-restraint. (I Timothy
2:7-15)

As we already noted, Paul begins by saying that his mission was to the
Gentiles. In the next line, he says, *"Therefore I want the men in every place to pray,
lifting up holy hands, without wrath and dissension."* Evidently Paul's desire for the
men to pray was connected to his mission to the Gentiles. Because he was a
preacher, apostle and teacher of the Gentiles, Paul wanted the men "therefore" to pray in every place on behalf of all people (I Tim 2:I) since "God
our Savior" desires all people to be "saved" (I Tim 2:4).

Apparently the men in Ephesus were not being faithful to pray. Apparently
they were fighting in "wrath and dissension" (I Tim 2:8). Thus I'm inclined
to guess that Paul wanted the men to pray for the people, false teachers and
all, rather than be angry at them. For it's likely that Paul was sympathetic
since he had once been a "blasphemer" and a "persecutor" and a "violent
aggressor" (I Tim I:13). And it's likely that he was hopeful because Paul
knew firsthand that "the grace of our Lord" is "more than abundant" (I Tim
I:14) even to save the "chief" of sinners (I Tim I:15).

In the next verse Paul says, *"Likewise I want women to adorn themselves with proper
clothing, modestly and discreetly, not with braided hair and gold or pearls and costly garments;
but rather by means of good works, as befits women making a claim to godliness."* The text
implies that certain women were clothing themselves with immodest attire
instead of clothing themselves in good works.[5] Hypocritically these women

---

[5]Though Paul is talking to Ephesian women, not Roman women, we do know that it was extremely time-
consuming for wealthy Roman women to preen themselves. As Professor Balsdon said, "The arranging
of her hair naturally occupied a large part of a woman's time and thought." See J. P. V. D. Balsdon, *Roman*

were making a "claim to godliness." But their indiscreet behavior failed to meet the standard of their claim. As a result, they were failing to love "from a pure heart" (1 Tim 1:5) without hypocrisy (Rom 12:9).

This is what I imagine Paul was saying to the Christians in Ephesus, because it is not loving for women to dress immodestly. It's not loving toward men, and it's not loving toward women. It's selfish. When women dress immodestly, most men can't think straight. I know a pastor who had to look down at the floor during an entire worship service in his home church because one of the women singing on the stage was wearing platform shoes and tight leather pants with a starched white shirt that was cut just short enough to expose her very slender suntanned navel. Other women were distracted by her too. (Apparently I was one of them.)

Flamboyance of dress is not a sure way to worship God. I have never dressed immodestly as an act of humble obedience toward the Lord. Every time I have dressed in a culturally acceptable yet immodest way, it's always been for the sake of my vanity. Christian women are not so naive that we haven't figured how to please the eyes of the men. We know it when we're trying to look pretty, even if we're honestly and sincerely thinking about God at the same time. What we forget is that we're making a claim to godliness in hypocrisy.

In the next line Paul says, *"Let a woman quietly receive instruction."* Here again, the biblical clue indicates that women in Ephesus were not being quiet during

---

Women (London: The Bodley Head, 1962), p. 253. There seems to be some conjecture as to whether or not the "towering splendour" of a woman's high piles of curls was a wig. Of special note, Balsdon adds, "Writing in Africa two centuries later than Ovid wrote in Rome, the Christian Tertullian is his perfect foil. Ovid glorified and sought the refinement of every pleasure which the flesh affords; Tertullian would have the rest of humanity as ascetic as himself. Women must be reformed like everybody else; among other things, they must stop devoting so much time and thought to the arrangement of their hair. 'All this wasted pains on arranging your hair—what contribution can this make to your salvation? Why can you not give your hair a rest? One minute you are building it up, the next you are letting it down—raising it one moment, stretching it the next. Some women devote all their energy to forcing their hair to curl, others to make it hang loose and wavy, in a style which may seem natural, but it is not natural at all. You perpetrate unbelievable extravagances to make a kind of tapestry of your hair, sometimes to be a sheath to your head and a lid to the top of you, like a helmet, sometimes to be an elevated platform, built upon the back of your neck'" (pp. 257-58). We also know that according to Pliny, women spent more money on their ears, in the purchase of pearl earrings, than on any other part of their person. Seneca said scathingly that some women wore on a single ear the value of two or three estates (Balsdon, p. 263).

instruction. As a professor, I know how unlikely it is for people to be quiet when they are being taught something revolutionary that undermines the framework of their thought. For example, undergraduates today tend to murmur the first time they hear it said that "truth is objective." It stirs them up because the culture has taught them to see truth as relative, not fixed. The students argue with me not because they're being inappropriate but rather because the concept of objective truth upsets their paradigm. Thus, by analogy, it's feasible to believe that the women in Ephesus were somewhat argumentative whenever they heard the gospel. It didn't fit their former paradigm.[6]

More specifically, however, Paul says, "A woman must quietly receive instruction with entire submissiveness." I'll say more about this in the next chapter. Here I want to highlight Paul's concern for the women to learn to recognize the true gospel in contradistinction from heresy. In order to do this, they would have to be specially equipped. For no one can discern between heresy and truth without first being taught (Rom 10:14-17). Anyone can go outside and look at the stars and intuit there is a God (Ps 19:1), but none of us can intuit by looking at the stars that God created Adam before Eve.

"But I do not allow a woman to teach or exercise authority over a man, but to remain quiet." The text implies that someone had the idea of allowing a woman to teach a man.[7] For all we know, it may have been Paul's idea. It could also have been Timothy's. Timothy might have reasoned that since his mother and grandmother had reared him in the faith (2 Tim 1:3), they would be good teachers for other men and women as well. It's feasible that Paul was saying, "But I—unlike you, Timothy—am not allowing a woman right now to teach or exercise authority over a man, but to remain quiet."[8]

---

[6]Scholars on both sides of the debate agree that the women in Ephesus were being taught false doctrine by the teachers in town. Thus it's common to believe the framework of their faith was faulty.

[7]Thomas Schreiner agrees. He says, "it is likely that the prohibition is given because some women were teaching men" (Thomas Schreiner, "An Interpretation of 1 Timothy 2:9-15: A Dialogue with Scholarship" in Women in the Church, ed. Andreas Köstenberger, Thomas Schreiner and H. Scott Baldwin [Grand Rapids, Mich.: Baker, 1995], p. 141).

[8]Scholar Don Williams is typically credited for drawing attention to the present participle in the Greek text (see Don Williams, The Apostle Paul and Women in the Church [Ventura, Calif.: Regal, 1979], p. 112).

Apparently Timothy didn't know that Paul was prohibiting "a woman."[9] How could he know? Paul had labored with other women in Philippi (Phil 4:2), Cenchrea (Rom 16:1) and Rome (Rom 16). It wasn't like Paul to prohibit a woman. More specifically, it wasn't like Paul to prohibit a woman from teaching in Ephesus. Though it is often overlooked, the historical fact is that Paul allowed Priscilla—a woman—to correct Apollos in the city of Ephesus, where Timothy was when he received 1 Timothy 2.

Am I the only person to be stunned by this? Priscilla taught Apollos in Ephesus!

I cannot imagine that Timothy, Paul's colleague, was unaware of this (Acts 18:23—19:22). Nor do I believe that Apollos was the only man Priscilla ever taught. When Priscilla lived in Rome, she and Aquila hosted a church in their house (Rom 16:5). Surely Priscilla—the teacher of another great teacher —did not shut down or be silent in the church that she and her husband led. The way Luke tells the story in Acts 18, it does not seem extraordinary that a husband and wife corrected a man who was "mighty in the Scriptures."

Notice once again that 1 Timothy 2 does not say, "I do not allow a woman to teach a man unless she is partnering with her husband." There is no caveat in the passage. No room for a woman to teach men on the radio or in books or in partnership with her husband. No room for a woman—any woman— to teach a man.[10]

In principle, it must have been acceptable for Priscilla to teach Apollos and exercise authority of correction over him. [11] Indeed, I have never met a

---

[9]Keener's view is similar, though based on a different line of argumentation. He says, "What is most significant about the wording of the passage . . . is that Paul does not assume that Timothy already knows this rule. . . . Paul often reminds readers of traditions they should know by saying, 'You know,' or 'Do you not know?' or 'According to the traditions which I delivered to you' " (Keener, *Paul, Women and Wives*, p. 112).

[10]Though I have been using the term "a woman" throughout this book, I acknowledge that Paul's alternation form the plural in 1 Timothy 2:9 ("I want women") to the singular in 1 Timothy 2:12 ("I do not allow a woman") illustrates that Paul was talking about all women. As Schreiner rightly says, "The singular 'woman' *(gynē)* is generic, and thus should not be limited to an individual woman" (Schreiner, "A Dialogue with Scholarship," p. 121).

[11]It is silly to suggest that Apollos was corrected by a woman who was sinning when she and her husband

Christian or heard of a church father who ever ventured to say that Priscilla
was sinning on the day she taught Apollos.[12]

ANOTHER EXCEPTIONAL WOMAN

Here's a related question. Do deacons count as leaders in the church?

Phoebe was a deacon. Paul commended Phoebe as a "deacon in the
church" (Rom 16:1). Not only that, but he instructed the Roman Christians
to "receive her" and "help her in whatever matter she may have need" (Rom
16:2). Paul didn't say that Phoebe was a secretary who was coming to Rome
in order to be an assistant of the men. On the contrary, he told the church
to help her.

Some might argue that Phoebe was a deaconess,[13] not a deacon.[14] But
the Bible says in Greek she was a deacon (*diakonos*). As a *diakonos*, Phoebe was
a minister like Paul (Col 1:23). The Bible says Paul was made a *diakonos*, not
for the purpose of distributing Communion and collecting the offering as

---

corrected him. It is even sillier to suggest that all three of them were sinning: Priscilla, Aquila and
Apollos.

[12]Chrysostom, for instance, justifies Priscilla teaching Apollos. He says, "It is worth looking into the reason why, when Paul greets them, he places Priscilla's name before her husband's. For he did not say,
'Greet Aquila and Priscilla,' but 'Priscilla and Aquila.' Now he did not do this unwittingly, for it seems
to me that he knew she was more pious than her husband. And that interpretation is not just a guess,
one can learn it from the Acts of the Apostles. Apollos was an eloquent man, skilled in the Scriptures,
but he knew only the baptism of John. This woman took him, instructed him in the way of God, and
made him a perfect teacher (Acts 18:24-28). . . . But why then does he write, 'I do not permit a woman
to teach, nor have authority over a man' (1 Tim 2:12)? This is the case whenever the man is reverent,
holds the same faith, shares in the same wisdom. But if the man is an unbeliever, wandering in error,
Paul does not deprive her of the power of a teacher. Paul writes to the Corinthians, 'If a woman has an
unbeliever as a husband, let her not leave him. For how do you know, wife, if you will save your husband?'
(1 Cor 7:13-16) But how can a believing woman save an unbelieving husband? Quite clearly, through
her instructing, teaching, and leading him to the faith, just as Priscilla did for Apollos." See Chrysostom's homily "Greet Priscilla and Aquila," translated and quoted by Elizabeth A. Clark, *Women in the Early
Church*, ed. Thomas Halton, Message of the Fathers of the Church 13 (Collegeville, Minn.: Liturgical
Press, 1983), p. 158.

[13]The Greek word "deaconness" is not a biblical word. But a separate order known as deaconesses did
develop toward the third century in the Eastern church, though not in the Western (see Tucker and Lie-
field, *Daughters of the Church*, p. 86).

[14]Even if someone argues that the word *women* in 1 Timothy 3:11 refers to "deaconesses" (a nonbiblical
word), my point still stands. For the women in 1 Timothy 3:11 are called "women." Phoebe is called a
"deacon."

contemporary deacons might do. On the contrary, he was made a *diakonos* in order to "carry out the preaching of the word of God" (Col 1:26; cf. Eph 3:7-8). Likewise, Paul says he was made adequate as a *diakonos* of the new covenant (2 Cor 3:5). Was Paul not a leader when he introduced people to the new covenant? Was Paul not a leader when he preached?

A *diakonos* is a leader who serves. A *diakonos* is a leader who acts as a minister of God's Word. A *diakonos* is a leader who understands what leadership is. In Mark 9:35, Jesus said to the twelve apostles, "If anyone wants to be first, he shall be last of all, and *diakonos* of all." That's what Jesus said to them as leaders. He said leaders are "deacons of all."

Phoebe was deacon in the church of Cenchrea (Rom 16:1). She was a leader like other well-known leaders who helped Paul to minister the gospel.[15] Phoebe was a *diakonos* like Apollos (1 Cor 3:5) and Tychicus (Eph 6:21; Col 4:7) and Epaphras (Col 1:7). The word is exactly the same.

How are we conservatives going to choose to respond to that? Are we going to tell ourselves, "Well, it appears that we have another exception on our hands. Priscilla and Phoebe were exceptional women. The order of creation—that universal principle—doesn't apply to them." Is that what we're going to do?

I can't do that anymore in good conscience. It's illogical for Christians to say that a universal principle doesn't have to be applied to every woman. If former President Bill Clinton had ever tried to tell the American people that a "universal principle doesn't necessarily apply to all situations," most conservative Christians probably would have strongly disapproved. We might even have said that Clinton was being dishonest. But now here we are faced with our own indicting question: What does our logic reveal about our hearts?

I feel so convicted to repent from my former blindness. It's not that I can't remember why I used to think that women aren't allowed to be pastors or

---

[15]Complementarian Foh says, "Certainly Phoebe being a deacon would make her a leader in the church" (Susan Foh, "A Male Leadership View," in *Women in Ministry: Four Views* [Downers Grove, Ill.: InterVarsity Press, 1989], p. 79).

preachers. It's that I can finally see that my reason for thinking that hinged upon my presuppositions. In the past, I stood in solidarity with many other conservatives, telling myself that 1 Timothy 2 prohibits women from only this one thing—teaching and having authority over men. And yet, simultaneously, it was during that time that I assumed without thought that women were prohibited altogether from being pastors and preachers. Because of my preset mindset, I failed to see that God himself has given "some" women as "pastors" just as he has given "some" as "apostles"[16] and "prophets"[17] and "evangelists"[18] and "teachers"[19] (Eph 4:11).

It's conspicuous that so many of us believe that women can't be given as apostles, pastors or preachers. Where did we get that idea? Not from 1 Timothy 2! Had we gotten that idea from 1 Timothy 2, then it never would have occurred to us that women can't be pastors of children and other women. But it did occur to us, and even to this day, some of us are saying that God does not "genuinely [call] women to be pastors."[20] This tells me that our paradigm is tainted. This tells me that our paradigm needs to be revised.

In the name of 1 Timothy 2, we say that women can't be pastors, and yet they can be teachers. This kind of inconsistency ought to wake us up. I am aware that many of us temper our belief on women's teaching with other Bible passages such as

- ■ Titus 2:3, "Older women are to be reverent . . . teaching what is good"

---

[16]Many scholars believe that Romans 16:7 refers to a female apostle named Junia. The verse says, "Greet Andronicus and Junia, my kinsmen, and my fellow prisoners, who are outstanding among the apostles, who also were in Christ Jesus before me."

[17]Both sides of the debate acknowledge that women can be prophets. Indeed, the Scriptures explicitly identify women such as Miriam, Huldah, Philip's seven daughters, and others as "prophetesses."

[18]Most complementarians believe that Christian women can communicate the gospel to unbelieving men. When I was in seminary, Wayne Grudem told me that he thought it would be acceptable for me to share the gospel with unbelieving men or to teach theology to unbelieving men in a secular college.

[19]There isn't one contemporary Christian I know of who believes that God gave men only to be teachers.

[20]Piper and Grudem jointly say, "We do not believe God genuinely calls women to be pastors" (John Piper and Wayne Grudem, "An Overview of Central Concerns: Questions and Answers" in *Recovering Biblical Manhood and Womanhood*, ed. John Piper and Wayne Grudem [Wheaton, Ill.: Crossway, 1991], p. 77).

- Proverbs 31:26, "and the teaching of kindness is on her tongue"
- Proverbs 1:8, "Hear, my son, . . . and do not forsake your mother's teaching"

And yet we do not—for some reason—temper our belief with other relevant passages such as

- 2 Timothy 2:24, "And the Lord's bond-servant [male or female] must be . . . able to teach."
- 2 Timothy 4:2, "Preach the word."
- Matthew 28:19-20, "Go . . . and make disciples . . . baptizing them . . . teaching them."

Consequently many of us contend that it's unbiblical for a woman to baptize children and other women. I used to think that too. About ten years ago, I led a little boy named Tony to Christ, and though he wanted me to baptize him, I didn't—because I thought that would be unbiblical. I was still of the mindset that 1 Timothy 2 prohibits women from baptizing anyone even though the text of 1 Timothy 2 says nothing of the sort—and even though Jesus commands the opposite. The craziest thing about this is that all my life I have believed the Great Commission applies to me.

How could I be so blind? How could I have overlooked the Great Commission all these years? Well, somehow I did. But now my blindness has been taken away, and now I am able to communicate with others in order to let them know that Christ says something different from church tradition. It was Tertullian—not Christ—who boldly proclaimed, "For how credible will it seem that Paul gave a woman the power of teaching and baptizing!"[21] Christ commands all Christians to "go therefore and make disciples of all the nations, baptizing them in the name of the Father and the Son and the Holy Spirit, teaching them to observe all that I commanded" (Mt 28:19-20).

The irony in this story, at least for me, is that I am now persuaded that Paul prohibited women for the sake of the Great Commission.

---

[21]Tertullian, "On Baptism," chap. 1 (ANF 3:677) as quoted in Tucker and Liefeld, *Daughters of the Church*, p. 105.

DISCUSSION QUESTIONS

1. When you read I Timothy 2:8-15 with the expectation that it says something other than that men only should be leaders, what fresh ideas come to mind?

2. How long have you known that Phoebe was a deacon *(diakonos)*? What kind of help do you think Paul might have wanted the church to give her?

3. Have you ever noticed that Paul calls himself a deacon, not an elder? Note also that neither Barnabas nor Silas nor Timothy is ever referred to as an elder. What do you make of this? Do you think Barnabas and Silas and Timothy were leaders in the church?

4. Review Ephesians 4:11. What evidence do you find in the biblical text that God has given "some" women to be apostles, prophets, evangelists, pastors and teachers? What evidence is there in church history? What evidence can be found in the church today?

20

THE SIGNIFICANCE OF ADAM BEING
CREATED FIRST

*Let a woman quietly receive instruction with entire submissiveness. But I do
not allow a woman to teach or* authentein *("exercise authority") over a man,
but to remain quiet. For it was Adam who was first created, and then Eve. And
it was not Adam who was deceived, but the woman being quite deceived, fell into
transgression. But the women shall be preserved through the bearing of children
if they continue in faith and love and sanctity with self-restraint.*

I TIMOTHY 2:12-15

We know I Timothy 2 means something. It is also clear that Paul was
prohibiting something. Indeed, it is clear that Paul was prohibiting "a
woman" (or wife) from doing something.[1] Unfortunately, however, we don't
know for sure what that something was, for none of us know with certainty
what the Greek word *authentein* means. Nor can we decide if *authentein* in this
passage carries a positive or negative or neutral connotation. Nor can we
agree on the grammar. Granted, we have access to the context of I Timothy
2 as well as extrabiblical literature. Nevertheless, for a variety of reasons,
scholars haven't reached consensus on this. Defining *authentein* is one of the
many difficulties of this passage. As Thomas Schreiner says, "Virtually every
word in verses 11-12 is disputed."[2]

Consequently we don't know if Paul was prohibiting women from having

---

[1]In Greek the word for "wife"*(gynē)* is the same word for "woman" *(gynē).*
[2]See Thomas R. Schreiner, "An Interpretation of I Timothy 2:9-15: A Dialogue with Scholarship," in
Women in the Church, ed. Andreas Köstenberger, Thomas Schreiner and H. Scott Baldwin (Grand Rapids,
Mich.: Baker, 1995), p. 114.

authority or exercising authority or usurping authority over a man.[3] We don't know if he was telling them not to teach false doctrine or not to teach the gospel of grace.

That's the problem—we don't know.[4] We don't know how to translate I Timothy 2, much less interpret it correctly or apply it appropriately to today. That's why this passage is so humbling; to some extent it has stumped us all, scholars and practitioners alike. My best answer, then, is to publicly confess that I don't know. Indeed, there isn't a commentator in all of church history who has fully figured out the meaning of I Timothy 2.[5]

Part of the difficulty is that the normal Greek word for "authority" is not used. The apostle Paul didn't say *exousia*. He used the word *authentein* instead. The word *authentein* is not used anywhere else in the New Testament. That's

---

[3]While the NIV, NASB and RSV translate *authentein* either as "have authority" or "exercise authority," the KJV and the Authorized Version translate it as "usurp authority." The New English Version translates it as "domineer."

[4]The current debate is one of conflicting opinions. Again, the words of Mortimer Adler are instructive. Adler says, "And usually, in the case of opinions, what makes up our mind one way or the other is not the thing we are thinking about, but our emotions, our desires, our interests, or some authority upon which we are relying. . . . And when one is holding mere opinion, one finds the emotional content very high indeed. Precisely in proportion as the opinion is not well founded in fact or evidence, one tends to support it with one's emotions and to be obstinate in holding onto it as one holds onto a prejudice. I know this in my own case when I find that I am saying, 'No, no. That is not so. That isn't so.' . . . I suspect that I am holding an opinion without much evidence to support it. And I am putting in my emotions, making up by my emotions for the lack of evidence" (Mortimer Adler, *How to Think About the Great Ideas,* ed. Max Weismann [Chicago: Open Court, 2000], p. 26).

[5]I recognize, as Harold O. J. Brown puts it, that "for about eighteen centuries I Timothy 2:12 as well as I Corinthians 14:34 and related texts, was assumed to have a clear and self-evident meaning" (Harold O. J. Brown, "The New Testament Against Itself: I Timothy 2:9-15 and the 'Breakthrough' of Galatians 3:28," in *Women in the Church,* ed. Andreas Köstenberger, Thomas R. Schreiner and H. Scott Baldwin [Grand Rapids, Mich.: Baker, 1995], p. 197). I can also see *why* these texts seemed self-evident. The reason is because church tradition held that women, by nature, were inferior to men. It was this presupposition that made the text seem so clear. It didn't make verse 15 clear, but it did make verses 13-14 clear. Verse 15 historically has been assigned an awkward translation that is so unconvincing that many scholars on both sides of the debate disagree with it today. Neither complementarians such as Thomas Schreiner, Douglas Moo, T. David Gordon, Paul Levertoff and Andreas Köstenberger nor egalitarians such as Craig Keener, David Scholer or Richard Clark Kroeger and Catherine Clark Kroeger embrace the historical idea that verse 15 somehow refers to the birth of Christ. Indeed, as Schreiner says, the historical interpretation is "quite improbable." Not only are there grammatical reasons for rejecting this interpretation, there is also a basic theological reason—that we are saved by Jesus' death, not his birth. See Schreiner, "A Dialogue with Scholarship," p. 148.

why it's hard to define. Another challenge relates to the fact that we, as readers, bring so many assumptions to the text.

For instance, many of us unwittingly have assumed it is acceptable for men to *authentein* women. In reality, it may be just as sinful for a man to *authentein* a woman as it is for a woman to *authentein* a man.[6] Similarly it seems that others of us have assumed that men have *exousia* ("rightful authority") over women. But that can't be supported by any biblical text. The Bible says clearly that all authority *(exousia)* has been given to Christ. Jesus put it plainly: "All *exousia* has been given to Me in heaven and on earth. Go therefore and make disciples of all the nations, baptizing them in the name of the Father and Son and the Holy Spirit, teaching them to observe all that I commanded you; and lo, I am with you always, even to the end of the age" (Mt 28:19-20).

Unless we're ready to say the Great Commission applies only to men, then we're going have to admit that men and women are commanded to "go and make disciples" by virtue of the authority of Christ. For in keeping with his character, the Lord Jesus used his authority *(exousia)* to commission every believer. Thus it's inconceivable to think that Paul would order Timothy to prohibit Christian women at the expense of the Great Commission. It appears instead that all of the exhortations in 1 Timothy 1—2 have something to do with Paul's mission to the Gentiles (1 Tim 2:7). Paul "urged" Timothy to stay in Ephesus "in order to instruct certain men [people] not to teach strange doctrines" (1 Tim 1:3), presumably so the true gospel would go out. Moreover, he urged that "entreaties and prayers, petitions, and thanksgivings be made on behalf of all men [people]," noting that "this is good and acceptable in the sight of God our Savior, who desires all men [people] to be saved" (1 Tim 2:1, 3-4).

LET A WOMAN REMAIN QUIET

Although we can't know with certainty the full meaning of 1 Timothy, we can obtain some fairly accurate insights by way of observation. For instance, it is evident in the text that 1 Timothy 2:11-12 are closely related, for in both

---

[6]Campus Crusade staff member Holly Sheldon offered this insight to me.

verses Paul says he wants the women to be "quiet."[7] He says in verse 11, "Let a woman *quietly* [emphasis added] receive instruction with entire submissiveness"; he says in verse 12, "But I do not allow a woman to teach or *authentein* over a man, but to remain *quiet* [emphasis added]." From this, we can gather that the women in Ephesus were talking when they should have been listening. Whether or not the men were present with them, we do not know.[8] If they weren't, that would constitute one plausible explanation of why Paul commanded women, not men, to be silent.

This is where the discussion gets interesting. It's interesting because it's so hopeful. It's promising that a consensus has been reached with regard to women being allowed to speak. Many different scholars on both sides of the debate have firmly established that women are not required to be wordless or soundless at church.[9] Neither side of the debate believes a right application of I Timothy 2:11-12 is for women literally to be "quiet."[10] We don't believe this because we know from other verses that God wants women to join in the singing, praying and prophesying of the general assembly (I Cor 11:5).[11]

---

[7]Grammatically this syntactical structure is called an "inclusio." That is, verses 11-12 in Greek begin and end with the phrase *en hysēchia* ("in silence"). "*Gynē en hysēchia . . . en hysēchia.*"

[8]There is biblical precedent for women meeting without men. In Philippi, for instance, the women were gathered on the sabbath day at a riverside praying. Apparently no men were there until Paul and his fellow travelers started speaking to them (see Acts 16:13).

[9]In Luke 14:4 and Acts 22:2, this same Greek word, *hysēchia*, does refer literally to "silence." Scholars agree, however, that in the context of I Timothy 2:11-12, the word *quiet* describes the kind of demeanor a woman should have. Notably, most scholars are not saying that women should be "silent"—even though a strictly literal reading would charge women to say nothing at all.

[10]Cf. I Corinthians 14:34-35, "Let the women keep silent in the churches; for they are not permitted to speak, but let them subject themselves, just as the Law also says. And if they desire to learn anything, let them ask their husbands at home; for it is improper for a woman to speak at church." According to many complementarians such as Wayne Grudem, D. A. Carson and James Hurley, the Corinthian passage does not literally mean that "women must keep silent in the churches." For instance, Carson says, "In a Greek *ekklēsia*, i.e., a public meeting, women were not allowed to speak at all. By contrast, women in the Christian *ekklēsia*, borne along by the Spirit, were *encouraged* to do so" (D. A. Carson, " 'Silent in the Churches': On the Role of Women in I Corinthians 14:33b-36" in *Recovering Biblical Manhood and Womanhood*, ed. John Piper and Wayne Grudem [Wheaton, Ill.: Crossway, 1991], p. 153).

[11]Another reason is that Paul could have used a stronger Greek word such as *phimoo*, meaning "to muzzle," as is found in I Peter 2:15.

Yet oddly enough, the only imperative in I Timothy 2:8-15 is Paul's instruction that a "woman must quietly receive instruction with entire submissiveness." This is significant because evangelicals are not arguing over whether or not that particular imperative literally understood applies to women today.[12] Together we are saying it does not. Yes, we believe that women are to be allowed to learn, but we do not demand that women learn in silence without asking any questions in public.[13] On the contrary, we allow women to learn just as openly and freely as men.

What does that say about us?

It tells me that none of us can say with integrity that we, unlike others, are embracing the clear and obvious meaning of I Timothy 2. It also tells me that both sides of the debate, hermeneutically speaking, are perhaps more similar than we think.[14]

A CLOSER LOOK AT PAUL'S PROHIBITION

Though many Christian feminists have argued that the emphasis of I Timothy 2:11 lies on women learning,[15] I agree with complementarian Thomas Schreiner, who rightly explains that "the focus of the imperative is not on women learning, but *the manner* and *mode* of their learning."[16] I disagree, however, with Schreiner's statement that "the permission for women to 'learn' is

---

[12]As Schreiner points out, "Most scholars today argue that this word ["quiet"] does not actually mean 'silence' here, but refers to a quiet demeanor and spirit that is peaceable and not argumentative" (Schreiner, "A Dialogue with Scholarship," p. 123). Historically, however, this was not always the case.

[13]In other words, evangelicals understand that I Corinthians 14:34-35, "Let the women keep silent [*sigatōsan*] in the churches . . . and if they desire to learn anything, let them ask their husbands at home," was intended for a particular situation. (Even so, we are unsure of what Paul meant. For as Anne Atkins astutely observes, "We know some women were not married (I Cor 7:8); how can they ask their husbands? . . . We know some were married to non-Christians (I Cor 7:13); how can they ask them questions about the faith?" (Anne Atkins, *Split Image* [London: Hodder & Stoughton, 1998], p. 95).

[14]I have in mind those of us who recognize the authority and primacy of Scripture.

[15]It is quite extraordinary that Paul commanded something the Jewish rabbis of his day forbade. Jesus broke the Jewish norm when he invited Mary, a woman, to sit at his feet as his disciple. To read more on this, see Ruth Tucker and Walter L. Liefeld, *Daughters of the Church* (Grand Rapids, Mich.: Zondervan, 1987), p. 26.

[16]Schreiner, "A Dialogue with Scholarship," p. 122.

contrasted with the proscription for them 'to teach,' while 'all submissiveness' is paired with 'not exercising authority over a man.' "[17]

For Paul does not say, "Let a woman learn but not teach." Nor does he say, "Let a woman be submissive to a man but not in charge of a man." On the contrary, Paul couples learning with submitting and teaching with *authentein*. Thus it would seem more accurate, as well as more consistent with Schreiner's understanding of verse 11, to summarize the text like this:

- Paul allowed a woman to learn submissively.
- Paul forbade a woman to teach or *authentein* a man.

If we take seriously the connection between verses 11 and 12, then we might predict from the context that *authentein* refers to the semantic opposite of learning "with entire submissiveness." In other words, we might guess that since Paul allowed a woman to learn if she behaved acceptably, he likewise forbade her to teach if she behaved unacceptably. And the grammar of the sentence (in Greek, not English) as well as the word *authentein* appears to be able to accommodate this interpretation. Furthermore, if H. Scott Baldwin, my classmate at Trinity, is right, then *authentein* (as a transitive verb)[18] could rightly mean "to control" or "dominate."[19]

In light of this, someone might argue that Paul was prohibiting women from teaching in a dominating way. But even this by itself is not conclusive, for it is necessary grammatically to understand the two infinitives ("to teach"

---

[17]Ibid., p. 124.

[18]*Authentein* can also be intransitive. The grammar in 1 Timothy 2, however, calls for a transitive verb.

[19]Baldwin also includes the possibility that *authentein* (as a transitive verb) can mean either "to compel; to influence" or "to flout the authority of." We can eliminate these two definitions, however, because neither can be practically applied. To begin with, it's impossible for women not to influence men. Second, it has never been orthodox for Christians to believe that all men have inherent authority over all women. Thus it's unacceptable to understand the verse as saying, "I do not allow women to teach in such a way that flouts the [inherent] authority of men." Indeed, both sides of the debate openly agree that men in general do not have authority over women. Baldwin also explains, however, that *authentein* can mean "to assume authority over." If it does, then this would suggest that women can exercise authority over men as long as they don't assume it, that is, as long as the elders grant her permission to serve as a leader over men. See H. Scott Baldwin, "A Difficult Word," in *Women in the Church*, ed. Andreas Köstenberger, Thomas Schreiner and H. Scott Baldwin (Grand Rapids, Mich.: Baker, 1995), pp. 72-80.

and "to *authentein*") as either both being negative or both being positive.[20] Thus the verse most likely either means

- negatively, I do not allow a woman to misteach or domineer over a man but to remain quiet,[21] or
- positively, I do not allow a woman to teach or exercise authority over a man but to remain quiet.

If Paul meant the former, then it is self-evident why he made the prohibition.[22] If he meant the latter—that he prohibited a woman from teaching or exercising authority over a man—then we are back to the beginning of this book. That is, we are forced to go back and confront ourselves again with all the inconsistencies that this interpretation tends to foster.

I TIMOTHY 2:13-14

Moving on to I Timothy 2:13-14, there's something else important to point out. Both sides of the contemporary debate tend to embrace one verse more than the other.

For example, most complementarians strongly embrace a straightforward

---

[20]Complementarian Andreas Köstenberger is credited for having publicized this. See Andreas Köstenberger, "A Complex Sentence Structure," in *Women in the Church*, ed. Andreas Köstenberger, Thomas R. Schreiner and H. Scott Baldwin (Grand Rapids, Mich.: Baker, 1995), pp. 81-103.

[21]Alan Padgett has correctly pointed out Andreas Köstenberger's mistake of saying that the word *didaskein* "to teach" is always positive in Paul. As Padgett rightly shows, the word *didaskein* "to teach" is used negatively in Titus 1:11 and I Timothy 6:3. Padgett thus draws attention to the fact that Köstenberger himself has openly said that the two Greek words *didaskein* ("to teach") and *authentein* ("to _____ ?") in I Timothy 2:12 are either both viewed positively or both viewed negatively by the original writer of I Timothy. It is therefore grammatically feasible to understand Paul's prohibition as a means of preventing women from teaching false doctrine or exercising some kind of unsanctioned authority. See Alan Padgett, "The Scholarship of Patriarchy" (On I Timothy 2:8-15)," *Priscilla Papers* (winter 1997): 24.

[22]As to why Paul prohibited women, not men, my guess has to do with the context. For instance, it could be that Paul wasn't thinking about men—because the male false teachers were unbelievers. Hymenaeus and Alexander, for instance, "rejected" the faith (I Tim 1:19-20). It wasn't Paul's intention to restore these men. Indeed, the Bible says that Paul had "delivered" these men "over to Satan" (I Tim 1:20). By contrast, the women might have been Christian women who sincerely were deceived and therefore stood in need of correction. This might explain why Paul was careful to say, "Let a woman . . . receive instruction." It could have been that Paul wanted the Christian women to be delivered from their deception. For, indeed, "some [had] . . . turned aside to follow Satan" (I Tim 5:15). The distinction, then, is that while Paul had "delivered" certain men to Satan, the women had themselves wilfully "turned aside" to follow Satan.

reading of verse 13, "for it was Adam who was first created, and then Eve."[23]
Many of them see it as the abiding rationale to undergird a theology of male
leadership.[24] Men, as they see it, hold priority over women with regard to being leaders in the home and church precisely because God created Adam before he created Eve.[25] From a complementarian perspective, it is more than
clear that Paul's prohibition in I Timothy 2:11-12 is grounded in the order
of creation.[26]

By contrast, many biblical feminists tend to downplay verse 13.[27] As
Thomas Schreiner observes:

> Progressives [biblical feminists] back away from verse 13 because it calls into
> question the exegetical edifice they have built to justify women teaching men.
> For example, Mary Evans says the relevance of verse 13 for verse 12 is unclear,
> and that verse 13 merely introduces the next verse about Eve. Gordon Fee as-
> serts that the verse is not central to Paul's argument. Timothy Harris says that
> the verse "is difficult to understand on any reading." Craig Keener thinks the

---

[23]For instance, Douglas Moo says, "For Paul, the man's priority in the order of creation is indicative of
the headship that man is to have over woman. The woman being created after man, as his helper, shows
the position of submission that God intended as inherent in the woman's relationship to the man, a submission that is violated if a woman teaches doctrine or exercises authority over a man." (Notice that
Moo says nothing about women being quiet, even though Paul's prohibition does twice.) See Douglas
Moo, "What Does It Mean Not to Teach or Have Authority Over Men? I Timothy 2:11-15," in *Recovering Biblical Manhood and Womanhood*, ed. John Piper and Wayne Grudem (Wheaton, Ill.: Crossway,
1991), p. 190.

[24]Of note, Schreiner says that verse 12 alone "does not contain sufficient evidence" to prove that the Paul's
prohibition was timeless. For Schreiner, the universality of the "the principle of male leadership" is established, not by verse 12, but rather by verse 13 (Schreiner, "A Dialogue with Scholarship," p. 127).

[25]For example, Piper and Grudem say, "The contextual basis for this argument in the book of Genesis is
the assumption . . . that the 'firstborn' in a human family has the special right and responsibility of leadership in the family." With that, they say, "The question that evangelical feminists must come to terms
with is why God should choose to create man and woman sequentially" (John Piper and Wayne Grudem, "An Overview of Central Concerns: Questions and Answers," in *Recovering Biblical Manhood and Womanhood*, ed. John Piper and Wayne Grudem [Wheaton, Ill.: Crossway, 1991], p. 81).

[26]Moo speaks representatively when he says, "For by rooting these prohibitions in the circumstances of
creation rather than in the circumstances of the fall, Paul shows that he does not consider these restrictions to be the product of the curse and presumably, therefore, to be phased out by redemption" (Moo,
"What Does It Mean Not to Teach or Have Authority over Men?" p. 190).

[27]Moo further says, "It is very telling that most of the advocates of [biblical feminism] pass over verse 13
very quickly, explaining it as simply an 'introduction' to verse 14, or ignoring it entirely" (ibid).

argument here is hard to fathom. David Scholer protests that the text is unclear.[28]

In the eyes of biblical feminists, it doesn't make sense to understand verse 13 as a timeless rationale for subordinating women to men.[29] They do recognize that granting prominence to the firstborn was a common practice in Old Testament times, but they also note that Scripture often overturns primogeniture values.[30] Exceptions to the rule include Abraham, Isaac, Jacob, Joseph, Moses, Judah, David and Solomon, all of whom were preeminent and none of whom were the firstborn.[31]

With regard to I Timothy 2:14, however, most biblical feminists seem to be less wary. Granted, a literal interpretation would say that women are prohibited from teaching men simply because "Eve was deceived." But that is so unreasonable that neither side of the debate is willing to say it. It doesn't make sense to say in one breath that women are not trustworthy to teach sound doctrine to men, but they are trustworthy to teach sound doctrine to women and children. If women by nature are too easily deceived, then godly Christian women shouldn't be allowed to teach Christian doctrine to anyone.[32]

---

[28]Schreiner, "A Dialogue with Scholarship," p. 136.

[29]Commenting on the complementarian point of view, egalitarian scholar David Scholer says, "The Genesis allusion in 2:13-14 is often considered to be an especially authoritative sanction because it derives from so-called creation ordinances. Of course, this applies only to the first sanction (2:13); the second sanction (2:14) is drawn from the account of the sin that violated the original situation. An argument drawn from the Genesis 3 account of sin does not necessarily give a Pauline injunction universal validity" (David Scholer, "I Timothy 2:9-15 and the Place of Women in the Church's Ministry," in *Women, Authority and the Bible*, ed. Alvera Mickelsen [Downers Grove, Ill.: InterVarsity Press, 1986], p. 208).

[30]For those unfamiliar with the term, the practice of primogeniture refers to when the firstborn is granted prominence with the creative order of a family unit. For a more in-depth discussion of this, see William Webb, *Slavery, Women and Homosexuals* (Downers Grove, Ill.: InterVarsity Press, 2001), pp. 134-45, 257-62.

[31]Biblical feminist Rebecca Merrill Groothuis fortifies her argument by referencing this quote from John Calvin: "The reason which Paul assigns, that woman was second in the order of creation, appears not to be a very strong argument in favour of her subjection; for John the Baptist was before Christ in the order of time, and yet was greatly inferior in rank" (Rebecca Merrill Groothuis, *Good News for Women* [Grand Rapids, Mich.: Baker, 1997], p. 218).

[32]Groothuis extends the point by saying, "Other difficulties arise in the traditionalist treatment of verse 14. . . . If verses 13 and 14 are to be viewed as presenting a causal connection between the orders of creation and women's permanent subordination to the teaching authority of men, then the logic for verse 14 must go as follows: Since the first woman was deceived, this failing is somehow characteristic of *all*

Hence it is common for egalitarians to believe that the reference to Eve's deception in verse 14 points to the fact that women in Ephesus, being uneducated, were deceived by the false teachers as Eve was by the serpent in the garden.[33] And thus many egalitarians logically conclude that Paul prohibited women from teaching and leading men on a temporary basis until the women there were properly trained.[34]

Complementarians, however, tend to downplay verse 14, "And it was not Adam who deceived, but the woman being quite deceived, fell into transgression." It is notable, for instance, that while Schreiner almost exaggerates about how clear verse 13 is to him,[35] he backs away from verse 14, admitting *that* verse is "difficult."[36] As egalitarian Rebecca Merrill Groothuis points out:

> Some traditionalists [complementarians] today seem to [recognize] . . . the difficulties that arise in the traditional treatment of verse 14 . . . and [make] efforts to avoid them. Craig Blomberg solves the problem by detaching verse 14 from verse 13 and grouping it instead with verse 15. . . . Douglas Moo regards verse 13 as the causal basis for woman's permanent subordination to man's spiritual authority; he then switches to viewing verse 14 as illustrative—but with a strange twist. The issue becomes, in his view, not the woman's deception exactly, but her insubordination. Thus Moo proposes that "Eve was deceived . . . in tak-

---

women. Because of their propensity for deception, women are less fit than men to give spiritual instruction and leadership. But this reasoning assumes that it is worse to have a leader or teacher who can be seduced to sin (like Eve) than to have one who sins willfully with his eyes wide open (like Adam)" (ibid, p. 222).

[33]Gilbert Bilezikian puts it this way, "Eve was . . . the late-comer on the scene. Of the two, she was the one bereft of the firsthand experience of God's giving the prohibition relative to the tree. She should have deferred the matter to Adam, who was better prepared to deal with it since he had received the command directly from God" (Gilbert Bilezikian, *Beyond Sex Roles* [Grand Rapids, Mich.: Baker, 1985], p. 180).

[34]Bilezikian thus concludes, "At the core of Paul's strategy was the elimination of all unqualified or deviant would-be teachers. . . . Thus neither women nor all men could teach in Ephesus, but only a group of trained and carefully selected individuals. The restrictions placed on women applied also to most male members of the Ephesian church in the spirit of James 3:1, 'Let not many of you become teachers, my brethren'" (ibid., pp. 182-83; cf. Atkins, *Split Image*, pp. 104-7; C. S. Cowles, *A Woman's Place* [Kansas City: Beacon Hill, 1993], pp. 135-47; Groothuis, *Good News for Women*, p. 214).

[35]Schreiner says, "It seems that clarity is in the eye of the beholder, for the thrust of the verse [verse 13] has been deemed quite clear in the history of the church" (Schreiner, "A Dialogue with Scholarship," p. 136).

[36]Schreiner, "A Dialogue with Scholarship," p. 141.

ing the initiative over the man." . . . James Hurley also tries to avoid an interpretation of verse 14 that says women in general are more prone to deception.[37]

So there we have it: both sides of the debate championing one verse more than the other.[38] That in itself convinces me again that this debate, underneath the surface, is not about 1 Timothy 2.[39]

1 TIMOTHY 2:15

Perhaps the most significant point of agreement between both sides of the debate has to do with 1 Timothy 2:15. Most of us think it's best to understand 1 Timothy 2:15 as Paul's response to a specific heretical teaching.[40] Both sides of the debate increasingly agree that 1 Timothy 2:15 is not only "difficult"[41] but also quite indicative of the content of the heresies being taught in the church of Ephesus. Schreiner acknowledges this openly when he says, "Many scholars have rightly seen that the reference to childbirth was precipitated by the impact of the false teachers."[42] More specifically, he says, "The false teachers . . . prohibited marriage and certain foods (1 Tim 4:1-5). If marriage was banned, then bearing children was probably also criticized."[43]

---

[37]Groothuis, *Good News for Women*, p. 223.

[38]I am speaking in broad terms, knowing full well there are exceptions. Still, the point remains that 1 Timothy 2 is an unclear passage that doesn't make sense if we read it in a straightforward way. Moreover, I am saying that both sides of the debate are handling the passage in similar ways (i.e., they're practicing selective literalism) though reaching dissimilar conclusions.

[39]Harold O. J. Brown says something similar: "In the final analysis, the issue is larger than the analysis of ancient culture, word studies, Greek syntax, exegesis, and hermeneutics" (Brown, "The New Testament Against Itself," p.198).

[40]Schreiner, for instance, says, "Childbearing was selected by Paul, then, as a *specific response* to the shafts from the false teachers" (Schreiner, "A Dialogue with Scholarship," p. 150).

[41]For instance, Moo says, "We must say something about the notoriously difficult verse 15" (Moo, "What Does It Mean Not to Teach or Have Authority Over Men?" p. 192). Scholer uses the same words, "notoriously difficult," to describe verse 15 (Scholer, "1 Timothy 2:9-15 and the Place of Women in the Church's Ministry," p. 195). Susan Foh is not quite as willing to wrestle with the verse. Instead, she says verse 15 "is a puzzle and a sort of non-sequitur" (Susan Foh, *Women and the Word of God* ([Phillipsburg, N.J.: P & R, 1979], p. 128).

[42]See Schreiner, "A Dialogue with Scholarship," p. 150. Schreiner's list of "many scholars" includes complementarians and egalitarians: Barron, Fee, Gritz, Harris, Jeremias, Kelly, Kimberly, van der Jagt, the Kroegers, Moo, Padgett and Scholer.

[43]Ibid.

Granted, the two sides of the debate generally disagree on exactly what the heresy was,[44] but that is relatively insignificant. The critical point is that it doesn't make sense to say that verse 15 *must* be alluding to a local heresy and that verses 13-14 *can't* be alluding to a local heresy. Thus I am not persuaded by any argument that says 1 Timothy 2:15 alone is situational while 1 Timothy 2:11-14 are universal.

- Both sides generally agree that 1 Timothy 2:8-10 alludes to a local situation. (It's absurd to conclude that men, not women, must pray with lifted hands, and that women, not men, are prohibited from wearing gold, pearls, and braids.)
- Both sides generally agree that 1 Timothy 2:15 alludes to a local situation (i.e., to a local heresy).
- It is likely, therefore, that the verses sandwiched in between, namely 1 Timothy 2:11-14, also allude to a local situation, especially since both sides agree that all four verses, as traditionally understood, give rise to a number of difficulties.
- The question, then, is this: Was there any known heresy in first-century Ephesus? If so, then the conclusions of this summary are confirmed.

Figure 20.1. Summary of the current debate regarding 1 Timothy 2

THE SIGNIFICANCE OF ADAM BEING CREATED FIRST

For me, things started to add up when I combined my learning from Trinity with my observations of the current debate. In other words, once I begin to see that the biblical text of 1 Timothy 2 gives us hints about the historical situation—and that both sides of the debate generally agree that verse 15 refutes a very specific heresy—then it hit me as being probable that verses 8-14 might also have been written as refutes to certain heresies being promoted by the false teachers in Ephesus.[45] That explains why, in my study of 1 Tim-

---

[44]For instance, Craig Keener suggests that "the most natural way for an ancient reader to have understood 'salvation' in the context of childbirth would have been a safe delivery." According to Keener's research, pregnant women commonly prayed to a variety of deities for safekeeping of the delivery of newborns. Keener also says that Jewish tradition taught that particularly sinful women could die during childbirth as a consequence of the curse in Genesis 3:15. See Craig Keener, *Paul, Women and Wives* (Peabody, Mass.: Hendrickson, 1993), pp. 119-20.

By contrast, Moo says, "Probably Paul makes this point because the false teachers were claiming the women could *really* experience what God had for them only if they abandoned the home and became actively involved in teaching and leadership roles in the church" (Moo, "What Does It Mean Not to Teach or Have Authority over Men?" p. 192).

[45]Paul's concern to correct the false teaching is evident throughout 1 and 2 Timothy, especially in 1 Timothy 1:18-20; 4:1-8; 5:16; 6:3-10; and 2 Timothy 2:16-18; 3:1-9; 4:3-4, 14-15.

othy 2, I kept asking God, "Why is Paul so careful to remind Timothy that Adam was created first? And that Adam was not deceived?"

And then it dawned on me. Paul was emphatic about Adam and Eve because the false teachers in Ephesus were misleading people to follow Satan instead of Christ (1 Tim 5:15). In other words, the false teachers were lying to the people. They were stirring up the men, so that the men were more angry than prayerful (1 Tim 2:8). They were tempting the women, so that women were adorning themselves in provocative clothing rather than in good works (1 Tim 2:9-10). Moreover, they were allowing the women to be loud and argumentative whenever they sat to learn the false teaching (1 Tim 2:11).[46] Furthermore, they were raising up women false teachers to domineer over men in order to promote the heresy even further (1 Tim 2:12). To top things off, they were scaring the women by telling them they would die if they ever (again) tried to have children (1 Tim 2:15).

Perhaps the most insidious thing is that the false teachers, like Satan,[47] were twisting the Scriptures, lying to the people by saying that Eve was created first and that Eve was not deceived. This was their way of luring people toward Satan, not Christ.

In a flash, this all made sense to me as I remembered that in Romans 5:14-15, Paul compares the "transgression" of Adam with the "free gift" of Jesus Christ. He says further in Romans 5:17, "For if by the transgression of the one [Adam], death reigned through the one, much more those who receive the abundance of grace . . . through the One, Jesus Christ."

Similarly, Paul says in 1 Corinthians 15:22, "For as in Adam all die, so also in Christ all shall be made alive." In that same passage, Paul goes so far as to say that Jesus is "the last Adam" (1 Cor 15:45). He does not call Jesus "the last Eve."

This textual distinction makes all the difference in the world. What it indicates is the radical importance of setting the facts straight in the creation

---

[46]Paul, by contrast, wanted the women to be quiet and submissive when learning the true gospel (1 Tim 2:11).

[47]See Matthew 4:1-11, where Satan uses Scripture to tempt Jesus.

narrative. It is heresy to proclaim that Eve was created first. It is heresy because Christ is not "the last Eve."

The first man on earth was a man, not a woman. If we say the first person
was a woman, we lose the parallel between "the first man," who is "earthy,"
and the "second man," Jesus Christ, who is "from heaven" (1 Cor 15:46-47).
In other words, we lose a major indicator that Jesus is the Messiah. Paul's big
concern was for everyone to know that the Savior of the world is not a woman. The Savior of the world is a man.

Radical feminists in the United States stand in line at conferences to emulate Eve in partaking of the apple in the garden. They eat it symbolically as
a means of "enlightenment" to true knowledge. They see Eve as the first created and Eve as the giver of life. To them, Eve is a heroine who took the initiative to bring enlightenment to the world by partaking of the tree of
knowledge of good and evil. Worse than that, they enshrine Eve as a mediator.

It is not coincidental that only a few verses before Paul gives his reminder
of the creation narrative, he tells Timothy there is "one mediator," Jesus
Christ. Paul clarified the means of salvation in 1 Timothy 2 because the people there in Ephesus needed him to. The crisis of false teaching had overshad-
owed the fact that Adam foreshadows the Christ.

In Ephesus, where there was a crisis of false teaching, Paul laid out the
facts of the gospel. He wanted everyone to know that the first person God
created was a man—because Adam foreshadows the man Jesus Christ.

As Adam is the firstborn in the flesh, so Christ is "firstborn among many
brethren" (Rom 8:29). Jesus is the firstborn of all God's children in heaven.
If we ever forget that Adam was created first, then we become candidates to
stand in line with the radical feminists who worship a goddess and promote
the ancient heresy that Eve was firstborn and that Eve was enlightened, not
deceived.

It's not a huge surprise that in first-century Ephesus, the Ephesians were
worshiping a goddess. I didn't learn that from sources outside of the Bible.
Luke makes it clear in Acts 19:24-35. Remember the story? Paul had sent
Timothy and Erastus into Macedonia while he stayed in Asia. That's when

the riot began. A certain silversmith, Demetrius, who made silver shrines of Artemis, gathered all the craftsmen who were making a lot of money from their trade. Persuasively he convinced them that Paul was a threat to them financially. He said:

> Men, you know that our prosperity depends upon this business. You see and hear that not only in Ephesus, but in almost all of Asia, this Paul has persuaded and turned away a considerable number of people, saying that gods made with hands are no gods at all. And not only is there danger that this trade of ours fall into disrepute, but also that the temple of Artemis be regarded as worthless and that she whom all of Asia and the world worship will even be dethroned from her magnificence.

Luke reports that when they heard this, they were "filled with rage." That's when they began to cry, "Great is Artemis of the Ephesians!" (Acts 19:28).

I have a hunch that Paul's prohibition of "a woman" in Ephesus had something to do with his mission to the Gentiles in light of the goddess worship in town. For it is significant that in this particular historical context Paul deemed it relevant to remind Timothy that Adam was created first and that Adam was not deceived. My best guess is that Paul was trying to help Timothy clearly show the people that God is not a goddess and Artemis is not the Messiah.

First Timothy 2 makes a lot more sense when we see it this way, especially with regard to verse 15. Paul wanted Timothy to be firmly assured of the truth. Mothers can be saved, but only if they "continue in faith and love and sanctity with self-restraint." In other words, mothers can be saved, but only in accordance with the same ol' gospel that Paul had preached before.

DISCUSSION QUESTIONS

1. What do you think *authentein* means?

2. Read the whole book of I Timothy. What do you think is the most important thing that Paul wanted Timothy to convey to the church in the Ephesus?

3. What do you think the current debate is really about? First Timothy 2 or something else?

4. What aspect of this chapter was most helpful to you? Which scholar up to this point best represents your point of view? Review the footnotes, if necessary.

BUILDING

CONSENSUS

ON CHRISTIAN

LEADERSHIP

21

THE FAULT LINE

The Trinity is a mystery and must remain a mystery.
HAROLD O. J. BROWN, *HERESIES*

The heart of this debate pertains overall to the fundamental mystery of what it means to be a man or a woman. We know that women have babies and men do not. But other than that, the differences between men and women are not entirely clear. We also know that men and women have human bodies, human nature and human dignity. But other than that, our similarities are not entirely clear. Researchers in gender studies cannot solve the riddle of male and female; they can only uncover more mystery.[1] I believe this mystery is one of several mysteries of God.[2]

---

[1]See Anne Balsamo, *Technologies of the Gendered Body* (Durham, N.C.: Duke University Press, 1997.)

[2]Although John Piper finds it "stunning" and "a great sadness" to read that the late Paul Jewett (a biblical feminist) "does not know what manhood and womanhood are," he does not seem to bemoan Elisabeth Elliot's humble admission that "sexuality is a mystery." Quoting C. S. Lewis, Elliot says, "When we deal with masculinity and femininity we are dealing with the 'live and awful shadows of realities utterly beyond our control and largely beyond our direct knowledge' " (Elisabeth Elliot, "The Essence of Femininity: A Personal Perspective," in *Recovering Biblical Manhood and Womanhood*, ed. John Piper and Wayne Grudem [Wheaton, Ill.: Crossway, 1991], p. 397; see also John Piper, "A Vision of Biblical Complementarity: Manhood and Womanhood Defined According to the Bible," in *Recovering Biblical Manhood and Womanhood*, ed. John Piper and Wayne Grudem [Wheaton, Ill.: Crossway, 1991], p. 34).

My best way of describing these mysteries is to plot them on an imaginary fault line. Fault lines are dangerous. In geology, a fault line is a fracture in the crust of the earth along which earthquakes tend to happen. Fault lines demarcate where the earth's crust is broken and liable to rupture again. In southern California where my husband and I live, this phenomenon is more real than imaginary. Because we live on the San Andreas fault line, sometimes we experience earthquakes.

To put it analogously, the church sometimes experiences earthquakes with regard to various debates on Christian doctrine. In other words, there seems to be a fault line in theology, if you will, where breaches in the church tend to form. The fault line in theology reaches all the way up into heaven and all the way down into hell. Every major argument in the history of the church tends to erupt along this fault line. As table 21.1 shows, disunity results when Christians dissect the truth, falsely dividing it into two opposing parts, then favor one side of the truth over the other.

Church battles, then, are notoriously fought over questions about the nature of God (Is he one or three?), the nature of Christ (Is he divine or human?), the nature of humans (Are we predestined or free?), the nature of Christians (Are we saints or sinners?), the nature of Scripture (Is it flawed by the human authors or does divine inspiration make it inerrant?), the nature of the sacraments (Are the elements symbolic or real?), and also the nature of hell (Is it a place of final death or conscious suffering?).

Let's start with the nature of God. Is God one or three? In the earliest days of Christianity, this was not an easy question to answer. As many people know, the word *Trinity* is not a biblical word. The doctrine of the Trinity is a biblical concept, but the word can be found nowhere in Scripture. The apostle Paul probably never even heard of the doctrine of the Trinity. Paul apprehended God as Father and Son and Spirit, but he didn't speak of God in the same language that we do because he predated the time of the ecumenical councils when the doctrine of the Trinity was established. Nevertheless, Christians today believe in this doctrine so firmly that we use it as a litmus test to identify believers in the faith. As I tell my students, "You can't teach at Moody Bible Institute unless you sign a faith statement that says you're a believer in the Trinity."

Table 21.1   Fault lines in Christian theology

God	
One	Three
Christ	
Divine	Human
Humans	
Predestined	Responsible and free
Christians	
Saints	Sinners
Scripture	
Divinely inspired	Written by fallible human authors
Sacraments	
Physical/real	Spiritual/symbolic
Hell	
Conscious	Death

Occasionally in the classroom I will ask the trick question, "How many people in here understand the Trinity?" If any hands go up, I give a speech about the difference between accepting the doctrine of the Trinity and understanding the Trinity.[3] There's no way for a finite mind to comprehend infinite God; it's logically impossible to do. But we can still know God

---

[3]Harold O. J. Brown, offers the following insight: "Although it was necessary for Christianity to *formulate* the doctrine of the Trinity in order to come to grips with its convictions . . . it has proved impossible for Christians actually to *understand* the doctrine or to explain it in any comprehensive way. The doctrine of the Trinity speaks of the inner nature of the transcendent God, a matter that certainly surpasses our human ability to understand and that must be respected as a divine mystery" (Harold O. J. Brown, *Heresies* [New York: Doubleday, 1984], p. 128).

personally. We can know him because he reveals himself to us so personally.
Something similar can be said about Scripture. There is no way for our minds
to fully ascertain all the wisdom of the Bible. We can learn from Scripture
but not control it. I like the way one professor puts it, "The Bible is an un-
ruly book which, if we take it seriously, refuses to be locked up in any systematic cage."[4]

Who can understand the truths of the Christian faith? I can't. I believe
that God is three persons in one, but I don't understand how. I believe that
Christ is 100 percent human and 100 percent divine, but I don't understand
how. I believe that Scripture is 100 percent inspired by God and 100 percent
written by humans, but I don't understand how. We can ask undisciplined
questions (such as, Why can't God keep it simple?), but they won't do us
much good. For God will not cater to our human discontent. We can hope
for pat answers, but the Scriptures don't dispense them. We can press for simple truths, but the Bible offers paradox instead.[5]

There's a difference between a paradox and a contradiction. A paradox is an
apparent contradiction. It is not contradictory at the core. A contradiction, by
contrast, *is* truly contradictory. Contradictions are internally illogical. Para-
doxes, however, are logical. It is logical though incomprehensible to say that
God is three and one. It is illogical, by contrast, to say that God is three and
not-three. Three and not-three are mutually exclusive counterclaims. Either he
is three, or he is not-three. He can't be both. But he can be three *in* one.[6]

I have no idea how someone utterly dead in hell can consciously suffer for
eternity.[7] But then again, I have no idea how God can be three in one. The

[4]Josef Blank, "According to the Scriptures: The New Testament Origins and Structure of the Theological
Hermeneutics" in *Paradigm Change in Theology*, ed. Hans Küng and David Tracy (New York: Crossroad,
1991), p. 261.

[5]Robert Mulholland expresses similar thoughts in *Invitation to a Journey* (Downers Grove, Ill.: InterVarsity
Press, 1993), p. 148.

[6]Carl F. H. Henry explains it in mathematical terms: "the formula $3x = 1x$ does *not* describe the living
God. But 3x in 1y does." As Henry further explains, "Such a formula is both intelligible and noncon-
tradictory" (Carl F. H. Henry, *God, Revelation and Authority* [Waco, Tex.: Word, 1982], 5:165).

[7]There are two reasons why I don't see this as contradictory: because it's biblical and because no one really
knows what death is.

mystery of hell is just as baffling to me as the mystery of the Trinity in heaven. Indeed, the mystery of hell is acceptable to me precisely because it reminds me of the mystery of the Trinity. As a matter of fact, the mystery of hell reminds me of every Christian doctrine I know. The same sense of wonder overtakes me whenever I ponder the nature of God, the nature of Christ or the nature of Scripture.[8] To paraphrase G. K. Chesterton, when a finite mind tries to comprehend an infinite God, that finite mind is doomed to split.[9]

The Bible reveals that God is one *and* three. He is both. That's the mystery. Likewise, the Bible reveals that Christ is human and divine. He is both. That's the mystery. Both truths must be embraced. Both truths must be held in tension.[10] For the moment we attempt to demystify the mysteries, orthodoxy is lost.

MEN AND WOMEN ON THE FAULT LINE

Men and women, likewise, are paradoxical mysteries that cannot be defined. Defining a woman is no more possible than defining a man or defining the Spirit of God. God is not a definition. Neither is any person. People can describe someone; we can know someone. But we cannot define someone as if a person could be reduced to a definition. No mystery of truth can succinctly be defined. That's what makes it a mystery. Of course church tradition promoted the idea that men are superior and women are inferior, but that is not mysterious. As a matter of fact, that's what Muslims believe. It's in the Qur'an—the same book that openly denies that Jesus Christ the human is also fully divine.[11]

The beauty of the fault line is that it has a way of forewarning us about

---

[8]By this, I do not mean to insinuate that the doctrines of the faith convey no rational information about objective realities (contra neo-orthodoxy or dialectical theology). In fact, I believe it's reasonable to believe that God's wisdom surpasses human reason without negating it.
[9]See G. K. Chesterton, *Orthodoxy* (Allen, Tex.: Thomas More, 1985). This book stands among my top five favorite books of all time.
[10]For to separate the truths, one from the other, is to tear apart the mystery, converting it into something that reason alone can comprehend.
[11]"Men are superior to women" (2:228; 4:34).

where more debates are likely to ensue. Every generation will argue over something that appears along the fault line. In our day, one hot issue is the debate on men and women in the church. At varying levels, both sides of the contemporary debate are promoting women's equality. Both sides are also saying that men and women are distinct. But the words *equal* and *distinct* mean two different things to the two sides.

Complementarians are fond of the phrase "equal but distinct." For them that means women are not inferior, although they are required to be restricted. Egalitarians would probably rather have it said that men and women are "distinct but equal." In their view, women and men ought to function as equals despite their bodily differences. What I'm saying is that if all of us could agree that men and women are "equal *and* distinct," then perhaps we could reach a broad consensus.[12]

Unfortunately many of us tend to overemphasize one side of the fault line at the expense of the other. Egalitarians tend to overemphasize the equality of men and women and underemphasize their distinction. Conversely complementarians tend to overemphasize the distinction between men and women and underemphasize their equality. As a result, the biblical paradox is lost.

In reality men and women are always both equal and distinct. Both truths on the fault line must be kept intact (see table 21.2). Isn't that intriguing? How much less intriguing would it be if men and women were anything less than both?

Table 21.2. The men-women fault line

Men		Women	
Equal to women	Distinct from women	Equal to men	Distinct from men

---

[12]Hildegard of Bingen tried to do this in the twelfth century through different language and categories than the ones I am presenting. See Sister Prudence Allen, *The Concept of Woman: The Aristotelian Revolution 750 B.C.–A.D. 1250* (Grand Rapids, Mich.: Eerdmans, 1985), pp. 292-315.

God would be less mysterious if he were one and not three, or three and not one. Christ would be less mysterious if he were human and not divine, or divine and not human. To deny either side of the theological mystery is to deny the revelation of biblical truth. Heresies reflect this mistake. It is an age-old heresy to say that God is three and not one. It is an age-old heresy to say that Christ is divine, not human. It is an age-old heresy to say the Bible is human and not divinely inspired (see table 21.3).

Table 21.3

God	Christ	Scripture
Three	Divine	Human
Not One	Not Human	Not Divine

I'll say the same thing another way. To deny either side of the fault line is to attempt to demystify the mystery.

People are prone to do just that. We don't like having a fault line slicing through our beliefs.[13] We are threatened by the fact that life is mysterious and ultimately beyond our control. We want life to be tidy. It's hard to embrace the built-in balance of paradoxical truth. It offends our desire for control. It becomes even harder, I have noticed, to embrace the untamed truth when other people around us are protecting only one side of the line.

For instance, when egalitarians de-emphasize the differences between women and men, it becomes more difficult for complementarians to be willing to proclaim the similarities that men and women share. Typically complementarians react to the biblical feminists by stressing gender distinction instead. Very few complementarians acknowledge gender differences in the context of gender similarities. The opposite is true for egalitarians. Hardly an egalitarian will openly admit the differences between men and women.

When evangelical feminists contend for absolute equality between men

---

[13]Brown says, "Even when people admit [for example], that the doctrine of the Trinity is a mystery and must remain a mystery, they are tempted to try to explain it" (Brown, *Heresies*, p. 128).

and women, they radically reduce the mystery of the nature of men and women to something that is manageable and flat. In effect, they say that women, as full equals of men, have the God-given right to function just the same as men who are similarly gifted (see table 21.4).

Table 21.4

Women

Equal to men

Not distinct from men who are similarly gifted

Likewise, when complementarians extol Christian men as the leaders of women, they effectively do the same thing. They demystify the mystery. They say that men are designed for supervisory roles precisely because men are distinct from women (see table 21.5).

Table 21.5

Men

Distinct from women

Not equal, except before God

If, however, we accept the mystery of the nature of men and women *as a mystery*, then we can boldly say that the equality of men and women is necessarily interrelated to the distinctiveness of the two. As with all the other mysteries on the fault line, both sides of the line must be held harmoniously in tension.

DISCUSSION QUESTIONS

1. Summarize your understanding of the fault line in theology.

2. What is the difference between a paradox and a contradiction?

3. What is your view of "equal *and* distinct"?

4. Name one truth about men and women in the church that is hard for you to admit.

22
THOMISTS AND SCOTISTS

I solemnly charge you in the presence of God and of Christ Jesus and of His chosen angels, to maintain these principles without bias, doing nothing with a spirit of partiality.

1 TIMOTHY 5:21

The contemporary debate on men and women in the church might seem to amount to an argument over semantics. But the argument runs deeper than that. Beneath the surface, Christians are grappling with an underlying issue of order. Evangelicals, in particular, are asking the practical question How should Christian families and local church communities appropriately be organized and ordered? In other words, we're having a major dispute about who is eligible to do what. Some of us are saying that men but not women are eligible to do anything (the view of the complementarians). Others of us are saying that eligibility should be more open (the view of the egalitarians). To put it another way, we're asking, Should there be a policy in the Christian community that says men only can lead?

As you already know, the rhetoric of the debate can sometimes be confusing. To me, it's reflective of the difficult dynamics of communicating in marriage. In our first two years of marriage, my husband and I often failed to communicate effectively. Sometimes we would argue for hours, only to find out later that we hadn't even identified our real conflict. Complementarians and egalitarians seem to do the same thing. They talk past one another. I don't say this as a mere bystander who has followed the debate from a distance. I say it as one who has lived simultaneously in both theological worlds. For almost nine years I served as a member of Willow Creek Community Church, a Chicagoland megachurch led by egalitarian leaders. For six of those same years, I submitted to the authority of my professors at Trinity Evangelical Divinity School, a Chicagoland seminary led by complementarian leaders. Within this double context, I began to notice that complementarians and egalitarians often fail to speak in a way that shows the other side was heard.

The issue, as I see it, comes back to the notion of exactly what is meant by the terms *equality* and *distinction.* For egalitarians, the concepts of equality and distinction mean that women and men are equal as persons but distinct with regard to sexuality. It means, moreover, that roles should not be defined by gender unless the activities of the role are sexual, such as with a husband or wife. When the nature of the role is nonsexual, such as with a pastor or preacher, then roles should be defined by giftedness rather than gender.[1] As egalitarian Rebecca Merrill Groothuis explains it, "Evangelical egalitarians affirm all types of equality between women and men *except* the equality of identity or sameness. . . . Obviously, male and female are not identical, nor are male and female sexual roles interchangeable."[2]

For complementarians, the concepts of equality and distinction mean that men and women are equal before God as persons but distinct with regard to roles. It means, moreover, that proper roles for men and women are defined by gender distinctions, even though the tasks do not involve sexuality.

In spite of this particular disagreement, I believe it is possible for evangelicals to reach a broad consensus about men and women in the church.

THOMISTS AND SCOTISTS

I don't claim to see every aspect of this debate in perfect detail. But I can name

---

[1]See Rebecca Merrill Groothuis, *Good News for Women* (Grand Rapids, Mich.: Baker, 1997), pp. 48-49.
[2]Ibid., p. 48.

one reason for the gridlock that results when complementarians and egalitarians try to talk about church order. Their philosophy of order is not the same. Generally speaking, complementarians are Scotists[3] and egalitarians are Thomists.[4] Understanding the difference between these two philosophies of order is vital to interpreting the debate. Daniel Doriani explains it well:

> To speak in archetypes, there are Thomist and Scotist views of order. The Thomist says God's order must and does have a reason, and readily propounds natural and theological reasons why women may not teach and exercise authority in the church. The Scotist says we know God's will, but cannot explain it, for God orders the world as he wills, whether with, against, or beyond reason. The Thomist expects and examines a coherence between natural law and divine law; the Scotist does not.[5]

That means that while Thomists insist that God's commands and God's creation correlate directly with one another, Scotists believe that God's commands need to correlate with nothing but God's will.

Here's how the views play out. Egalitarians, being Thomists, assume it is obvious that God's plan for women accords with nature and reason. Complementarians, being Scotists, don't see that as necessary. By contrast, they assume that it is obvious that God's plan for women doesn't have to be connected to anything else in God's design. Consequently, what is obvious to one side is not obvious to other for the simple reason that they enter the debate presupposing two different things. That's why neither side tends to be persuaded by the other.

Neither complementarians nor egalitarians debate with these categories in

---

[3]The word *Scotist* derives from the name of Duns Scotus [A.D. 1266-1308], a theologian who was not a Scotist. As Doriani points out, Scotus himself was a Thomist. When Scotus made his case against women's ordination, he gave two reasons why: because Jesus did not ordain his mother and because women should suffer the punishment of the Fall by never enjoying eminence or authority. See Daniel Doriani, "Appendix I: A History of the Interpretation of I Timothy 2," in *Women in the Church*, ed. Andreas Köstenberger, Thomas R. Schreiner and H. Scott Baldwin (Grand Rapids, Mich.: Baker, 1995), pp. 232-33.

[4]The Thomist view is named after Thomas Aquinas (1225-1274).

[5]See Doriani, "Appendix I," p. 218.

mind. And yet, as far as I can tell, both sides project their view on the other. In other words, they assume that their thinking is the same as the other side's, even though it's not. Again, it's analogous to my marriage. When communicating with Jim, I assume that both of us are communicating in terms of generalities, because that's what I tend to do. But he assumes we are talking in specifics, because that's what he tends to do. We have thus developed a pattern. When I talk to him in terms of the big picture, he listens in terms of detail. When he talks to me in terms of detail, I listen in terms of the big picture.

Early in our marriage, neither of us realized this. We were not aware that I was thinking in terms of generalities and Jim wasn't. Instead, I thought he was stubbornly refusing to hear my overall point, and he thought I was deliberating evading the real issues. By analogy, it appears that Rebecca Merrill Groothuis perceives Wayne Grudem to be evading her overall point rather than addressing it openly. From Grudem's point of view, Groothuis is the one being evasive.

From my point of view, it is evident that the two are engaged in a miscommunication. Listen and see if you agree.

TWO DIFFERENT PHILOSOPHIES OF ORDER

Philosophically speaking, the Scotist doesn't need an explanation. God's will is all the Scotist needs to know. Hence any time a Thomist demands a rational explanation from a Scotist, it will surely lead to futility. Practically that's what happens when Groothuis takes Grudem to task with a Thomist line of argumentation. Though her argument is logical and carefully worked out, she fails to address Grudem's Scotist mind.

According to Groothuis, it is irresponsible to disregard the logical implications of the complementarian tenet of "equal worth and unequal rank." As a Thomist, she is compelled to emphasize "the ethical, social, and theological" implications of being equal as persons before God.[6] Though she believes in the authority of Scripture and the sovereignty of God's will just as much

---

[6]Groothuis, *Good News for Women*, p. 46.

as Grudem does, momentarily she turns to political philosophy in order to explain her case more rationally and fully. Specifically she says:

> According to the classical liberal thought of the eighteenth and nineteenth centuries, the equality of the individual entails equal rights under the law. In a society of equals in this sense, there is no legal basis for granting or denying social status on the basis of race, class, or gender. Everyone has equal opportunity to earn—by virtue of one's individual qualifications—equality of status with any individual of any social group, whereby the standard of achievement is the same for each member of each social group. This clearly is not the sort of equality traditionalists are thinking of when they insist that they value women equally. In reserving leadership positions for men, traditionalists deny women the opportunity to demonstrate their equality of ability and maturity, and thereby to earn equality of status and social value.[7]

To that she adds, "The classical feminism of the nineteenth century applied the principle of equality under the law to women, as well as to men."[8]

No wonder complementarians don't internalize her protest. By arguing on the basis of classical liberal thought instead of arguing exclusively with Scripture, Groothuis fails to engage the Scotist mind. She assumes that sensible Christians will automatically see the reasonableness of her point. But that is precisely her mistake.

Because Groothuis is a Thomist, she continually insists it's illogical to assume that God wills for women to be subordinate to men. It's illogical to her because God is the one who has anointed certain women to serve as gifted leaders.[9] Thus in Groothuis's mind it is a given that women and men "stand on equal ground before God." Moreover, she counts it as an "obvious fact" that creation reveals an overall equality between men and women in that both bear the image of God. Hence Groothuis contends that the divine perspective of men and women ought to be the human one as well.

With that, she protests Grudem's statement, "We must never think that

---

[7]Ibid.
[8]Ibid.
[9]Ibid., p. 43.

there are second-class citizens in the church."[10] She finds his case unconvincing, even when he says, "Whether someone is a man or woman, employer or employee . . . strong or weak, attractive or unattractive, extremely intelligent or slow to learn, all are equally valuable to God and should be equally valuable to one another as well."[11]

In Groothuis's mind, the question at stake in the debate "does not pertain merely to how God views people."[12] She agrees that "God values everyone equally" and affirms that "this is a wonderful truth that we should never forget."[13] But to her the central issue is how people view each other, and in this case, how people in the church view women.

When Grudem declares that people "should be equally valuable to one another as well," it sounds to Groothuis as though Grudem is saying that women should be equally valued, even though they aren't men's equals. Groothuis strongly protests against any theology that says men have exclusive access to higher rank in leadership "solely on the basis of their gender."[14]

If complementarians were saying that men have exclusive access to higher status leadership "solely on the basis of their gender," they would gladly concede that Groothuis is right. But that is not what are they are saying. Complementarians are touting no claim to gender superiority. On the contrary, they are trying to be submissive to God. From their perspective, they are submitting to the mandate of Scripture. It is not men's gender per se that leads them to believe that men should take the roles with higher status. It is the Bible, as they understand it, that inclines them to believe that men in the Christian community are exclusively entitled to the higher rank and role of executive leadership.

Complementarians such as John Piper and Grudem have tried to assure the egalitarians and the rest of the church that they do not believe women are

---

[10]Wayne Grudem, *Systematic Theology* (Grand Rapids, Mich.: Zondervan, 1994), p. 459.
[11]Ibid.
[12]Groothuis, *Good News for Women*, p. 46.
[13]Ibid.
[14]Ibid.

inferior to men.[15] They reiterate that men are not superior to women. As they see it, God is the one who authored the commandment for men to bear the primary responsibility for the family and church.[16] Why God did this is irrelevant. From a Scotist point of view, the only thing that matters is whether or not Scripture says it's true. Thus if it is truly scriptural that God wills for men, not women, to serve as spiritual leaders, no other reason is needed.

COMPARING THE ARGUMENTS

Let's compare the arguments. According to Groothuis, women are not second-class citizens in the church, but they are treated as second-class citizens in the church. According to Grudem, women are not second-class citizens in the church. (Notice what Grudem does not say.) For Grudem, it suffices to proclaim the theological truth—that women are not second-class citizens—irrespective of the historical truth of how women in the church are treated.

Do you see the gap? Grudem and Groothuis don't seem to be able to hear each other, though in one sense they agree. Both believe, theologically speaking, that women are not second-class in the church. Nevertheless they struggle to stand on common ground because Groothuis doesn't share Grudem's distaste for classical feminist thought and because Grudem doesn't share Groothuis's complaint about the church's disrespect for Christian women.

Groothuis contends that women will never be seen as first-class citizens until the women leaders who God has gifted and called are officially secured in executive leadership functions.[17] Groothuis does not want women to be given priority status simply because they are women. Rather, she wants Christian women to be given the same opportunity as Christian men to as-

---

[15]John Piper clearly states, "Mature masculinity does not presume superiority" (Piper, *Recovering Biblical Manhood and Womanhood*, p. 10).

[16]As Ray Ortlund Jr. puts it, "In the partnership of two spiritually equal human beings, man and woman, the man bears the primary responsibility to lead the partnership in a God-glorifying direction" (Ray Ortlund Jr., "Male-Female Equality and Male Headship: Genesis 1—3," in *Recovering Biblical Manhood and Womanhood*, ed. John Piper and Wayne Grudem [Wheaton, Ill.: Crossway, 1991], p. 95).

[17]One woman I met said the dictum of "equal but lower" is as illogical and unjust as the "separate but equal" Jim Crow laws that were contrived for African Americans in Birmingham, Alabama.

cend to "higher levels" of church leadership.[18]

Grudem disagrees. He says it's unnecessary for women to be eligible to be pastors in order to be first-class citizens in the kingdom. Grudem believes that true equality for women can be fully experienced within the context of female subordination. He believes true equality for women in the church precludes equal opportunity.

So now we have come full circle—back to the concept of equality. What is equality? For Groothuis, equality means equal opportunity and equal rights. For Grudem, equality means equal worth before God. Whereas Groothuis's view of equality obligates people to treat one another as full equals, Grudem's view of equality obligates no one but God.

Which view is correct? Shall we side with the egalitarians in the name of classical feminist thought? Or shall we side with the complementarians and never get around to the uncomfortable subject of how women in the church are treated?

In the preface of their book, Piper and Grudem sidestep the question of how women ought to be treated. Jointly they say:

> We hope that thousands of Christian women who read this book will come away feeling affirmed and encouraged to participate much more actively in many ministries, and to contribute their wisdom and insight to the family and the church. . . . Similarly, we desire that every Christian man who reads this book will come away feeling in his heart that women are indeed *fully equal* to men in personhood, in importance, and in status before God.[19]

Look closely at the quote. With italicized emphasis, they say women are "fully equal to men in personhood, in importance, and in status." But in the next phrase Piper and Grudem qualify women's status as "fully equal . . . before God." [20] They affirm the status of women in the presence of the Lord

---

[18]Notice that Groothuis affirms hierarchical leadership structures in church.

[19]Piper and Grudem, preface, *Recovering Biblical Manhood and Womanhood*, p. xiv.

[20]This same qualifying phrase "before God" appears in the 1998 amendment to the *Baptist Faith and Message* of the Southern Baptist Convention. The statement reads, "The husband and wife are of equal worth *before God*, since both are created in God's image" (emphasis added).

but not in the presence of God's people. It sounds pleasant for every Christian man to feel "in his heart" that God sees Christian women as men's equals. But it doesn't strike me as being challenging. It's easy to give assent to God's impartiality toward women. The biblical teaching is much harder. The Bible makes it plain that every believer is expected to become impartial too (1 Tim 5:21).

If I rightly understand Groothuis, her point is to say that women have no problem being recognized as equals by God. "It misses the point,"[21] she says, when complementarians assure women of their value "before God."[22] Complementarians, however, don't hear Groothuis because part of her appeal is to feminist thought. If I rightly understand Grudem, his point is that Christians are not obligated to align our beliefs with classical feminist thought.

So which of the two is right?

I believe they both have something right to say. Groothuis correctly insists that women should be equal before Christians, not just equal before God. And yet, Grudem correctly maintains that if Scripture reveals that God prohibits women from being pastors or preachers, then classical feminist thought is irrelevant. The authority of Scripture overrules.

DISCUSSION QUESTIONS

1. What is the difference between a Thomist view of order and a Scotist view of order? Which view most closely resembles yours?

2. Do you think women are treated with as much respect as men in the Christian community? How equitable is the pay for women who serve on church staffs?

3. What is the difference between feeling in your heart that women ought to be treated as equals and treating women as men's equals?

---

[21]Groothuis, *Good News for Women*, p. 46.
[22]The Danvers Statement carefully qualifies women's equality with the same two words, "before God." See Affirmation I in "Appendix 2: The Danvers Statement" in *Recovering Biblical Manhood and Womanhood*, ed. John Piper and Wayne Grudem (Wheaton, Ill.: Crossway, 1991), p. 470.

4. Discuss the significance of the claim that women are "equal before God."
   Does that imply that women are not equal before people on earth? If not,
   then why might the phrase be there?

23

JESUS *IS* THE LOGIC

In the beginning was the Word, and the Word was with God, and the Word was God.
JOHN 1:1

The more I pay attention, the more I become convinced that the current debate on men and women in the church effectively unearths people's buried thoughts about their sexuality, their concept of marriage, their view of the authority of Scripture, their theology of God and their philosophy of natural order. That's why this debate is so volatile and heated. It strikes at the core of people's most sacred beliefs. I appreciate the way one professor puts it. He says the issue of women in ministry can appropriately be referred to as a "presenting issue." A presenting issue is the one that gets presented, though several underlying issues are involved.

In evangelical circles, 1 Timothy 2 is a presenting issue. The deeper issues are those such as people's view of God and the Trinity, and manhood and womanhood. In other words, the deeper issues lie on the fault line. The deeper issues, moreover, prove to inform our behavior. In other words, these deeper issues explain why it is that women in the church are invited to speak and lead, even in Southern Baptist settings—and then told not to speak and lead too much.

In order to clarify what I'm saying, we need to revist our discussion about Thomists and Scotists, but this time at a little deeper level. I won't say as much here about egalitarians because they seem to be consistent in their Thomism. Complementarians, however, tend to be inconsistent in their Scotism; thus their beliefs are more complicated.

In the preceding chapter I said that complementarians are Scotists. That's true, but it's not that simple. Many complementarians are also Thomists. Remember what a Thomist believes?

Thomists believe that God has ordered things in such a way that his commandments have a built-in correlation with the logical order of creation or with the logical order of God within himself.

Most complementarian thinking derives from a belief in the logical order of God within himself. What does that mean? It means that complementarians aren't Scotists, though earlier I said that they are. In spite of their good intentions, they end up trying to be Thomists *and* Scotists. As Scotists, complementarians say that God wills for men only to be the leaders of the church, no matter if it makes sense or not. But as Thomists, they say church leadership ought to accord theologically with the logical order of God within himself. In other words, as Thomists, they say the relationship of men and women ought to reflect the relational dynamics of the Father and Son within the Trinity.

ENCOUNTERING A SCOTIST

Some time ago a complementarian told me on the phone that the Bible is "absolutely clear" on the issue of women in ministry. He said that he had "studied the subject carefully" and arrived at the conclusion that "women are not allowed to exegete the Scriptures in Sunday school or church or in any other place where there are men." Resolutely he said it's "unbiblical" for a woman to pastor or preach or teach theology or serve as a deacon or an elder. But then, gratuitously, he added, "My desire is for women to be able to do more. In fact, my wife would make a much better elder than I do. I really don't understand why God wants it this way."

In my estimation, this gentleman is a Scotist. As a Scotist, he can see his wife's ability to lead, but he doesn't consider her giftedness to be a valid clue of God's will. As a fellow conservative, I can appreciate his caution. He doesn't want to exchange the biblical revelation for some preference of his own human will. That's understandable and wise; I wouldn't want to do that either.

Logically, however, something seems a little off to him. But because he is a Scotist, he accepts the strange dissonance between his theology of women and common sense. Morally he sees no reason for the traditional prohibition upon his godly wife. But neither does he expect God's will to correlate necessarily with God's design. Justifiably, then, he can say to himself that the only reason why it's wrong for his wife to be an elder at church is because "God said so" in the Scriptures.

ENCOUNTERING CHURCH TRADITION

Although this elder sees his wife as a potentially good elder, church tradition by contrast says his wife is inferior. Church tradition says that she is not to be treated on a par with the men because she, being a woman, stands below. According to tradition, it makes sense for the status of the person to align with the status of the role. Therefore traditionally it has been thought that a woman ought to be assigned a subordinate role since she is an inferior being. This was the rule because this was the logic of tradition.

Counter to tradition, this elder says his wife is not inferior. Her essence, according to him, is equal to his own. Thus there is no correlation in his complementarian logic between his wife's equal essence and her subordinate role. Her equality as a person has no bearing whatsoever on her function. Consider the comparison:

Tradition: women as inferiors should always assume subordinate roles.
Complementarianism: women as equals should always assume subordinate roles.

Do you see what has happened? Complementarians, in their benevolent intention to be biblical and loving, dumped the traditional premise that women are inferior to men. Unwittingly, however, they continue to maintain the logical conclusion of that premise. It makes good sense to say inferior beings ought to assume subordinate roles; that's why the church fathers said it. But it doesn't make sense to say equal beings should always be subordinate too. It's more logical to say that equal beings share in equal status.

ENCOUNTERING ORTHODOX THEOLOGY

In complementarian theology, women are seen as equal to men in personhood but subordinate in function and role. Thomas Schreiner perhaps explains it best. Writing against egalitarianism, he offers the following argument:

> Evangelical feminists . . . conclude that a difference in function necessarily involves a difference in essence; i.e., if men are in authority over women, then women must be inferior. The relationship between Christ and the Father shows us that this reasoning is flawed. One can possess a different function and still be equal in essence and worth. Women are equal to men in essence and being; there is no ontological distinction, and yet they have a different function or role in church and home. Such differences do not logically imply inequality or inferiority, just as Christ's subjection to the Father does not imply His inferiority.[1]

It's sort of like a military set-up. Essentially every soldier in the army is equal in being to the general. Functionally, however, the soldiers are inferior to him. A similar dynamic exists relationally between lieutenant and colonel, deacon and elder, and vice president and president. The lieutenant, deacon and vice president are all equal in essence yet unequal in role relative to their superior. Even Rebecca Merrill Groothuis concedes to the logic of this. She says, "It is *possible* to be equal in being but different in role or rank."[2]

---

[1] Thomas Schreiner, "Head Coverings, Prophecies and the Trinity: I Corinthians 11:2-16" in *Recovering Biblical Manhood and Womanhood*, ed. John Piper and Wayne Grudem (Wheaton, Ill.: Crossway, 1991), p. 128.

[2] Rebecca Merrill Groothuis, *Good News for Women* (Grand Rapids, Mich.: Baker, 1997), p. 46. Arguing in a different direction, she says the Son can maintain his status because his subordination is only temporary. Groothuis believes that his status would be compromised if his subordination were eternal.

Similarly orthodox theology says the Father and Son are relationally distinctive and yet essentially equal in substance. The early creeds ascribe to the Son and Spirit an equality of being with the Father. The Athanasian Creed, for instance, says that "all three persons [essentially] are coeternal and coequal to themselves." Along with that, it also says, "we are compelled by Christian faith to confess each person distinctively to be *both* God *and* Lord." In other words, all three persons are equal in being as God and equal in status as Lord.

As orthodoxy puts it, the Son is fully God, "equal in status and power."[3] That is, the Son is equal to the Father though not the Father. For according to the Niceno-Constantinopolitan Creed (A.D. 381), the Son is of the very same essence (*homoousios*) as God. Indeed, the Son himself *is* God. Thus by no means is the Son less than the Father in his being.[4]

Though egalitarians have been known to argue otherwise, I believe that some complementarians truly do maintain an orthodox view of the Son's radical equality with God.[5] What I question is whether or not they truly believe in women's radical equality with men.

Though John Piper and Wayne Grudem sincerely believe that women are equal to men before God, it appears they have no adequate language to describe what they mean by a woman's essential equality. Accordingly, then, the Danvers Statement—which is the official public statement of the Council on Biblical Manhood and Womanhood—says that Adam and Eve were created "equal before God as persons."[6] Elsewhere in the document that same qualifying phrase "before God" is repeated. Nevertheless, the Danvers Statement is unclear. Theologically, my guess is that Grudem and others writers of the Danvers Statement *do* want to say that women are just as equal to men as the

---

[3]Cf. Alister McGrath, *Christian Theology* (Cambridge, Mass.: Blackwell, 1994), p. 20. Also see Charles Hodge, *Systematic Theology* (Grand Rapids, Mich.: Baker, 1988), p. 171.

[4]It is true, however, that Christ, the Son incarnate, lowered himself, taking on inferior humanity. But the Son within the Trinity is equal in status to God.

[5]Not every complementarian believes, as Grudem does, in the "eternal subordination" of the Son.

[6]See "Appendix 2: The Danvers Statement" in *Recovering Biblical Manhood and Womanhood*, ed. John Piper and Wayne Grudem (Wheaton, Ill.: Crossway, 1991), p. 470.

Son is to the Father. And yet neither the statement nor Grudem (to my knowledge) ever qualifies the Son's essential equality as something that exists before God.

Why, then, does the Danvers Statement consistently say that women are men's equals before God? If the writers truly intend to parallel the equality of men and women with the equality of the Father and Son, then it might be helpful for them to say without qualification, as Schreiner does, that "women are equal to men in essence and being."[7]

PIPER'S DEFINITION OF *MASCULINITY* AND *FEMININITY*

According to Piper, *femininity* is not defined by an "equality of essence and being." Rather, it is defined by a distinctive disposition to be subject to the leadership of a man. The same can be said about the way *masculinity* is defined. As Piper puts it, mature masculinity is "a sense of benevolent responsibility to lead, provide for, and protect women." Thus masculinity is not associated or defined in terms of its essential equality with femininity. On the contrary, masculinity and femininity are defined as essentially distinct from one another.[8]

It is heresy to say the Son is essentially distinct from the Father. There is no such thing as essential Sonship or essential Fatherhood or essential Holy Spiritness within the Trinity as if the Father and Son and Spirit were essentially distinct in their being. The Athanasian Creed says, "There are not three

---

[7]Schreiner also plainly says, "There is no ontological distinction." Furthermore, Schreiner appeals to Hodge's commentary on the Nicene Creed, quoting Hodge as saying, "The creeds . . . assert the distinct personalities of the Father, Son, and Spirit; their mutual relation as expressed by those terms; their absolute unity as to substance and essence, and consequent perfect equality" (Schreiner, "Head Coverings, Prophecies and the Trinity," pp. 131, 136). Notice that Schreiner and Hodge speak in terms of "mutuality" and "equality."

[8]Knowing Grudem personally, I can't help but believe that he would agree that masculinity and femininity both are full, as opposed to partial, expressions of the image of God. Likewise, I would imagine that he and Piper would readily say that men and women share the same essence of humanity, just as the Father and Son share the same essence of divinity. And yet it also seems that they might simultaneously say men and women *don't* share the same essence since, as they perceive it, masculinity itself, just like femininity itself, makes men and women essentially, not just functionally, different. But it is contradictory to say that men and women are and are not essentially the same. As the fault line shows, theological truth is paradoxical, not contradictory.

eternal Beings, but one eternal Being." What distinguishes each person within the Trinity is not the nature but the *relationship* among the persons of the Trinity.[9] The Father is not the Son insofar as the Father is unbegotten relative to the Son and Holy Spirit. Likewise, the Son is not the Father insofar as the Son *is* begotten relative to the Father and Holy Spirit. The Father and Son, then, are distinct in terms of their relationship to one another. Hence the Unbegotten is the one who sends, and the Begotten is the one who is sent. Essentially, however, the Father and Son equally and fully are God.[10]

In orthodox theology the identity of the Father is defined by his equality of being with the Son and Holy Spirit. The Son's identity likewise is defined by the equality of his being with the Father and Holy Spirit. But in Piper's and Grudem's theology, the identity of men and women is not defined by shared essential equality. Thus the analogy of men and women mirroring the Father and the Son ultimately breaks down for them.

A SCOTIST-THOMIST CONTRADICTION

In effect Piper and Grudem have structured a theology of manhood and womanhood on the basis of a Scotist-Thomist self-contradictory view. In doing so they can offer several explanations of why women should assume subordinate roles. On the one hand, they can say that the restrictions placed on women have

---

[9]Complementarian theologian Bruce Ware, president of the Council on Biblical Manhood and Womanhood, tries to make his point by asking, "Is not the Father-Son relationship within the Trinity indicative of some eternal relationship of authority of within the Trinity?" (Bruce Ware, *Tampering with the Trinity: Does the Son Submit to the Father?* <http://www.cbmw.org/resources/articles/trinity/pdf>). In other words, Ware suggests that the metaphor of Father vis-à-vis the Son suggests that the Father has more authority than the Son. Unlike Hodge, Ware seems to overlook the orthodox fact that the Father and Son share the same status.

[10]The theological concept of the three persons sharing the divine essence is called the "perichoresis," or synonymously the "circumincession." By extension, this idea, as defined in the *Pocket Dictionary of Theological Terms*, suggests that any essential characteristic that belongs to one of the three is shared by the others. Circumincession also affirms that the action of one of the persons of the Trinity is also fully the action of the other two persons. See Stanley J. Grenz, David Guretzki and Cherith Fee Nordling, *Pocket Dictionary of Theological Terms* (Downers Grove, Ill.: InterVarsity Press, 1999). For a more lengthy discussion, see Jürgen Moltmann, *History and the Triune God* (New York: Crossroad, 1992), pp. xi-xiii; see also Miroslav Volf, *After Our Likeness* (Grand Rapids, Mich.: Eerdmans, 1998), pp. 208-15; Donald Bloesch, *God the Almighty* (Downers Grove, Ill.: InterVarsity Press, 1995), pp.180-83, 193, 274.

nothing to do with the basic constitution of the female.[11] On the other hand, they can say that women are so constituted as to have a disposition to be subject to the leadership of a man. See the contradiction? They say that a wife should submit to her husband not just voluntarily as an equal[12] but also in accordance with her nature. Do you hear the tones of tradition in that claim?

Listen to something else Piper says: "When the Bible teaches that men and women fulfill different roles in relation to each other, charging man with a unique leadership role, it bases this differentiation not on temporary cultural norms but on the permanent facts of creation."[13] In this context Piper is trying to say that I Timothy 2 applies not only to the church in first-century Ephesus but also to every succeeding generation. Nevertheless there is a problem with the logical implications of Piper's teaching. What does he mean by "the permanent facts of creation"? That women are not designed for responsible leadership over men? That "the permanent facts of creation" mitigate against her being effective? That she lacks the essential qualities of a leader? Could it be that Piper is echoing the belief passed down by church tradition that says God "shows [men's] superiority" in his act of creating Adam first?[14]

Whatever the answer, the point stands: Piper is offering a reason for women's subordination as if he were a Thomist. He is not saying, as a Scotist would do, that women are supposed to be subordinate to men strictly because of God's will. Unlike the elder who openly says his wife is more gifted

---

[11]Jointly they say, "We do not build our vision on the assumption that the Bible assigns women their role because of doctrinal or moral incompetence. The differentiation of roles for men and women in ministry is rooted not in any supposed incompetence, but in God's created order for manhood and womanhood" (John Piper and Wayne Grudem, "An Overview of Central Concerns: Questions and Answers" in *Recovering Biblical Manhood and Womanhood*, ed. John Piper and Wayne Grudem [Wheaton, Ill.: Crossway, 1991], pp. 73-74).

[12]Even the phrase "submit voluntarily as an equal" is confusing in a complementarian paradigm. For though complementarians say that the wife submits voluntarily as an equally valuable person, they also contend that she submits voluntarily as one who is unequally ranked. In other words, she submits as a subordinate to her husband.

[13]John Piper, "A Vision of Biblical Complementarity: Manhood and Womanhood Defined According to the Bible," in *Recovering Biblical Manhood and Womanhood*, ed. John Piper and Wayne Grudem [Wheaton, Ill.: Crossway, 1991], p. 35.

[14]See Chrysostom, "Homilies on Timothy (Homilies 8-9)" in *Nicene and Post-Nicene Fathers*, first series, trans. Philip Schaff, 14 vols. (Peabody, Mass.: Hendrickson, 1995), 13:432-35.

for the role than he is, Piper is suggesting that "the permanent facts of creation" make it permanently impossible for a woman truly to be suited to serve officially as a pastor or preacher.[15]

No wonder conservative Christians are confused. We are given so many mixed messages. In one long breath, we are told that women are not inferior but that "the permanent facts of creation" reveal that women should assume subordinate roles; yet women are equal to men just as surely as the Son is equal to the Father, even though we don't share the same status with men as the Son does with the Father; and men are not superior to women because both are created in the image of God, although men are uniquely designed (though not necessarily gifted) to be women's leaders; and women are uniquely designed to nurture and affirm men's leadership over them even if they themselves are more spiritually gifted than the men who oversee them. All this, we are told, is to be honored—unless certain male leaders commission certain women to be exceptions.

Evangelical feminists may not have everything right,[16] but at least their vision is consistent. To them, it's simple: align people according to their giftedness and calling. But for complementarians, the matter is enormously more complex considering all of the exceptions and inconsistencies. For instance, some otherwise complementarian local churches have been known to invite a woman to fill the pulpit on Mother's Day Sunday morning. Perhaps even more confusing is the fact that most complementarian-led seminaries rou-

---

[15]Complementarian Paige Patterson, president of Southeastern Seminary, echoes the same thing when he says that "men and women possess distinct abilities and callings" (*CBMW* 3, no. 2 [1998]: 9). I agree with him if he means that only men are able and called to be fathers, and only women are able and called to be mothers. But it appears that he means something different. Indeed, what strikes me most about Patterson's position is that he never names anything specific—that has nothing to do with men's and women's bodies—to illustrate what he thinks only men or only women are able and called by God to do.

[16]As I have said before, I disagree with biblical feminists on several accounts. I don't think head (*kephalē*) means "source." Nor do I believe that the Bible teaches "mutual submission" as the primary dynamic in a marriage. Nor do I believe that Galatians 3:28 ("There is neither . . . male nor female; for you are all one in Christ,") means that sexual distinctions are irrelevant to ministry. Nor do I believe that women have the right to be leaders in the church. Nor do I agree with those egalitarians who say it's theologically permissible to address the Lord God as "Mother." Nor do I believe that it's necessary to blend a feminist worldview with a Christian worldview in order to be supportive of women pastors and preachers.

tinely accept large amounts of tuition money from female seminary students who go there to gain formal pastoral training.

If we categorize this in terms of Scotist and Thomist claims, we can sort things out again. As Scotists, complementarians can make the unassuming statement that the only reason why women can't lead is because "that's God's will." In a way, complementarians can't say otherwise. For if they say God forbids women from leading the congregation because women aren't strong enough for the job, then inadvertently, by default, they champion church tradition. But that's precisely what they don't want to do. As Scotists, therefore, many complementarians are careful to say that women as equals must assume subordinate roles because "that's the way God has ordained it."

Now consider how they sometimes speak as Thomists. As Thomists, complementarians say that women as equals before God must assume subordinate roles on the basis of an analogy with the Trinity. And yet, as we have seen, the comparison between women's equality with men and the Son's equality with the Father turns out to be inexact for complementarians. Openly they celebrate the Son's full equality with the Father. But subtly they limit women's equality with men. They say women are equal to men, but only before God. I believe that is misleading. Piper and Grudem also say that women, as women, must assume subordinate roles because women are not designed to lead, protect or provide for a man. They say a woman of "mature femininity" is naturally inclined to be subject to the leadership of a man.

Perhaps it would help to summarize these ideas in a list.

Complementarians as

- **Scotists** say women *as equals* should assume inferior roles *only* because it's "God's will."
- **Thomists** say women *as equals before God* should assume inferior roles on the basis of a quasi-analogy of the Trinity.
- **Thomists** say women of *mature femininity* are naturally predisposed to assume interior roles.

- **Thomists** say women *as women* should assume inferior roles in accordance with the permanent facts of nature.

What does the summary reveal? It shows that Piper and Grudem are more Thomist than Scotist.[17] It also shows why complementarians need their Scotism. They can't give up their Scotism because it provides them with their only way simultaneously to affirm women's equality without forfeiting their claim that women should assume subordinate roles. Without their Scotism, Piper and Grudem have no means by which to deny the traditional belief that women are inferior to men.

None of this is to say that Piper and Grudem are sneaky Thomist-Scotists who deliberately mean to talk out of three or four sides of their mouths. I do not believe that. On the contrary, I believe that complementarians such as Piper and Grudem are devout Christians who have rejected the idea that women are inferior to men and replaced it with a view that says women are not inferior to men. But that's the point. Many conservative Christians, like Piper and Grudem, have revised the basic premise of church tradition without revising the conclusion of that premise.

It's reasonable to say that women should be limited, if women are inferior to men. But it doesn't make sense to forward the church tradition of prohibiting women leaders within the Christian community if everyone agrees that women are not inferior after all. If church tradition was based on Scripture, then so be it. But church tradition regarding women is based on the church fathers' belief that women are inferior to men. That's why Christian women have been prohibited all these years. Indeed, Christians in the past did not stand up and say, "Women are men's equals, but God says to prohibit them anyway." They said, "God said women are to be prohibited precisely because women are inferior."

JESUS IS THE LOGIC

The greatest commandment in Scripture says to "love the Lord your God

---

[17]As you may recall, Duns Scotus was also more Thomist than Scotist.

with all . . . your mind" (Mt 22:37). It is sinful not to love God mentally. It is un-Christian to diminish the importance of meaning and reason and logic. In spite of this reality, sometimes evangelicals are so intent on being biblical that we forget about striving to be logical. It is logical to believe in the miracles of God since God is a God of miracles. It's also logical to believe in the paradox of biblical truth. It is illogical, however, to believe in blatant contradictions such as a Thomist-Scotist view of men and women. Indeed, logic itself compels us to believe that the mysteries of God are higher than, not lower than, our reason.

According to the Scriptures, Jesus *is* the Reason and the Meaning and the Logic. Look at John 1:1. Here's how it reads with the Greek word inserted into the English translation: "In the beginning was the *Logos,* and the *Logos* was with God, and the *Logos* was God."

The Greek word *Logos* is usually translated into the English language as "word."[18] Our English Bibles thus say, "In the beginning was the Word, and the Word was with God, and the Word was God." Scholars know that it is also fair to translate the Greek word *logos* into the English word *reason.* Translated this way, the verse says in English: "In the beginning was the Reason, and the Reason was with God, and the Reason was God."

There's another way to look at it too. The Greek word *logos* also connotes the idea of the English word *meaning.* Hence we can say, "In the beginning was the Meaning, and the Meaning was with God, and the Meaning was God."

Isn't that neat? Jesus is the Meaning of life.

Logos also means "logic." You can see the similarity between the Greek word *logos* and the English word *logic.* And you can surely guess that John 1:1 also legitimately means "In the beginning was the Logic, and the Logic was with God, and the Logic was God."

The truth of Christianity is not illogical. Truth can't be illogical, because

---

[18]Noted scholar F. F. Bruce says, "No doubt the English term 'Word' is an inadequate rendering of the Greek *logos,* but it would be difficult to find one less inadequate" (F. F. Bruce, *The Gospel of John* [Grand Rapids, Mich.: Eerdmans, 1983], p. 29). Bruce contends that "Reason" is a more misleading translation than "Word" because "Reason" comes across as more impersonal.

Christ *is* the Logic and the Truth, and he is not against himself. The Logos plainly told us, "I am . . . the truth" (Jn 14:6). Therefore Christians are responsible to develop sound theology that honors the Logic *and* the Truth.[19] The onus lies on us to labor with our minds, as an act of love for God[20] and by the help of the Holy Spirit, to reason through our reading of his Word.

By simultaneously adopting two theories of natural order that are mutually exclusive, some of us have promoted a lack of logic. It can't be true that the only reason why women are to assume inferior roles at church is because God said so, if indeed the permanent facts of nature also explain the reason why. I believe it's unintentional, but many of us Christians in the evangelical community have unknowingly adopted a Scotist-Thomist view and called it biblical. With that, we have trumpeted a mixed-up view that says women, as equals, are allowed to speak and lead, but only unofficially as subordinates.

So here are we again, facing another call to repentance.

Dear Lord, please enlarge our hearts. Help us to love one another. Help us also to be merciful, not judgmental, of one another. I pray that all of us will be diligent to become better listeners and to hear what each other is saying. O God, we need to be touched by you. Grant us the grace to honor men as men and women as women, and yet show us what it means for the church to be united in spirit (Phil 2:2). We want so much for our marriages and families to flourish. Lord, bless our children, and bless us as the family of God.

DISCUSSION QUESTIONS

1. Explain what it means for a Thomist and Scotist view to be mutually exclusive. Make sure everyone in your group understands why it's illogical to be assume a Thomist-Scotist view of women in ministry.

2. What other observations can you make from the list on page 292?

---

[19]The dictum *sola Scriptura* does not mean that Christians are to disregard reason in our reading of the Word. It means, rather, that all Christian doctrine should be founded on the Word of God. See Lutheran theologian John Theodore Mueller, *Christian Dogmatics* (St. Louis: Concordia, 1934), p. 85.

[20]The great commandment is to "love the Lord God with all your heart, with all your soul, and with all your *mind*" (Mt 22:37, emphasis added).

3. Do you think the complementarian analogy of women's equality with men before God parallels with the Son's equality with God? Why do you think the Danvers Statement uses the phrase "before God"?

4. Take time to pray, confessing your sins and asking God to help you repent.

24

BROTHERS AND SISTERS IN CHRIST

But we have the mind of Christ.
I CORINTHIANS 2:16

My husband, Jim, leads a small group of serious-minded men who earnestly want to be holy. One of their goals is to purify their minds and exercise fidelity, physically and mentally, to their wives. Jim has told me time and time again that Christian men need Christian women to minister to them by dressing modestly. He isn't blaming women for men's weakness. Openly he confesses that it's the men's responsibility to learn not to objectify women. My husband is well aware of his own sin. I am aware of mine too. I have a past of dressing and behaving immodestly.[1]

Jim and I talk about this with our friends. For example, when we first moved to California, we went on a double date with a Bible professor and his wife whom we had recently met. In the car that night before we left, we decided to share prayer requests and pray. Jim said, "Please pray that I'll be sexually pure." Believe me, that was not my favorite moment in life. I felt embarrassed and

---

[1]Jim has been instrumental in helping me to find my security more wholly in the Lord than in trying to be sexually appealing in the way that I dress. Older women have helped me too. I used to pray every morning at 6:00 a.m. with a group of women who required each other to wear modest clothing, even though no men were around. Modesty, I have learned, is an expression of personal dignity and humility.

humbled. I would prefer to think of myself as the end-all woman for Jim. I wish he would be so enthralled by me that he never had a thought about anyone else. It's a pride-buster for me to face the truth about Jim's sin. It's even harder, however, for me to face the truth about myself. Jim and I have always been physically faithful in our marriage, but we are not sexually pure.

I say this because I think it should be normal for people in the church to fight together for sexual purity. Most of the time the subject is so taboo that we feel way too ashamed to admit our temptations, much less to confess our sin. Thus we isolate from each other rather than ministering to each other. We practically pretend that none of us has any live hormones. Consequently, many Christian men are rarely held accountable for the suggestive and demeaning kinds of things they sometimes say to Christian women. And women in the church are rarely held accountable for the way they dress.[2]

Unfortunately it is common for Christian women to bare their backs and legs, so common in southern California that one man told me going to church is almost as exciting for him as going downtown to a bar. Yet many Christian women refuse to dress modestly.

How can the people of God win the world for Christ when we are unwilling to modify the way we express our sexuality? Most of us know that the issue of sex and modesty is a hypersensitive subject in the church. It is such a sensitive subject that people feel afraid to ask Christian women to cover themselves up; we're scared they'll think we're judging them in self-righteousness. We're scared they won't like us anymore or that they'll blame us and say that's it's our problem, not theirs. We're afraid, moreover, to talk to Christian men about their attitudes toward women. We're scared they'll think we're suing them for sexual harassment or that we're being overly analytical and reading something into their behavior. No Christian man wants to be labeled as a "dirty old man" or a "creep." Thus very, very few Christian men are willing to confess the struggle that they have—daily—with sexual sin.

---

[2]I believe men should dress modestly too, and that women should speak wholesome words to men. I phrased it this way because I see far fewer scantily clad men than women, and I know more stories about inappropriate remarks made by men than women.

I am convinced that it would be less controversial for men to partner with women in church leadership if it weren't for the church's sexual sin. Moreover, I believe that the church could greatly recover from a lot of our sin if Christians would be more willing to confess our sins out loud and repent. But as it is, we have acquired certain nonsensical habits. For example, we say that it's acceptable for a pastor to hire a female secretary but dangerous for him sexually to hire a female associate.

I know of one woman who in her early thirties applied for a coveted position to work at an upstanding evangelical institution where she emerged as the leading candidate. A few weeks into the job search, she received an invitation to visit privately with the chair of the hiring search committee, who told her that she brought "too much physical beauty" into the work environment. It wasn't that she dressed immodestly. It was rather that she dressed more fashionably than professionally, a problem that easily could have been corrected. Even so, the Christian men found themselves unable to cope. The chair of the search committee told her what the men had said behind her back. In closed quarters, after her initial interview, he said that one man remarked to the others, "What are we going to do with that?" She became a "that," an object of beauty, not a sister.

This kind of story is hard for a woman to tell. It's hard because when she tells it, she sounds like a victimized feminist who has an axe to grind. She hardly has an avenue for holding men in leadership accountable. The same frustration is equally true for Christian men. It's difficult for men to find a good way to say that they're offended when women dress immodestly at church. It's difficult because if he says it, he sounds like a member of Sexaholics Anonymous. There is no standard way in evangelical circles for Christian men politely to ask Christian women to be more modest.

BEING VULNERABLE TO SIN AND DEATH

It's a sad, unspoken fact that many Christian men, including senior pastors, are stuck in lonely isolation. At least in this one sense, many Christian men can hardly be distinguished from unbelievers. Every year the church hears stories of prominent Christian leaders who are asked to step down due to sexual misconduct. In almost every case, the man who falls was isolated spiritually and personally disconnected from others in the Christian community. Most men feel too embarrassed and ashamed to ask for and receive real help. It is humiliating for a Christian man to admit he is unable to control his private thoughts and behavior. Men as men are supposed to be more competent than that. I have been told that this is true especially for male pastors. Thus male pastors often hide. Habitually they hide, taking advantage of the unfortunate fact that being in charge typically exempts prominent Christian men from the kind of accountability they need.

Speaking of this, I am reminded of the time when I led a retreat for a twenty-five-person church staff. The people were divided into small groups of two or three to air out their confessions and pray for one another in support. I coupled the senior pastor with another senior pastor who had joined them as a guest. At the end of the exercise, the staff had become refreshed. They had verbalized their grievances and articulated their sin to each other and the Lord. But not the two senior pastors. They engaged in small talk for almost an hour. It wasn't safe for them to let down their guard and still be leaders. That showed me again that trust in the Christian community is not well developed, especially between Christian men.

Once you get them talking, however, it is not unusual for men to recount childhood memories of having a father who was so caught up in trying to impress his little son that he never even noticed how miserably he failed to give encouragement to his son. Many unencouraged boys grow up to become unencouraged teenagers and then unencouraged husbands and fathers. I wonder how many men in the Christian community feel as though they don't measure up. It doesn't help them out when mothers and wives and daughters wistfully look at them as Bible Answer Men and spiritual leaders who stand above the line of temptation.

IMMODESTLY DRESSED WOMEN
Some time ago I was invited to speak to a small group of undergraduate

Christian men who, like my husband, are trying their best to be holy. One thing I told them is that women just want to be pretty. I said, "You know when women dress in ways that wreak havoc for you?" Oh, yeah, they knew.

I said, "They're not trying to tell you they want to be taken advantage of. It appears that's what they're doing. But they're too vain to know that you're not thinking about who they are whenever you look at them. When you look at their body, you're looking at their body. They think you're looking at them. When you sin against them mentally, they take it as a personal compliment. As you already know, once you're skilled enough to sin against women in a subtle, nice way, they won't be offended at all."

Then I told them my testimony of how Christian men have helped me to become more godly and appropriate in the way I relate to men. At Baylor there was a guy in my Bible study who let me know that the jogging shorts I wore to Wednesday night Bible study were "plenty short." He didn't rebuke me. He simply mentioned it, but it really hit me. I repented to some extent in those days, but not entirely. Even into my thirties, I was still wearing my jogging clothes to the grocery store and other public places where I run errands. Several years ago my husband, Jim, finally persuaded me to start making the extra effort to stay more covered.

I feel a little protective of my husband when I say this for fear that some people might be tempted to judge him. However, I believe it's a good thing for Jim to be forthright about the truth. No doubt there are those who may wonder to themselves about Jim's and my personal issues. The point is not to talk about myself or my husband but rather to attempt to steer everyone's attention to the reality of what happens in grocery stores every day. Women dress immodestly, and men in the grocery store look.

I was floored when Jim told me his observations. There we were, he in his jeans and I in my running clothes. My mind was focused on the apples. I was engrossed in the mundane task of selecting the best apples to take home while Jim stood there watching other people. Very matter-of-factly he said, "That guy just caught a glimpse. Yep, and that one too."

I turned around and said, "What guy? I didn't even see him!"

Jim answered, "Women don't see what men do. We're experts at stealing self-indulgent glances. We try not to be pigs who just stand there and gawk, although we do that too." Then he shrugged with a bit of frustration, "Women don't even know what men do. But I know because I'm a man, and I do it. And I know men."

Jim's uncompromising view has opened my eyes to a new world. No other man has ever been so honest and candid with me about the way men operate sexually. After listening to him, I asked several of my Christian men friends if they agree with Jim. They do. But they don't go around saying it. Most men are afraid to be known in their sin. They're afraid their wives will throw a fit, or give them the cold shoulder, or even file for divorce. Consequently, many Christian men go around feeling guilty while many Christian women (who are dressed immodestly) go around hoping that people will think they're pretty.

Here again I am optimistic that the Christian community can change. For I firmly believe that many Christian women will be internally motivated to alter the way they dress as soon as they decide to squarely face the truth about all the Christian men who are struggling and failing sexually. It's nice for the female ego to attract little glances from men, but it doesn't build security when a wife finds out that her husband enjoys a lot of "little glances" of other Christian women who dress the same way that she does.

MEN AND PORNOGRAPHY

A couple of years ago I was asked to speak in chapel at Azusa Pacific University (APU) on the subject of pornography. That's the hardest talk I've ever had to give. I stood there and spoke about the need for Christian community, how people can't be holy by themselves. We all need people to pray for us and listen to our confessions and steer us back into God's grace. We can't build Christian community when people isolate. But that's what happens when someone indulges in pornography.

Pornography destroys togetherness. I know a woman whose marriage ended in divorce due mostly to her husband's infidelity made manifest in a pornography addiction. When she asked her husband why he preferred to be with women by proxy on the Internet or through magazines, he answered without emotion, "Because the women on the pages don't talk."

I also know an alumnus from APU, a non-Christian at the time, who came into my office a few years ago and made a first confession about his terrible addiction to pornography. He was in a state of desperation. The air was heavy in the room. I sat in silence and waited for him to open up. His bottom lip was quivering. Finally he managed to cough up the words, "I've seen a lot of pornographic pictures of women over the years. But lately, I've begun to look at men. I am so scared that I'm turning into a homosexual. All I can think about is how much I want to experiment sexually with a man."

Tears were streaming from his eyes. This young man was a virgin. He and I had been friends for a couple of years. I introduced him to my husband as well as to my mother when she came into town for a visit. He was confused about his sexual identity, but he was also ready to be helped. Over the next few weeks, the Lord provided him with a weekly small group composed of Christian men and women. Some were married, and some were not. It was an ideal group for him. He also started seeing a Christian counselor. After several months of having stopped hiding, his desire to be with men began to fade. About a year later, he put his faith in Christ. Over time, by God's grace, he was also freed from his addiction.

I believe the only way for men and women to stay repentant from sexual sin is by experiencing true fellowship with each other. Christian men and women need to be known and accepted and loved by one another. We need to be prayed for. We need to find times to confess. We need to worship God together authentically in spirit and truth (Jn 4:24). We need to hear God's Word and learn to apply it in our sex lives. Can you imagine the impact it would have on a woman if she confessed to men her sin of wanting to look sexy in her Sunday worship clothes? And if a man confessed his sin to women that when he sees them dressed immodestly, he thinks about sex, not God?

One of the husbands in my men's group at Willow Creek celebrated with his wife that I was the first "attractive" woman he didn't lust for. He was amazed that he had the capacity to view a woman outside of his family as a sister.

He kept saying to me, "I hope it doesn't hurt your feelings that I don't have any thoughts about you."

I said, "It doesn't hurt my feelings at all. I feel dignified by your high regard for me. Now you know that it is possible for you to look at other women the way you look at me."

This was a major breakthrough. Here was a man well into his forties who had never in his adulthood been friends with a woman without confusing his feelings of endearment for her with feelings of sexual attraction.

One of my goals when I minister to men is to help them understand that lust is not an innate male reflex; it is a condition of the heart. Lust toward women is not entirely natural. Much of it is learned. How else could it be that men in America tend not to lust for their sisters? I lived with my brother for five years as an adult during our mid to late twenties. Though he struggled to be pure sexually as a godly Christian bachelor, he didn't have an issue with me. For him it was taboo to think of me, his sister, as a potential sexual partner. I was "just Sarah" to him. He thought of me as "Sis." So far was he from feeling any impulse to exploit me that he felt protective of me.

That's what happened with the gentleman in my class. I became his spiritual sister. He thought of me with pure motives because he made the decision to think of me with pure motives. His mindset was not so out of control after all. In the context of our relationship, he caught a glimpse of what it means to "have the mind of Christ" (1 Cor 2:16).

Christ viewed women as women, not sex objects. Thus Jesus was able to spend unhurried time with the woman at the well (Jn 4), Mary of Bethany (Lk 10:39) and the woman who kissed and caressed his feet (Lk 7). Jesus was undistracted by the sexual beauty of women. Because Jesus cultivated the right mind, he was free from self-indulgent desire. Perhaps that explains why Jim says the most powerful ammonia to awaken him out of lust is for him to throw himself fully into spiritual battle and fight against the flesh by crying out the name of Jesus Christ. For Jesus, as a sympathetic High Priest (Heb 4:15), can help men and women to have a right view of each another.

I have come to realize that the sin of lust is analogous to the sin of greed. The miser and the playboy have a problem in the way they view other people. Both see people as something to be had and used and exploited. Whereas the miser uses people to make money for himself, the playboy uses women to make himself feel powerful and manly. The same applies to women who are misers and to women who use men sexually. In either case, both fail to see that every individual is someone, not something. Through the power of the Lord, a miser can become a giver, and a playboy can be transformed into a brotherly minister of women.

PRACTICAL WAYS TO PROTECT ONE ANOTHER

As a matter of wisdom, Christian men and women need to be careful to honor certain boundaries. We are brothers and sisters, but we're also sexual, and that can be dangerous in light of our propensity to sin. Thus it is good to practice habits that can help us to be biblical and true to our commitment to Christ. Though I don't like the idea of becoming legalistic, it's wise to be mindful of ways to protect one another and also keep ourselves from falling into sexual sin. Here are some suggestions:

- Dress appropriately.
- Treat the people around you as brothers and sisters, not potential lovers.
- Don't wear so much perfume that it might be distracting.
- Make sure your body language is wholesome rather than suggestive.
- Meet with people in public places, such as a restaurant, coffee shop, conference room or office rather than somewhere private. (I say "people" because in this fallen world, some are attracted to the same sex. Setting boundaries with the opposite sex is not enough. Thus for anyone who has homosexual tendencies, the rest of the suggestions below

should be modified accordingly.[3])

- As a general rule, don't discuss marital problems with someone of the opposite sex if you're alone with them and your spouse is excluded from that relationship.
- Honor people who do not feel the freedom to ride in the same car with you or share a meal with you alone in a restaurant. It's better to be careful than reckless.
- Don't hold hands if you're praying alone with someone of the opposite sex.
- Don't hug the opposite sex with a full-body hug that may be sexually arousing.
- Stay accountable to someone, especially your spouse if you're married. Better yet, stay accountable to a small group. Don't hide if you get off track.
- Ask people to pray for you to be sexually pure.
- Pray for yourself and others to be sexually pure.
- Pray for other people's marriages to flourish, especially if you feel attracted to someone who's married.
- Memorize Scripture.
- Read Mike Mason's *The Mystery of Marriage*. More than any other book I know, except the Bible, it makes you want to be sexually pure. It helped me tremendously when Jim and I were engaged.
- Sing praise songs when you feel sexually vulnerable to sin.
- If you can't control your sexual energy, do some physical exercise.
- Give other people the benefit of the doubt. There's no need to be paranoid or suspicious about others' sexuality. Just be sensible and wise.
- Cultivate the mind of Christ, so that you don't sexualize relationships inappropriately.
- Thank God for your sexuality. If you feel sexually aroused at times,

---

[3]To read an excellent book on the biblical teachings regarding homosexuality, see William Webb, *Slaves, Women and Homosexuals* (Downers Grove, Ill.: InterVarsity Press, 2001). Webb shows clearly that the Bible consistently condemns homosexuality as a sin. He also shows, however, that the Bible teaches Christians to love homosexuals just as we love ourselves (Mt 22:37-39).

you're normal. This is the gift of God. Your job is to manage and enjoy your sexuality, not kill it.[4]

DISCUSSION QUESTIONS

1. What should a man do if he is distracted by Christian women who are dressed immodestly at church?

2. What should a woman do if a Christian man says something inappropriate or looks at her inappropriately?

3. Read Luke 7:40-50 and then describe what it must have been like for Jesus to be greeted with such love and affection by a woman prostitute.

4. What suggestions can you add to or subtract from the list on pages 305-7?

---

[4]When Christians confuse sexuality with lust, we mistakenly conclude that sexual feelings felt outside of marriage are sinful. It is not sinful to feel sexually alive. Sexual energy is a good thing. What Christians need to learn is how to cope wisely with our God-given sexual energy. Otherwise, the evil one may deceive us into thinking that human sexuality is a bad thing that suddenly turns into a good thing on the day a person gets married. By contrast, lust is a sin because lusting is a form of coveting.

25

FOLLOWING IN THE STEPS OF JESUS CHRIST

For you have been called for this purpose, since Christ also suffered for you, leaving you an example for you to follow in His steps.

1 PETER 2:21

In 1984, at the end of my junior year in college at Baylor, the college pastor of the First Baptist Church in Waco, Texas, meandered over to where a few of us were standing outside of the sanctuary and nonchalantly asked me, "Sarah, how would you like to become the first woman ever to teach the Action class on Sunday mornings?"

I couldn't believe my ears. The Action class was this really cool class of five hundred juniors and seniors. Only guys had ever been privileged to stand up in there before and say anything official out loud. Only guys had ever been asked to give announcements. Only two or three guys, all Baylor football players, had ever been invited to share part of their testimony or offer a vignette as an "intro" to the college pastor's lesson. No college guy had ever been asked to be the teacher. But that changed when I was twenty-one years old.

Starting my senior year, I became a teacher for the Action class, trading off biweekly with the pastor. For a while we cotaught as a team. Next he asked me to fill in for him and lead a retreat for some middle-aged adults from a church about a hundred miles away. The outcome of that endeavor was positive enough that I became a keynote speaker. (Now you can see why I was unaware of this debate. Though I knew it was unprecedented for a woman to teach our college group, I had never seen anyone argue over the matter.) It's funny for me to think about this, considering where I am now. God used a Southern Baptist pastor to situate me in my first public teaching role. This, I believe, was God's providence.

WALKING FORWARD IN OBEDIENCE AND PAIN

From 1985 to 1990, I was invited to speak to various groups around the country. Outside the church, I spoke to adults. Inside the church, I taught children. After that, from 1991 to 1995, I led a women's Bible study at Willow Creek Community Church in South Barrington, Illinois. For five years I devoted myself weekly to them. I loved those women. I agreed when Kathy Dice, who at the time served as the director of women's ministry, would frequently say that women's ministry was "the most exciting ministry" at Willow. Unchurched women often came to Christ while others became spiritually mature. Had anyone suggested that I was limited in ministry because I taught in women's ministry, I would not have comprehended the point. My cup overflowed.

In 1995, I joined the paid staff at Willow Creek. That was the year that I started being asked to preach on Sunday mornings in various local churches nearby. In 1997, after I joined the faculty at Azusa Pacific University, still more doors began to open for me to minister. By 2001, something else unprecedented happened. I was asked to join the preaching team in Jim's and my local church. I'd like to tell the story of how it all came about because it illustrates one way that a church can successfully bring a woman speaker into leadership. In our church, it was a process of slowly walking forward toward a change.

It's not easy to walk forward in obedience to Christ. Obedience to Christ is painful. Even Jesus learned obedience painfully from that which he suffered (Heb 5:8). Doing the right thing, making the right decision, often entails pain for a Christian. It hurts to be struck on the cheek (Mt 5:39). It's not very fun to turn the other cheek, so that *that* cheek can be struck too. But there's a power to be found when someone becomes willing to absorb the pain of being hit and then continue to walk forward in the same direction as before. When a person takes a risk to follow Jesus, he or she must be willing to suffer. Christians must be willing to suffer and not revolt.

I am reminded once again of the words of Peter: "For you have been called for this purpose, since Christ also suffered for you, leaving you an example for you to follow in His steps . . . and while being reviled, He did not revile in return; while suffering He uttered no threats, but kept entrusting Himself to Him who judges righteously" (1 Pet 2:21, 23).

Remember, it was Simon Peter to whom Christ said, "Simon, Simon, behold, Satan has demanded permission to sift you like wheat; but I have prayed for you, that your faith may not fail; and you, when once you have turned again, strengthen your brothers" (Lk 22:31-32). Jesus also said to him, "Truly, truly, I say to you, when you were younger, you used to gird yourself, and walk wherever you wished; but when you grow old, you will stretch out your hands and someone else will gird you, and bring you where you do not wish to go" (Jn 21:18). The Bible says Jesus was signifying the kind of death that Peter would die. It also says that "when He had spoken this," Jesus said specifically to Peter, "Follow Me!"

The call of Jesus Christ is for us to follow him. We are commanded to go where we do not wish to go. We are also commanded not to revile back when we are reviled, but to suffer for his sake.

The feminist movement is not famous for producing women who do not revile back. That particular glory is reserved for the women of the church. There is power in becoming a suffering servant. There is power in speaking the truth. There is power to be found whenever we entrust ourselves to him who judges righteously.

I am not saying that any woman should continue to be physically abused or financially destroyed if someone is attacking her body or squandering her provision. In those kinds of cases, a woman is responsible to expose the hidden truth and protect herself along with any children she might have. It isn't biblical for wives or mothers and children to subject themselves to violent or reckless behavior. On the contrary, the biblical command is for women to speak the truth in love (Eph 4:15). No one enjoys confronting the truth when there is something dreadful to hide. But the one and only way for people to be freed is by the truth. Make no mistake—love doesn't set people free.[1] Truth sets people free. Jesus said it plainly, "And you will know the truth, and the truth will make you free" (Jn 8:32).

THE NEXT STEP OF MY JOURNEY

Relative to many, I have hardly suffered. But I do have a story to tell. The story is about the process of my church making a significant shift. Perhaps I should begin with a little bit of background information.

My husband became a Christian in Chicago in 1994, about a year before I met him at Willow Creek. Within days of his conversion, he heard the Lord calling him into full-time ministry. But he couldn't see a way to make that happen. How does one become a paid minister at age thirty-seven without any knowledge of the Word? Jim couldn't become a minister, at least not yet. But he could prepare to be one later.

For two years, Jim attended church functions five days a week. His appetite for the Scriptures was voracious. He couldn't learn the Bible fast enough. When I met him, he had a reputation for being "the most on-fire new Christian at Willow Creek." For almost a year Jim and I were friends. We had no intention of ever dating. But suddenly we realized that we had fallen in love. Neither of us had ever been married or engaged, though he was thirty-nine and I thirty-three.

One day unannounced he greeted me matter-of-factly, "Sarah, we gotta

---

[1]God loves everyone, and yet not everyone is free. Many people souls are deeply loved by other people, and yet they are still not free.

get married." It seemed like the most natural thing in the world for him to say. Casually I replied, "Jim, I'll marry you in two days, two weeks, two months or two years. I don't want you to feel rushed or detained. Just let me know when the wedding day is, and I'll be there." Seven months later we were married.

In 1997 we became members of New Song Church in California and started meeting weekly with a small group. There wasn't any opening on the New Song staff, so we assumed God had a plan for Jim to serve somewhere else. Soon Jim was hired by an evangelical Formosan church to serve as the part-time assistant youth pastor to English-speaking kids on Friday nights and Sunday afternoons. Being an assistant youth pastor was a hand-in-glove ministry fit for Jim, especially at that time in his development.

The hours of the job for Jim were excellent. But a few months later, New Song discontinued the Saturday night service, and his youth group started meeting on Sunday mornings. For us, that meant attending two separate churches. Circumstantially we were forced to reconsider our original decision. I especially wondered if God was calling me to join with Jim. But every time I prayed, I sensed God was telling me no. It wasn't practical for me to attend a church with people who spoke Mandarin Chinese. Only the kids spoke English.

Apart from that, it felt right for me to be at New Song. I could tell in the first ten minutes of our first visit there that it was to be our church. The odd thing is that Jim did not enjoy the same sense of peace about it that I did. We realize now that his sense was unclear because God didn't call him to be at New Song on the weekends during that window of time. Jim and I prayed about what to do next, and both us heard the same answer. Together we agreed that God was leading us to continue to serve in two different church communities.

Thanks to our small group, Jim and I were able to share a common experience of being with other Christians each week. As for our weekends, they worked out well. It helped my husband to develop as a leader by serving in a context that was separate from me. He benefited greatly from the opportunity to discover his own rhythm and style. Had I been there, he probably would have attributed all the credit to me for the fruitfulness born through him. But God prevented that from happening. No mistake could be made. Jim had emerged as the only youth leader in the church. The other youth pastor, Jim's supervisor, had encountered some personal problems and quit somewhere along the way.

God also prevented something else. He used my husband to protect my development as a leader. Somewhere in the middle of our two-church period, I decided out of guilt that it would probably be best if I would start teaching young Taiwanese children where Jim was. My idea was for him to be the leader of the older students and for me to be the leader of the younger ones. Jim, however, knew that my heart was still at New Song. Without telling me, he approached the lead pastor at New Song, "warning him," as Jim put it, that I was about to leave.

The whole thing seemed to be orchestrated by God because Frank Selvaggio, our lead pastor at the time, had already felt convicted to invite me to participate in the preaching. Jim's little push became Frank's confirmation to go forward with the plan he already had. Up to this point, however, neither Jim nor Frank had spoken about it to me. I had no idea that Frank was about to ask me to join him in the pulpit. I had been serving in the nursery.

A day or two later, Frank phoned. He wanted me to sit down with him and explain my theology of women. I was slightly taken aback. Needless to say, Jim wasn't. Jim still hadn't told me about his conversation with Frank; he simply encouraged me to meet with him. So I did. I spent two solid hours trying to communicate as succinctly as I could a gospel paradigm of women in ministry leadership. At the end of my presentation, Frank's mood seemed to be more somber. He had a look of consternation on his face.

I was all set for him to wish me all the best and tell me goodbye, but instead he asserted a sober-minded request: "Would you be willing to sit down with every elder in our church and explain this theology to them?"

I knew this was a bold move. New Song Church is loosely affiliated with the Conservative Baptist denomination. To have a woman preach would most

likely be offensive to certain established families in our community. No wonder Frank was concerned. He was troubled to think about the potential upset, about losing key members and about setting me up to get hurt. At the
front of his mind was an episode that had happened several years back when
a woman at New Song had spoken on Mother's Day Sunday morning. The
response to her was so negative that she left the church soon after.

Frank was resolved not to repeat that story. He was also resolved to act
on his conviction to do his part to clear a space for me to minister to our
church. When Frank tried to assure me of his heartfelt conviction, I didn't
hesitate to believe him. The great blessing for us is that we were likeminded
step by step throughout the process. Both of us cared deeply for church unity.
And both of us were willing to be patient.

In the summer of 1998 Frank invited me for the first time to copreach
the sermon with him. He set it up so that I would do most of the talking.
The idea was for him to interview me, as Dr. Sarah Sumner, on my doctoral
dissertation as a special guest from within the regular membership of our
church. In seminary I had conducted an extensive Bible study on the subject
of godly anger. Frank asked me to share two or three of my conclusions.

For me, copreaching brought back memories of coteaching the Action
class with the college pastor in Waco. All of the sudden, I realized that God
had prepared me for this moment. I was glad to cooperate by easing the congregation into a new sense of normality. Frank and I decided we should both
sit on stools in order to try to minimize the shock of seeing a woman up
front.

To make a long story short, we preached our co-ed sermon, the tapes sold
out, so we did part two the next week. Once again, the sermon tapes sold out
right after the service. That's when a few people panicked. One couple in particular began to scrutinize me. They were faithful, however, to confront me
privately and tell me their concerns face to face.

Over a period of several months, we discussed I Timothy 2 and other passages. The wife even wrote a paper on women in ministry; that's how diligent
she was. Then one night she had a nightmare. She dreamt in her sleep that I

was a "queen locust" who would eventually destroy our church. Again, she was faithful not to spread any rumors. Instead, she and her husband, Jim and I, the chair of our elder board, the prayer pastor, and Frank met together to try to bring things out into the open in order to attempt to build trust. The meeting was conducted in an exemplary way. Silently the prayer pastor prayed and prayed throughout our long conversation. Everyone remained calm. We spoke in quiet tones, but the words were intense. The woman who called the meeting looked me in the eye and told me she was worried that I was secretly having an affair.

Somehow my husband kept his cool and said nothing.

I felt relieved. I relaxed once I heard that her main worry was neither biblical nor theological. Nor was it true for that matter. When I asked her how it was that she had arrived at this conclusion, she said that it was merely "a hunch." She felt disconcerted because I was spending time with the elders.

So I explained to her, "I spend much more time with men at APU than here at New Song."

Innocently she exclaimed, "You do?"

I said, "Yes. I'm the only woman on our faculty. If you think that's something, you should see how many men I went to seminary with. I was the only woman in practically every class that I had."

Almost instantly, she retracted her accusation. She also sincerely apologized. But a few weeks later, on a whim she appeared in my office and confronted me again.

She said, "Sarah, I'm worried about you. Do you have any women to talk to? I was thinking how lonely you must be not having any female friends."

I must admit that she caught me off guard that day. Exposing my vulnerability, I answered her in a pained voice, "It hurts to hear you say this. You don't even know me. Anyone who does knows that I have more women friends than I can keep up with. What are you going to say to me next?"

At that point, she started to cry. As she wept, she began to pour out her story. She told me that she wished that *she* could live my life. She never knew it was possible for a woman to do the things that I was doing.

I sat there watching her eyes burn with tears that were dripping all over her lap. We talked more. We talked more again for hours one day on the phone. I learned that her top spiritual gift is leadership, that she is more of a leader than her husband, and that her greatest fear is to talk to her husband about that.

She said, "I would never ask my husband to be vulnerable with me about his weaknesses."

I said, "Then how can you be intimate with him?"

She replied, "Oh, we're very intimate. It's just that we don't talk about *that*."

I tried to persuade her to take a risk and express herself more openly to her husband. But she wasn't willing. I never heard from her again.

In May 1999, Frank said it was time for me to preach alone on Sunday. The elders unanimously agreed. I'll never forget how affirmed I felt when the lead elder, Dave, phoned to remind me he was praying. At church that weekend, he took Frank and me aside to pray for us again in person.

Overall, the response from the congregation was favorable. Some people, however, felt slightly alarmed. But the issue, by that point, was not so much about a having a woman preach as it was about having a woman attain to the rank of teaching pastor.

In order to shepherd the people, the elders decided to schedule an after-church meeting. Approximately a hundred people showed up. That was a fairly significant turnout considering the fact that New Song is composed of about six or seven hundred adults. The associate pastor, George, moderated the meeting. Five male elders lined the stage. Very directly it was explained that our church constitution had been honored. There was nothing in the document that prohibited a woman from preaching.

Someone sitting in the back raised his hand and interjected, "The question is not whether it's constitutional for a Conservative Baptist church to allow a woman to preach. The question is whether or not it's biblical."

Frank replied, "All right, would the community be pleased if we selected a representative committee to research our view and then offer a recommendation to the elders, and then have the elders make a decision?"

Yes. That satisfied our group.

Immediately Frank appointed George to chair the committee. A year and a half later, George submitted to the elders a formal recommendation from the committee along with a paper presenting a biblical case for the New Song preaching team not to be limited to men. After several minor revisions, the paper was accepted by the elders.

During that period of eighteen months, I copreached with either George or Frank about four or five times, but standing and not sitting on a stool. I didn't preach alone until after the congregation had been given time (about six or seven weeks) to digest the decision of the elders. When the church met again to discuss the final paper that the elders had approved, only twenty or thirty people showed up. The meeting was uneventful. No one voiced a word of dissent.

All in all, New Song probably lost four or five families, including one man on the elder board. The remaining elders and staff, however, solidified on the issue; we never did face a church split. For us, the transition lasted almost three years (June 1998 to March 2001). It required hundreds of conversations with individuals behind the scenes, eighteen months of study by the committee, careful deliberation by the elders and ongoing fervent prayer.

This story, I believe, is a story about God and his powerful movement through a group of godly men at New Song. From my perspective, it was amazing to discover, first of all, that God was at work, stirring the heart of my husband. I think it's so biblical that my husband was the one who, as my head, initiated the process privately and quietly behind the scenes. I also think it's amazing that God had been preparing Frank Selvaggio providentially for a number of years. There was a time in Frank's life when he firmly disagreed with having women serve as pastors or preachers. But through a series of events and long hours spent with God as well as deep meditation on God's Word that preceded Jim's and my arrival, things came together so that Frank had a change of heart. It was less than one year after Jim and I came to New Song that Frank and Dave and rest of the elders began to feel convicted to prayerfully consider that God might be raising up a woman.

There's one more detail to mention. In September 1999, my husband was hired on staff at New Song to serve part time in children's ministry while he finished graduate school. In the fall of 2001, he became the full-time children's pastor, and he still serves today.

THE GIFTS AND CALLINGS OF GOD

Do I now have the right to serve as a teaching pastor in my church? Of course not. It is not my right even to be recognized as such. Christ wasn't recognized for who he really was. God does not command us to be recognized in our spiritual giftedness. He commands instead to exercise the giftedness we have (I Tim 4:14).

If you think about it, Jesus wasn't obligated to prove himself to every last skeptic in town. His duty was to serve as the Messiah. Analogously, it is not Anne Graham Lotz's spiritual obligation to sit down with the leaders of the Southern Baptist Convention and convince them that God gave her as a preacher. Her identity does not depend on them. If God gave her as a preacher, then she is preacher, even if someone claims that that's impossible.

None of us have to prove who we are in order to *be* who we are. You are who you are no matter what.[2] You are gifted and called by God in the way that you are gifted and called. The Bible says the gifts and callings of God are irrevocable (Rom 11:29). God decides your calling. God decides your spiritual giftedness (I Cor 12:18). No one can steal your identity in Christ (Jn 10:28-29). If the Spirit of God has given you as a pastor, you are a pastor, even if you're not employed as one.

WHAT ABOUT WOMEN'S ORDINATION?

When people ask me whether or not I believe in women's ordination, my an-

---

[2]This is partly what it means to be made in the image of God. God said, "I am who I am." The same is true for us. We are who we are. We are who God created us to be. That doesn't mean that we can make excuses for our sin. It means, rather, that God has given us each a self. It would be a cop-out for someone to say, "I can't help but be a stingy person because God made me to be a selfish type of person." It might be truthful, however, for someone to say, "In my fallenness, I tend to be stingy. Nevertheless, by the help of Jesus Christ, I can be very generous though I don't have the spiritual gift of giving."

swer has to do with whether or not I believe in ordination.[3] It's biblical for Christians to lay hands upon those whom the Holy Spirit has set apart for a special ministry (Acts 13:2-3). But it's not biblical for the church to be divided into two different tiers of believers. Few should be teachers (Jas 3:1), and only some of us qualify biblically to be elders. Even so, there is no such thing as a premier member of the church. Nor does the New Testament ever introduce the familiar terms *laity* and *clergy*. On the contrary, the Bible says that all of us in Christ are priests (1 Pet 2:9). John MacArthur Jr. puts it this way:

> Peter identified believers [both male and female] as holy priests, but many Christians don't really know what that means because priests aren't part of our culture as a whole. . . . Faithful priests had a positive impact on believers and unbelievers alike. Malachi 2:6 says they "turned many back from iniquity." Verse 7 adds that "the lips of a priest should preserve knowledge, and men should seek instruction from his mouth; for he is the messenger of the Lord of hosts.[4]

It is biblical to believe that the "lips of a priest," whether male or female, "should preserve knowledge" and that people should seek instruction from his or her "mouth" since a priest should be a "messenger of the Lord." Indeed, both sides of the debate believe that. Thus as far as I'm concerned, the ordained and unordained both are to "go" and "make disciples" and "baptize" and "teach" (Mt 28:19-20). If they're not, then the Great Commission applies to only a few and the priesthood really isn't of all believers.

When the church operates as a "priesthood of believers," it tends to be more functional and larger. Just look at Willow Creek. No one calls Bill Hybels "Reverend" or "Bishop," but everybody knows he is the leader. It's his job as the leader to mobilize more leaders in order to allow the church com-

---

[3]I do not hesitate to support men and women who either are already or are currently being ordained. As a seminary professor, I am entrusted with the responsibility of helping men and women become properly prepared to serve effectively as ministers in the church. It is hard for me to imagine how *any* seminary professor could be anti-ordination and yet still remain in the job. Seminary professors get paid, in large part, from the tuition money that comes in from students who are fulfilling their ordination requirements.
[4]See John MacArthur's Daily Devotional on Sunday July 7, 2002, at <www.gty.org/Daily Devotional>.

munity to grow. The fact that Willow Creek attracts approximately twenty thousand people every weekend is connected to Bill's willingness to rely on other leaders, both men and women.

Along with that, it's telling that Christians in America never seem to argue over who has the right to follow in the steps of Jesus Christ (1 Pet 2:23). We tend to argue about who has the right to lead (contra Mk 10:42). If someone is a leader, all he or she has to do is lead. People follow leaders, even when they're not ordained. Bill Bright is eighty-one years old, and he still is not ordained. But the last I heard, Campus Crusade for Christ has more than thirty-two thousand paid staff members and five hundred thousand trained volunteers worldwide. Bill started that ministry about fifty years ago. He started it by leading, not by being ordained. There is no commandment in Scripture for anyone to be ordained. The commandment is for each one of us to follow in the steps of Jesus Christ (1 Pet 2:21).

If you are gifted and called to be a leader in the church, then get out there and lead. Plant churches. Start from scratch. Enroll in seminary. Initiate a new ministry effort. Ask a few men and women to partner in ministry with you. Get people praying about the project in your heart. Ask for help. Ask more people for help. Use your freshest energy to cast a compelling vision to people you would like to join your team.

It's exhilarating to imagine what God might do. Do you know your spiritual gifts? Have you prayed about what to do? Are you willing to take a risk by faith?

Take heart. The harvest is plentiful. It's the workers that are few. Jesus said, therefore, to "beseech the Lord of the harvest to send out workers into His harvest" (Mt 9:37-38). If men and women alike will step up to the plate and take a swing for Jesus, the church will score more points. Don't forget, we're on the same team. Thus when a woman brings in a big harvest, it doesn't count for her. It counts for the kingdom of God. If Anne Graham Lotz is ever invited to preach a Billy Graham Crusade and things turn out well, not one man in the church will thereby be declared a loser. There won't be any losers because she won't be a winner. There is no contest for Anne Graham Lotz to win.

I wish the worldwide church had an intercom that would broadcast directly into every Christian's living quarters bright and early every morning and remind us again that we are not contesting against each other. Can you imagine that? "Good morning, Christians, this is your daily reminder that you are not in a spiritual contest trying to outdo the brother and sister next to you. I repeat. This is not a contest. As a matter of fact, it is a sin to become boastful, challenging one another, and envying one another (Gal 5:26). Now relax, and go have a good day."

If today we decide to enshrine the Great Commission as our boss verse (Mt 28:20), then perhaps we might be willing to stop playing tug-of-war with each other. As it is, proponents of male leadership are tugging hard on one side, arguing that only men have the right to be church leaders. On the other side, evangelical feminists are tugging hard too, arguing that women have the right to be church leaders. I keep praying that the church will drop the rope. When we look at the bigger picture, it's more than evident that complementarians and egalitarians are teammates, not opponents. We've all been assigned to the same Great Commission. We cannot afford to be divided.

WHO HAS AUTHORITY TO RULE?

Have you ever noticed that Adam was never commissioned all by himself to be fruitful and multiply and fill the earth and subdue it and rule? God knew that it was impossible for Adam alone to expand the human race. Adam couldn't have babies apart from Eve. Have you noticed that before?

In his pre-Eve days, Adam cultivated and kept the garden (Gen 2:15). He was not commissioned to fill and subdue the earth. Until God created Eve, Adam apparently didn't even know that the two of them were supposed to fill the earth. Until God brought him a helper, Adam wasn't told that he and his wife were meant all along to be in charge.

A lot of Christians mistakenly believe that God commissioned Adam to subdue and rule the woman. I'd like to challenge that assumption. If you think about it, that assumption invalidates God's statement, "It is not good for the man to be alone" (Gen 2:18).

It was God's idea to commission Adam and Eve to "fill the earth and subdue it and rule." Genesis 1:28 says, "And God blessed them, and God said to them." He told them together to "rule." That is significant. If it was unrealistic for Adam to attempt to fill the earth without Eve, then it must have been unrealistic for him to attempt to subdue it. Granted, Adam named all the animals in the garden (Gen 2:19-20). But that is not the same as ruling all the animals in the earth.

Adam could no more rule the earth all by himself than he could fill it. He was incomplete until God created him a "helper" (Gen 3:18). I believe that the woman was created "for the sake of the man" (1 Cor 11:9) because the man was inadequate to fulfill the will of God all by himself. Apart from his helper, Adam was unable to multiply. Apart from his helper, Adam was inadequate to rule. Thus God said, "It is not good for the man to be alone."

FATHERLESS HOMES AND MOTHERLESS CHURCHES
If you're skeptical of this, then consider what it takes to build a family. It takes a man *and* a woman to get pregnant. There is no way for two men or two women to "multiply and fill." It takes a father *and* a mother to complete a parenting set. Children should be reared, or ruled, if you will, ideally by both. Nevertheless, some of us have it in our heads that fathers aren't needed at home. The Christian community relies almost entirely on mothers to serve as the primary caregivers to our children. Very few fathers prioritize their kids. Even fewer fathers volunteer to serve at church in children's ministry. Thus kids grow up thinking parenting is feminine, that it's something meant for women to do. Why else would little boys be instructed not to play with dolls?

The flip side of this is that children perceive that the church is supposed to be motherless. Women do the most of the work at church, but men do most of the leading. So there you have it: fatherless homes and motherless churches—and a whole lot of Christians who wonder why we aren't a healthy family.

MANHOOD AND WOMANHOOD
It is worthwhile to mention that when Jesus ascended, he told the apostles

not to leave Jerusalem but to wait to for what the Father had promised (Acts 1:4). Thus they gathered not just as the Eleven but rather as a group of 120 people that included the apostles, "the women, Mary the mother of Jesus, and . . . His brothers" (Acts 1:12-15). The church began with men *and* women. The Bible says, "When the day of Pentecost had come, they were all together in one place" (Acts 2:1).

I believe the women there were mothers in the church, just as the men there were church fathers. When women rise up as leaders such as Deborah did, it's appropriate to refer to them as "mothers." In Judges 5:7, the prophetess Deborah says, "The peasantry ceased, they ceased in Israel, until I, Deborah, arose; until I arose, a mother in Israel."

The conclusion of this book is that men and women should be leading the Christian community, partnering as fathers and mothers. Whenever I preach at New Song, I preach as a mother in the church. I can't preach as a father because I am not a man. Nor can George preach as a mother because he is not a woman. The same can be said of Billy Graham and his daughter Anne Graham Lotz. Anne may preach with spiritual authority, but she does so as a mother, not a man. There's nothing masculine about her mothering the church. It's one of the most feminine things that Anne Graham Lotz could ever do.

Perhaps the church could learn a lesson if we interviewed our kids and asked them to tell us if they can sense the difference between a father and a mother. I am confident that they can. It's not just a matter having a mother wash the dishes and a dad take out the trash. In the eyes of a child, a mother is still a mother, even when she carries out the garbage.

Mothers are different from fathers because mothers are women and fathers are men. A child can intuit the difference. It's silly for us to say that manhood and womanhood cannot be defined without contriving categories for various activities to be limited to just men or just women. Jesus said he came to give us life abundantly (Jn 10:10). Because of his promise, we are invited to live. It's not his way to say that parenting is for women and preaching is for men. It's his way, rather, for us to say that mothering is for women and fathering is for men. That daughtering is for women and sonning is for men. That sistering is for women and brothering is men. That aunting is for women and uncling is for men. That wifing is for women and husbanding is for men. Isn't that nice and simple? The distinction between us does not lie primarily in our activities. It's rather to be found in our relationships.

In summary, the big idea is for Christian men and women to dwell as the family of God. The best way for us to do this is to follow the Golden Rule and love one another as ourselves (Mt 22:37-39). What encourages me most is that love "believes all things" (1 Cor 13:7). Thus I am resolved to wait in hope for men and women in the church to build a consensus on Christian leadership. I pledge allegiance to trust in God to enable us to unite against a common enemy, the devil, the serpent of old, who seeks to "devour" us by pitting us against one another (1 Pet 5:8). As far as I'm concerned, we are on the brink of a new day.

CLOSING REMARKS

For all those who accept this gospel paradigm, there's a certain word of caution to heed. As women are welcomed into leadership with men, I hope we will remember that the overall vision is not to turn the church upside down.[5] As Christians, our goal is to turn the church right side up.

There's nothing unbiblical about women being mothers and men being fathers in the church (1 Tim 5:1-2). It is right for the Christian community to function as the family of God. God alone is our Father, but there are also church fathers and church mothers. These terms refer to church leaders. The fathers of the faith are those such as Ignatius, Irenaeus, John Chrysostom, Augustine and Jerome, while the mothers include Amma (meaning "mother") Theodora, Amma Sarah, Melania the Elder, Melania the Younger and Macrina, the sister of Basil, whom Gregory of Nyssa called "the Teacher," just to name a few.

It is not a new thought that the people of God need to be fathered *and*

---

[5]Though we might hope to turn the world upside down (Acts 17:6).

mothered. Babes in Christ especially need to be fed. Not just milk but meat (Heb 5:12-14). Analogously speaking, a two-year-old can eat a piece of steak if it's cut into small enough pieces. Many babes in Christ aren't being nurtured in the faith. So many people in the Christian community have never been guided or led. What else is there to say? The church needs fathers and mothers. Every local church needs fathers and mothers to help feed and discipline and encourage the body of Christ to persevere.

There's also nothing new about the call for God's people to repent. All of us need to repent from the sin of partiality. We all play favorites. We all have a tendency to champion ourselves and forget about the plight of other people. But, as believers, we also know what it means to repent and how it feels to be forgiven by God. There is so much hope for everyone involved in this debate. We are a people of hope because we serve a God of grace.

Today can be a day of repentance. Today can mark the moment when you ask God for forgiveness. Wouldn't it be awesome if a massive wave of Christians would return to the Lord and worship him in spirit and in truth (Jn 4:24)? Can you imagine what would happen if men and women in the church made it our priority to listen to each other and straighten out our miscommunications? What would happen to the divorce rate in the church if husbands would stop thinking they're entitled and wives would stop refusing to submit? What kind of healing would happen if women were committed to dress and behave more modestly? How would your church change if men treated women as their peers? What would worship be like if there were strong bridges of genuine trust built between men and women?

The Bible says, "Behold, how good and how pleasant it is for brothers [meaning brothers and sisters] to dwell together in unity! . . . For there the LORD commanded the blessing" (Ps 133:1, 3). The blessing—the blessing that could be ours—is waiting to be had by complementarians and egalitarians and all of us who love the Lord Jesus. But we must strive together to be of the same mind (1 Cor 2:16), "maintaining the same love, united in spirit, intent on one purpose" (Phil 2:2).

In signing off, I would like to close with a reminder. The reminder is

this—that you are created in the image of God (Gen 1:27). You were designed to usher in the kingdom of the One who soon will return (Mt 25:14-
31). The good news of the gospel is that everyone who waits upon the Lord
Jesus Christ is guaranteed to gain new strength. "They will mount up with
wings like eagles. They will run and not get tired; they will walk and not
faint" (Is 40:31). All of us in Christ are marked as his. No matter who you
are, you won't be left out, if you put your faith in Christ. There is "no partiality" with God (Rom 2:11), for the beauty of his image is imprinted on
the wings of men and women alike. Now may God grant us grace to soar to
new heights, and may the world see his glory when we fly.

Discussion Questions

1. Discuss what it means for the distinction between men and women to be
   found in our relationships.

2. What do you think of the idea of the church having fathers but not mothers? What do you think of Deborah's proclamation in Judges 5:7?

3. Have you ever noticed that God did not command Adam alone to rule
   and subdue the earth? For what reasons do you think it was "not good
   for the man to be alone"?

4. What action is God calling you to take in response to having read this
   book?

For Further Reading

Atkins, Anne. *Split Image: Male and Female After God's Likeness.* Grand Rapids, Mich. : Eerdmans, 1987.

Barger, Lilian Calles. *Eve's Revenge: Women and a Spirituality of the Body.* Grand Rapids, Mich.: Brazos Press, 2003.

James, Carolyn. *When Life and Beliefs Collide.* Grand Rapids, Mich.: Zondervan, 2002.

Köstenberger, Andreas J., Thomas R. Schreiner and H. Scott Baldwin, *Women in the Church: A Fresh Analysis of I Timothy 2:9-15.* Grand Rapids, Mich.: Baker, 1995.

Mason, Mike. *The Mystery of Marriage.* Portland, Ore.: Multnomah, 1985.

Webb, William. *Slaves, Women and Homosexuals: Exploring the Hermeneutics of Cultural Analysis.* Downers Grove, Ill.: InterVarsity Press, 2001.